A BETTER WORLD IS POSSIBLE

A BETTER WORLD
IS POSSIBLE

THE GATSBY CHARITABLE
FOUNDATION AND SOCIAL PROGRESS

GEORGINA FERRY

PROFILE BOOKS

First published in Great Britain in 2017 by
PROFILE BOOKS LTD
3 Holford Yard
Bevin Way
London WC1X 9HD
www.profilebooks.com

10 9 8 7 6 5 4 3 2 1

A CIP catalogue record for this book is available from the British Library.

ISBN 978 1 78125 916 0
eISBN 978 1 78283 385 7

Typeset in Palatino by MacGuru Ltd
Printed and bound in Great Britain by Clays, St Ives plc

FSC
www.fsc.org
MIX
Paper from
responsible sources
FSC® C018072

'tomorrow we will run faster, stretch out our arms
farther ... And then one fine morning – '
Nick Carraway in *The Great Gatsby* by F. Scott Fitzgerald (1925)

CONTENTS

ILLUSTRATIONS

Colour plates

A series of reports on mental health care published by the Sainsbury Centre for Mental Health and its successor, the Centre for Mental Health. (Sainsbury Centre for Mental Health/Centre for Mental Health)

Cecilia Ogony, one of the farmer teachers trained by the International Centre for Insect Physiology and Ecology in Kenya. (Green Ink/Gatsby)

Raising trees from cuttings at the Tree Biotechnology Project in Kenya. (Neil Thomas/Gatsby)

Tea cultivation in Tanzania and Rwanda supported by a partnership between Gatsby and the Wood Foundation. (Neil Thomas/Gatsby)

Gatsby's Tanzania cotton programme works with cotton processors and farmers to increase yields and improve quality. (Neil Thomas/Gatsby)

Research at The Sainsbury Laboratory, Norwich, into how stomata respond to pathogen attack. (Robatzek Laboratory/TSL)

The Two Blades Foundation has a lab within The Sainsbury Laboratory, Norwich, and is developing a variety of tomato protected against bacterial spot. (2Blades)

The Sainsbury Laboratory Cambridge University (SLCU), designed by Stanton Williams Architects. (Hufton+Crow)

Detailed plant anatomy revealed by high-performance
microscopy at SLCU. (Devin O'Connor/SLCU)

Training technicians is central to Gatsby's work in education.
(Paul Worpole/Technicians Make it Happen)

The National STEM Centre at the University of York.

The National STEM Learning Centre (previously the National
Science Learning Centre) at the University of York.

The Sainsbury Wellcome Centre for Neural Circuits and
Behaviour (SWC), designed by Ian Ritchie Architects Ltd.
(Grant Smith)

The SWC is designed with double-height labs. (Grant Smith)

Researchers at the SWC combine biochemistry and microscopy
to image connections in the brain. (Andy Murray/SWC)

Eyewire, an online game developed with Gatsby support,
recruits citizen scientists to help refine the mapping of brain
circuits. (Eyewire)

Tristram Hunt MP speaking at an event co-hosted by the
Centre for Cities in Manchester in 2016. (Paul Swinney/
Centre for Cities)

The Institute for Government building in Carlton Gardens.

The Sainsbury Centre for Visual Arts (SCVA), designed by
Norman Foster. (Pete Huggins)

The Living Room at the SCVA, displaying items from the
Robert and Lisa Sainsbury collection. (Nigel Young, Foster +
Partners)

Curtain call after one of the first productions staged in the
remodelled Royal Shakespeare Theatre in 2011. (Stewart
Hemley © RSC)

The Chamber Orchestra of Europe on tour in Japan in 2016.
(Nick Asano-Naoyuki)

The *Weeping Window* from the installation 'Blood Swept Lands
and Seas of Red' on tour at Caernarfon Castle. (Craig Owen,
Wales for Peace)

Black-and-white illustrations

FOREWORD

In 1967, at the age of 26, I received a large number of shares in the family business. This enabled me to set up the Gatsby Charitable Foundation, and this year, almost exactly fifty years later, the amount of money given to charity by the Foundation reached £1 billion.

I thought this was a good moment to review the performance of the Foundation, and to see what lessons we could learn about how charitable giving can contribute to social progress. I also wanted to record the achievements of the clever and dedicated people who have helped me run the Foundation and the projects we have supported.

I commissioned a history of the Foundation to be written, and I am delighted at the brilliant job that Georgina Ferry has done, recording both the Foundation's successes and those areas where we have been less successful.

Managing the Trust has been for me and my wife an immensely enriching experience, and I hope that this account of what we have done will encourage other people to use their charitable giving to try to make the world a better place.

David Sainsbury
Lord Sainsbury of Turville Hon FRS
May 2017

PREFACE

On 17 March 1967, David Sainsbury, then aged 26, walked into the office of Ethel Wix, the formidable family solicitor, and handed over a cheque for £5. This represented the founding settlement of his personal charitable trust, which he named the Gatsby Charitable Foundation – F. Scott Fitzgerald's *The Great Gatsby* was his favourite book at the time.

The same day he transferred to Gatsby 110,000 ordinary shares in J. Sainsbury Ltd, the family supermarket chain that had come under the control of himself and his three cousins. It was the beginning of a personal quest to capitalise on the fortune of birth by taking on just a few of the social, economic and scientific challenges that face humanity in the modern age. By 2009, David Sainsbury had transferred more than £1 billion in cash and Sainsbury shares to Gatsby, making him the first Briton to join the super-league of billionaire donors. In recent years, Gatsby has spent of the order of £50 million annually on its charitable activities. In 2017, the fiftieth anniversary of its foundation, Gatsby will itself have passed the £1 billion spending mark.

No two charitable foundations are exactly alike: there are more than 10,000 in the UK, over 100,000 in the USA, and stories to be told about all of them. But, as Gatsby reaches its half-century, there are good reasons to choose it as a case history in modern philanthropy. It comes from a strong tradition of family foundations that have passed a commitment to social action down the generations along with the family business. It has grown from relatively modest beginnings to become one of the top ten UK foundations by assets and spending.[1] And it epitomises the principle that the effectiveness of a charitable body depends critically on the level of engagement of the person putting up the money.

Learning from its past successes and failures, Gatsby now almost exclusively funds projects that it has either initiated or continues to run directly. They have highly ambitious goals: reducing poverty in Africa; increasing government effectiveness; raising the standard and standing of technical education; answering fundamental questions about how plants grow and fight disease; and finding out how the brain works. Many have been running in one form or another for decades.

As Gatsby reaches its half-century in a world facing many problems, David Sainsbury's example provides many ideas and case studies for philanthropists who want to make the world a better place.

Georgina Ferry
May 2017

A TIME OF GIFTS

David Sainsbury and the rise of modern philanthropy

> Wealth is not new. Neither is charity. But the idea of
> using private wealth imaginatively, constructively, and
> systematically to attack the fundamental problems of
> mankind is new.
>
> John W. Gardner, 1912–2002, President of the Carnegie Corporation
>
> 1955–65

Philanthropic donation has a very long history. There has probably never been a time when the more fortunate did not offer help to the less fortunate. Every religion offers some variation on the theme that 'it is more blessed to give than to receive'.[1] From alms to the poor to multimillion-dollar research laboratories, donations have always formed part of the way people identify themselves as among the better-off.

Our age – the age in which Gatsby has come to maturity – is distinguished, however, by the sheer number of what are now commonly called 'high net worth individuals'. 'Millionaire' no longer quite captures the exclusivity of this concept. Between 2008 and 2015 the number of American households worth more than $1 million, not including their homes, rose by 54 per cent (to over 10 million), while those worth more than $25 million rose by 73 per cent – to 145,000.[2] The numbers of the ultra-wealthy are also rising elsewhere, not only in the older industrialised countries and the oil-rich Middle East, but also in the new economies of China, India and Brazil. While, for some, ostentatious displays of spending on yachts, jets and diamonds are part of what it means to be rich, for many others great wealth brings an obligation, and an opportunity, to give something back.

The number of people in the world living below the international poverty line (redefined by the World Bank in 2011 as $1.90 per person per day) has been falling consistently in recent decades, and in 2012 it reached 897 million people – 12.7 per cent of the global population.[3] Yet many more than this are still in great need, and the disparity between the poorest and the wealthiest is more startling than ever: in 2017, Oxfam estimated that just eight people commanded as much wealth as the bottom half of the world's population.[4] At the same time, taxpayers are unwilling to contribute more to public services, and economic turbulence has left government coffers depleted. The pressure to cut government budget deficits has seen austerity programmes rein in spending on areas such as welfare, housing and the arts. The demands of ageing populations mean that providers of state health care, though still absorbing high levels of government funding, are often under-resourced. There is therefore an ever-strengthening 'pull factor' of causes, from wildlife trusts to shelters for people with mental illness, seeking alternatives to government funding. While politicians debate the merits of higher taxation and renewed investment versus further tightening of the purse strings as the route to economic prosperity, the privately wealthy step into the gap.

Giving has become a major industry. Charitable foundations have proliferated. There are bodies that collect and publish data on the wealthiest individuals and foundations, networks of charitable organisations that lobby for giving to be made easier, and a worldwide cohort of highly paid philanthropy

2

consultants both advising charities on how to persuade the wealthy to part with their money and advising the wealthy on how to spend it.

In 2015, giving by American individuals, foundations and corporations reached $373.25 billion,[5] up from the previous record of $358.38 billion in 2014, and equal to almost 10 per cent of the Federal budget of $3.8 trillion. Because of differences in methods of data collection, it is difficult to come up with an exactly comparable figure for the UK, where the tradition of philanthropy is less pervasive and there has been a greater expectation that the state will fund everything from health care to culture. Different bodies provide different snapshots of the sector. The Charities Aid Foundation's 2014 survey gives a figure of over £10 billion for giving by UK adults, but this mainly covers donations by the general public to fundraising charities such as the British Heart Foundation or Children in Need, and excludes most major giving by individuals, corporations or foundations. The Coutts *Million Dollar Donors Report* for the same year suggests that charitable causes in the UK received close to 300 gifts of more than £1 million, adding up to £1.6 billion.[6] UK foundations spent £3.4 billion in total. The spending of the top 300 British foundations has risen steadily in real terms since 2003, with only a brief plateau following the stock market crash of 2007/08.[7]

In the USA, almost a third of all charitable giving goes to religious organisations, while 8 per cent goes to health.[8] Again, the figures for the UK are not strictly comparable, but 14 per cent of funds raised from the general public goes to religious institutions, while 33 per cent of donors give to medical care and research.[9] Education also receives a large proportion of donations in both countries: British universities are doing their best to inculcate the tradition of giving annually to your alma mater that has long been established in the USA, and run professionally staffed development offices in pursuit of donations from individuals, corporations and foundations.

Not surprisingly, the likelihood of giving is positively correlated with wealth on both sides of the Atlantic. In 2010, Microsoft
founder Bill Gates and investor Warren Buffett launched
The Giving Pledge, with forty American billionaires publicly
pledging to donate at least half their wealth. Many more have
since signed up.[10] However, researchers consistently find that, of
those who give, those on lower incomes give more than twice as
much as a percentage of their income than those at the top end
of the wealth scale.[11] There is clearly scope for greater generosity
among the wealthy.

The biggest names in the field of philanthropy are well known.
Many contemporary donors have been inspired by the example
of Andrew Carnegie, the nineteenth-century steel magnate who
emigrated from Scotland to the United States, built up a huge
fortune and spent the last two decades of his life giving most of
it away. His donations at the time of his death in 1919 totalled
$350 million, worth close to $80 billion in 2015 dollars. He not
only founded 3,000 public libraries in the USA and elsewhere,
but gave generously to universities, the arts and the sciences.
Significantly, he was an outspoken evangelist for philanthropy,
holding that 'the amassing of wealth is one of the worst species
of idolatry'. The Carnegie Corporation of New York continues
his legacy, as it supports the causes of education and international peace.[12]

In the UK, the pharmacist Sir Henry Wellcome died in 1936,
leaving a will that vested the share capital in his successful pharmaceutical company in a charity, the Wellcome Trust, for the
purpose of advancing medical research. Today Wellcome is by
far the largest foundation in the UK: it expects to spend £4 billion
between 2014 and 2019, overtaking the state-funded UK Medical
Research Council as the leading source of funds in the field of
biomedical science. No other British foundation comes close to
Wellcome's spending power, but alongside Gatsby other well-
known top ten UK foundations include the Nuffield Foundation,

the Wolfson Foundation, the Leverhulme Trust and the Garfield Weston Foundation.

As in the nineteenth century, the business opportunities of the late twentieth and early twenty-first century have created great wealth very rapidly, and the dotcom billionaires and financial speculators have also entered the philanthropic arena. The Bill and Melinda Gates Foundation, founded in 2000, is now the largest foundation in the world, with assets of over $40 billion (and counting). It aims to tackle some of the most intractable problems in international development, from eliminating malaria to raising the status and education of girls. Warren Buffett, described by *Forbes* magazine as the world's richest person in 2008, has pledged to give away 99 per cent of his fortune, mostly through the Gates Foundation. Since 2010, Facebook founder Mark Zuckerberg and his wife Priscilla Chan have made a similar pledge, their Chan Zuckerberg Initiative aiming to spend billions to improve education, health and inequality.[13]

These are only the highly visible tip of a very large iceberg. There are over 100,000 private grant-making foundations in the USA, not counting those with incomes of less than $25,000.[14] The top 100 of these each gave more than $70 million in 2013/14.[15] There are more than 10,000 foundations in the UK, with the top 300 accounting for 90 per cent of the spending. The top 100 of these each gave more than £5 million in 2013/14.[16] New entrants are joining almost every day.

For those with substantial sums to give, there are many advantages to setting up a foundation. Charity and tax laws are explicitly designed to encourage giving by this means. If you transfer a substantial portion of your assets to endow a foundation, those assets cease to form part of your personal tax liabilities, and within a charitable foundation they are not subject to tax. Unless you are very unscrupulous (and the Charity Commissioners are vigilant on this point), this is not in any sense a 'tax dodge', because you have given away more money than you will gain through any tax reliefs. However, your foundation has more money to spend on your chosen causes than you would have had if you had made donations directly from your pocket.

As it is likely that you will have oversight of the causes your foundation supports, you retain control over how the money is spent (within the constraints of charity law), which would not be the case had you given it to the Treasury in tax. Some argue that this gives the wealthy too much control in matters that should be determined by the state, but at 0.4 per cent of government spending (in the UK), the overall financial clout of charitable foundations is modest.[17]

From alms to 'venture philanthropy'

Giving money away is on the face of it altruistic, but the enthusiasm of donors depends on their feeling that they also get something out of the deal. Many, like Carnegie, recognise that they have much more than they need, and that wealth is corrupting. They feel thankful for their good fortune: they recognise a responsibility to help others, and it makes them feel good to do so. Some might have a specific reason to give: grateful patients give to hospitals that have saved their lives, or charities that conduct research into diseases they or their relatives have survived. Undoubtedly some like the recognition that comes from doing good: having a concert hall or a university department named after you is an even more public statement of your success than buying a yacht. In wealthy circles in the USA, stinginess carries the risk of social ostracism.

Yet more and more people, particularly those who have made their fortunes from innovation in business, seek the satisfaction of using their power as donors, combined with their commercial acumen, not just to give handouts but to effect transformational change. They see donation as an investment that can bring a measurable social return. The terms 'venture philanthropy' or 'the new philanthropy' have recently come into use to describe such activities, though there are many examples that long pre-date these coinings.[18]

Doing it the Gatsby way

Gatsby's fiftieth anniversary provides an opportunity to study in detail how one donor has developed such an approach to giving, based on years of experience. 'One of the luckiest things that happened to me', says David Sainsbury, 'was that I was able to set up my charitable trust early in my life, and this enabled me to learn how I could best run it long before it had a lot of money to give away.' He has formulated a set of questions that illustrate the lessons he has learned.

What can you do with charities that you can't do in other ways?
Gatsby is committed to doing things that most governments find difficult. 'The idea that you can use charitable spending as a substitute for social welfare is wrong,' says Sainsbury. 'The amounts are too small, and there's no evidence it's done better.' What charities can do, he argues, is to take risks and innovate in ways that are very difficult for governments, effectively becoming the R&D arm of government. 'The Treasury always says, "Can you prove that this will work?", which is inimical to innovation,' he says. 'It's not so much about supplying needy children with education, but finding new ways to educate.'

Charities can also take a long-term approach. The time horizon of government projects is bounded by the career of a minister, which leads to 'the curse of the three-year project'. Sainsbury is happy to fund projects for the long term: 'I think if you are going to change something significant, you probably need ten years of concerted effort,' he says. The following chapters describe a number of initiatives that have been running for twenty years or more, or that have been launched with a time horizon exceeding that figure.

What sort of projects should you fund?

It makes most sense to focus on just a few areas, rather than getting out your chequebook for every worthy cause that comes along. They should, first of all, be areas where there is an opportunity to make a real difference. 'In some areas', says Sainsbury, 'it's not clear that you can change things, without spending huge sums of money; and in some cases you may not be able to change things at all.' For example, Gatsby looked into supporting prison reform, but decided there was nothing it could do that would have a lasting impact, because the system in the UK is set up with a focus on punishment, not rehabilitation.

Second, they should be things that you think are valuable and interesting. 'It's important that you do things that you personally care about,' says Sainsbury, 'because you'll then put the effort into finding the projects, developing them, and recruiting the people to do the work. There are quite enough problems to go round – trying to decide which are the most important ones is a waste of time.' The Princeton ethicist Peter Singer has promoted an alternative approach: that the most effective way to give is through a hard-nosed, rational analysis of the impact, in terms of lives saved, of every pound or dollar spent.[19] This utilitarian philosophy has become a movement, known as 'rational giving' or 'effective altruism', that since 2007 has given rise to organisations such as GiveWell and The Life You Can Save in the USA, and Giving What We Can in the UK.[20] Their chief tool is a league table of charities, ranked by effectiveness. The Against Malaria Foundation consistently tops their rankings by distributing insecticide-treated bed-nets to children in sub-Saharan Africa and other malarial regions of the world.

However, few large donors and family foundations are attracted to such an impersonal approach. Like Gatsby, they are prepared to invest time as well as money in finding and pursuing projects about which they care deeply. One of the things that make Gatsby interesting as a case study is that during its history it has funded carefully selected projects across the spectrum of charitable causes. In the area of medicine and health, for example, Gatsby's initiatives have played a major role in the reorientation of mental health provision towards community-based care (see Chapter 3). In education, it has had a long-term focus on supporting teachers of science and technology to prepare the next generation for an economy based on industrial innovation (Chapter 6). Projects in international development (Chapter 4), science (Chapters 5 and 8), public policy (Chapter 9) and the arts (Chapter 10) complete the picture.

How do you find and assess projects?

Unlike many foundations, Gatsby does not rely on appeals coming through the door to determine what it funds. 'We came to the conclusion that you had to employ people who really knew about the areas that you wanted to put money into,' says Sainsbury. 'To the extent that Gatsby's been successful, it's because it has had some really bright people advising on the key areas.'

At the same time, Sainsbury realised that, once you have decided to support an area, it was important to get involved quickly but on a modest scale. 'You fund a number of small projects, and you don't agonise too much about whether they are the best projects,' he says. 'After about three years, people know you are in the field; and you know who the good guys are, who delivers and what is interesting. I call it "splashing around in the shallows".'

For example, learning that research into how plants grow and fight disease was seriously underfunded in the UK, Gatsby began to offer small grants to those working in the field, and to encourage young scientists to specialise in that area. This small beginning identified a group of highly talented young researchers, and led to the foundation of both a world-leading laboratory for research into plant diseases and a state-of-the-art institute for research into plant growth and development (Chapter 5). Unstinting support to key individuals, who develop personal relationships with Sainsbury and the Gatsby team, has been a feature of most Gatsby projects.

Sainsbury is quietly amused by some of the new 'entrepreneurial philanthropists', who demand guaranteed outcomes from their charitable donations. Far from being a 'businesslike' approach, this is the opposite of what they would have done when they were setting up highly speculative new business ventures.[21] 'There are no simple formulas that tell you what will be successful,' he says. 'You have to start somewhere, and be prepared to fail, just like an entrepreneur.'

How can you evaluate your foundation's impact?

The Centre for Giving and Philanthropy at the Cass Business School in London conducts an annual report into the activity of the top 300 foundations in the UK. In its 2015 report, its authors argue that 'independent charitable foundations – at their best – provide an efficient, transparent and intentional way of irrevocably transforming private wealth into public benefit. Their annual spending power is small … but foundations often punch far above their weight.'[22] The greatest asset of private foundations is that they are independent. This gives them the capacity to take risks, funding projects that offer no certainty of success, however that might be measured, and backing unfashionable or otherwise neglected causes.

Independence and risk-taking are at the heart of all that Gatsby does. It is proactive in its approach, seeking out the causes it wishes to support, often setting up new organisations to implement its programmes. With this mindset, it can operate more like a think tank, NGO or social enterprise than a traditional grant-maker. By selecting areas that are otherwise underfunded, it can effect transformational change; by experimenting with different models of support it can help to change the wider funding landscape. It does not burden its beneficiaries with bureaucratic obligations to meet arbitrary short-term targets, but it does maintain a longer perspective on the effectiveness of its programmes and is not afraid to terminate them if they no longer seem to be reaching their objectives.

For example, Gatsby's newest venture, the Institute for Government (see Chapter 9), is a leading think tank with a strong record of research and a stream of publications to its credit. But output alone is not enough when it comes to evaluating its performance. The IfG has the clear objective of making the machinery of government – from local councils to the prime minister's office – work more effectively. Accordingly, it has to present its trustees with quarterly reports on the impact it has been able to achieve on how government is practised. For example, it has encouraged the Treasury to strengthen its control over the accounting procedures of government departments and to appoint an accountant within the Treasury to take control of them.

What will happen to your foundation after your death?
Many foundations continue long after the original settlor has died. Sainsbury cites the Wellcome Trust as an example of a successful legacy foundation, and the Carnegie and Rockefeller Foundations are others. But he himself has declared publicly that Gatsby's funds will be spent out in his lifetime. Other billionaire donors, including Bill Gates and George Soros, have also decided not to be Carnegies or Rockefellers. 'If you are interested in innovation and risk-taking, lifetime is the way to go,' says Sainsbury. 'The danger with a legacy foundation is that it becomes more cautious, more traditional, funding things according to the criteria of the original settlor, which may have become out of date. The problems of society change.'

Involving your children in the foundation to carry on after you have gone may well not be the answer: even if they are competent and willing to do so, there is no guarantee that they will be interested in the same things. Had there been a single Sainsbury Foundation, says David Sainsbury, it would have been a 'recipe for disaster', as different family members had different and decided views about what to support. However, the Sainsburys have collaborated to the extent of operating a single family office, the Sainsbury Family Charitable Trusts (SFCT), which share many of their personnel and most of their administrative overheads. Currently there are seventeen trusts run from the office: members of the 'fifth generation', including David Sainsbury's three daughters, all head their own foundations. In this way, the tradition of philanthropy continues down the generations, while the choice of what to fund remains very much a personal one for each family member.

This book is the story of the choices that David Sainsbury made. Others will make different choices, but will face many of the same challenges in achieving their aims.

2

FAMILY BUSINESS

From grocery to Gatsby

On 20 April 1869, a newly married young couple – Mary Ann 'Polly' Staples and John James Sainsbury – opened a dairy shop in Drury Lane, in the heart of London's Covent Garden. They made good on their claim to sell 'the best butter in London', and four years later opened a second shop in Kentish Town. From such small beginnings, the Sainsbury's supermarket empire began to grow. By 1900, Sainsbury's ran a chain of provisions shops across Greater London: smart, clean and well furnished, they were increasingly stocked with competitively priced fresh goods produced under their own name. During the twentieth century, Sainsbury's grew into a national supermarket brand, with hundreds of shops throughout the UK. The company consistently held a market-leading position on its promise that 'Good Food Costs Less at Sainsbury's'.[1]

The earlier generations of Sainsburys – John and Mary Ann had six sons, all of whom went into the business – were not part of the wave of Victorian philanthropy that saw successful family firms such as the Cadburys, the Rowntrees and the Levers give generously to paternalistic social housing projects, cultural and religious causes and wider projects for social reform. But since the third generation of Sainsburys came to lead the company in

The first J. Sainsbury shop, in Drury Lane, London.

the mid-twentieth century, family business and family philanthropy have gone hand in hand. John's grandsons, Alan and Robert Sainsbury, who between them managed and chaired the company between 1938 and 1969, set an example of giving that now extends to their own grandchildren.

For Polly and John Sainsbury's great-grandson David Sainsbury, the success of the business brought great wealth, but also great responsibility. He knew he was lucky: he also knew that, having far more than he or his family could possibly need, he would give most of it away. But to whom, and for what purpose? Much of Sainsbury's life has been spent working out the answer to that question. Through his experiments in philanthropy, he has developed an approach to giving that does not simply meet immediate needs, but commits long-term investment to projects that will continue to have an impact long after the money has been spent. He has taken risks, most of which – but not all – have paid off. The lessons accumulated over fifty years offer a unique induction to anyone setting out today to tread a similar path.

In the family way

Sainsbury's remained wholly family-run for over a century. John and Polly's eldest son, John Benjamin, who had been born above the Drury Lane shop, joined his father as partner in 1915, and chaired the firm from 1928 until his death in 1956. His sons Alan and Robert Sainsbury became joint general managers in 1938, and one after the other succeeded their father as chairman.

Robert Sainsbury married Lisa van den Bergh, a cousin from his mother Mabel's Dutch-Jewish family. Lisa was herself an heiress – her family's successful margarine business eventually became part of Unilever. The couple lived modestly, but permitted themselves one indulgence: scouring the galleries of Europe for the work of exciting, up-and-coming artists, many of whom they befriended. They bought for pleasure, not investment, and in 1973 they gave most of their priceless collection of modernist and world art to the University of East Anglia. It is now the core collection of the Sainsbury Centre for Visual Arts, the strikingly modern gallery designed by Norman Foster for the UEA campus (see Chapter 10).

Although neither was observant in the Jewish faith, the religious obligation to donate a substantial part of their income to charity was very much part of their outlook on life. Lisa Sainsbury gave generously but less publicly to Kew Gardens (she had a passion for orchids), and to causes related to nursing. As a girl, she had wanted to train as a doctor, but was dissuaded by her family and instead worked as a medical social worker at St Thomas' Hospital in London before her marriage. She later became an early supporter of the world's first purpose-built hospice, St Christopher's, founded by her friend Cicely Saunders, as well as Trinity Hospice.

David Sainsbury, born in 1940, was Robert and Lisa Sainsbury's second child and only son (they also had three daughters). While the family was wealthy, they shunned ostentation or extravagance, and inculcated a strong sense of duty towards the company, the family and society. David's uncle Alan's social reforming sympathies led him to join the Labour Party in 1945, and he took the Labour whip in the House of Lords from 1962. The story goes that when his three sons – John, Timothy and Simon – joined the business in the 1950s, Alan Sainsbury was so anxious that they should not be 'overburdened' with wealth that he limited them to an allowance of £30 a week – for which they had to present themselves at the offices of the family accountant, Jack Lindsey.

As a boy, growing up in a tall, narrow house in Smith Square, Westminster, David saw nothing unusual about having a Henry Moore sculpture under the washbasin in his bedroom – Moore was his godfather. He treasures a postcard sent from Paris by his parents when he was fifteen, and signed additionally by 'Henry, Alberto and Sandy'. Sitting in a café, Bob and Lisa had been discussing with the sculptors Henry Moore, Alberto Giacometti and Alexander Calder whether or not David should be allowed to read *Lolita*.

Science, on the other hand, was a topic of conversation that simply never arose during David's upbringing. Educated at Eton, with a strong bias towards the arts and humanities, he went to King's College, Cambridge, to read history. There he encountered scientific ideas for the first time, and was caught up in the excitement of new discoveries about the workings of the brain. He switched to natural sciences for the final two years of his degree course and took the psychology option (for more about his interest in research on the brain, see Chapter 8). On his graduation from Cambridge in 1963, he did what was expected and joined the family firm, initially in the personnel department, later moving into finance, and finally, from 1992 to 1997, as chairman.

David Sainsbury's parents, Robert and Lisa, with two of Francis
Bacon's portraits of Lisa in their house in Smith Square, London.

From Cambridge he took away two ideas that would determine
his later approach to philanthropy: the excitement and interest of
scientific research, and the importance of economic growth. He
was excited by Harold Wilson's speech to the 1963 Labour Party
conference, when the future prime minister talked about Britain
being 'forged in the white heat' of the scientific revolution.
'My political interests had begun to develop around economic
performance,' he says. 'I thought Harold Wilson's speech was
fantastic. The idea of the relevance of science and technology
to economic growth was at the core of the development of my
charitable fund.'

In 1966, preparing for the succession of the next generation,
Robert Sainsbury transferred his stake of 45 per cent of the shares
in Sainsbury's to his only son. At the same time, Alan Sainsbury

split his 45 per cent shareholding equally between his three sons: the eldest, John Davan Sainsbury, became Deputy Chairman in 1967 and Chairman and Chief Executive in 1969. 'At the time the shares yielded very little,' says David Sainsbury. 'It wasn't about the money – it was about control of the company.'

In 1967, he made the modest settlement that established the Gatsby Charitable Foundation – £5 in cash, plus 110 shares in Sainsbury's, valued at £412,500. It was something that members of his family had done previously: his parents and uncle had set up charitable trusts in the early 1950s, and his cousins all set up trusts around the same time that he did. Until 1973, Gatsby's endowment generated dividends of £5,500 a year, which, together with some cash donations from David Sainsbury's parents' and uncle's trusts to get him going, were all that the charity had to spend.

In those first six years Gatsby made small grants to a handful of other charities. For part of the time David Sainsbury was away at Columbia University, studying for an MBA. He freely admits that his foundation was not the first thing on his mind, and on his return from America in 1971 he had the additional responsibility of a directorship of Sainsbury's. Most of Gatsby's early beneficiaries reflected a family bias. The Israeli Students Aid Association, St Thomas' Hospital, the Pestalozzi Children's Village Fund, the Perseverance Trust (a nursing charity, close to his mother's heart): Ethel Wix, the family lawyer who represented the trustees, probably had more to do with these choices than Sainsbury himself. A contribution of £100 towards scholarships to his old college, King's Cambridge, was a more personal gift. A few early donations did, however, begin to indicate some of the directions that Gatsby was to take in the future.

A developing world
One day in 1969, Sainsbury happened to read a newspaper article about the Liverpool School of Tropical Medicine (LSTM).

Founded in the late nineteenth century by the shipping magnate Sir Alfred Lewis Jones to cope with the influx of tropical diseases into Liverpool's thriving international port, LSTM had grown to be a world leader in the subject. The article concerned work by a former Medical Officer of Health in Kenya, Professor Rex Fendall, on community health care in Africa.

Fendall had joined HM Overseas Medical Service in 1944, working in Nigeria, Malaya and Singapore before moving to Kenya in 1948. He was promoted to be the country's director of medical services, a position he held until Kenya achieved independence from British colonial rule in 1964. In this capacity, Fendall was a leading contributor to an investigation by the Rockefeller Foundation, published in 1969 as *Health and the Developing World,* by the American specialist in community medicine Jack Bryant. The book set out new, community-based approaches to delivering health care in poor rural areas, largely based on Fendall's experience, that were ultimately to influence global health policies and inspire a generation of students in public and international health. After Fendall returned to the UK, he took up the Middlemass Hunt Chair of Tropical Community Health at the LSTM, which he held until his retirement, and used the post to raise the profile of primary health care.

As a student in the 1960s, Sainsbury had become aware of the challenges facing a post-colonial, increasingly globalised world, from access to technology to economic and social progress. Learning of Fendall's work, and thinking it sounded worthwhile, he sent him a cheque for £50 out of his own pocket, shortly before setting off for New York to do his MBA. 'When I came back,' he says, 'I found a letter saying, "Would you like to give more?"' Sainsbury went up to Liverpool and met Fendall. He remembers Fendall telling him that at the clinics where he worked in African villages, 'if God turned up asking for help, he'd be told to go to the back of the queue.' Suitably impressed, through Gatsby Sainsbury donated £10,000 to LSTM in 1970, the largest grant it had ever made.

Fendall argued passionately that the time lag between the acquisition of medical knowledge and technology in industrialised countries, and its application among the world's poor, was shameful. He was particularly exercised about high levels of infant mortality: between a third and a half of all babies born to poor mothers in the developing world would die before their fifth birthday. One solution he proposed was the training of many more medical auxiliaries, health workers who had not undertaken the lengthy training required of doctors and nurses. He wrote:

> Much of the time lag between the discovery of knowledge and its extensive application lies in the reluctance and inability to admit that lesser-trained persons can carry out routine tasks in medicine. Yet such lesser-trained persons must be selected, appropriately trained, and utilised if we are to achieve a total outreach of medical and health care within the parameters of the financial and manpower resources of the disadvantaged peoples of this earth.[2]

This philosophy led Fendall to develop new training courses at LSTM that focused on health service delivery and did not require a medical qualification. He was tireless in his campaigning to raise the profile of primary care as a fundamental prerequisite for global health. In 1978, the World Health Organization (WHO) declared at its Alma-Ata conference that primary care should be central to the goal of 'Health for All by the Year 2000'. Fendall welcomed the declaration, but was sceptical: 'I doubt if primary health care reaches more than 10% of the peoples of developing countries even today,' he wrote. 'Given that the population will practically double by the year 2000 what prospect have we of achieving 100% coverage unless we are realistic?'[3] The Health for All goals were widely adopted, and although the 100 per cent target was indeed missed as Fendall predicted, access to at least some aspects of primary health care, particularly childhood immunisation and maternity services, was widespread by 2000.

Fendall's vision of social progress delivered through practical, community-based initiatives appealed strongly to David Sainsbury's own instincts. He was sufficiently impressed by the work at LSTM to agree to join its governing body for a few years. After Fendall's retirement in 1984, Gatsby continued to support his successor, Professor Kenneth Newell, with increasingly generous grants for courses, fellowships and research. Under Newell's leadership the department was designated as a WHO Collaborating Centre for the development of health systems based on primary health care.

Gatsby's funding of programmes at LSTM, which eventually totalled more than £1.5 million, came to an end with Newell's untimely death in 1990. By this time, the Gatsby trustees had made a new commitment to supporting economic development in Africa, leaving health care to the many other charities and NGOs working in that field.

Over the period that Gatsby was funding work in community tropical health at LSTM, the health status of people in many developing countries began to be transformed. To take one example, WHO estimated that in 1975 only 69 countries, representing 30 per cent of the global population, had an infant mortality rate below 50 per 1,000 live births. By 1997, 106 countries, representing 64 per cent of the global population, reached this target. Much of this was due to the development of local health networks that could deliver effective antenatal care and childhood vaccination,[4] as advocated by Fendall and Newell. Their commitment was vindicated when WHO titled its 2008 World Health Report *Primary Health Care: Now More Than Ever*, positioning primary health care as central to health equity. For David Sainsbury, twenty years of close association with these two visionary

21

leaders inculcated a strong message about the need to develop from the ground up. It was a message he would take forward as Gatsby began to develop its own programme of support for economic development in Africa (see Chapter 4).

Going public

After more than a century as a private company, on 12 July 1973 the Sainsbury's supermarket business was floated on the stock market. It was the largest flotation to that date in the UK, and sent the value of the shares soaring. The family collectively had retained an 85 per cent shareholding: David Sainsbury found himself in the ranks of the super-rich, despite having already transferred more shares, worth over £5 million, to Gatsby during the previous year.

The share offer transformed the scale of Sainsbury's charitable activities. Within a few years, the amount Gatsby had available for grant-making increased a hundredfold, and the other Sainsbury family trusts were in a similar position. The trustees could no longer manage without the help of a dedicated administrator, and in 1973 Sainsbury's cousins John, Timothy and Simon Sainsbury hired Hugh de Quetteville as director of their trusts. De Quetteville was an advertising executive from Ogilvy & Mather who had been at Eton with Simon Sainsbury and was a long-standing friend of John's. But he was well aware of the risks of excessive familiarity. 'I determined from the start', he says, 'that just because they were amiable, I should not make the mistake of getting too close. They were my employers, I their employee. I think if you are too loyal – if you lose an astringent objectivity – you become a crony, and that's fatal.'

David Sainsbury immediately saw the merit in having some help with managing Gatsby, and approached de Quetteville to ask if he would take it on. When his mother heard that he was proposing to combine Gatsby's management with that of the other Sainsbury trusts, she insisted on having de Quetteville independently vetted. She sent him to be interviewed by Bryan Woods, Clerk to the City Parochial Foundation. 'He reported back that I wasn't interested in embezzling funds,' says de Quetteville drily, 'and she didn't take the matter any further.' Tall, spare, patrician and sharp as a tack, de Quetteville was to play a crucial role in fashioning the principles by which the Sainsbury trusts operated: minimal bureaucracy, low overheads, personal scrutiny of potential beneficiaries, long-term support for and close contact with those who met the trustees' criteria, and little or no publicity. The model remains to this day.

In 2016, the offices of the SFCT manage seventeen foundations, representing settlements by three generations of Sainsburys, sharing the costs roughly in proportion to the size of the funds: Gatsby's is the largest. The number of staff has increased to some dozens, but it still remains a tiny operation compared with many better-known charities.[5]

It has also retained something of the combination of rigour and informality that characterised de Quetteville's approach. 'I would hold a meeting once a month with each of the settlors individually,' he says. 'I would prepare the most elementary figures on each trust's projected annual income, how much had been spent, how much cash in hand we had to be allocated at the meeting. After the meeting I would ring up [the accountant] Jack Lindsey and ask for a cheque for whatever had been agreed. It was amazingly informal.' De Quetteville's role initially was to assess the various appeals for grants that came into the office, and allocate them to the most appropriate trust; he also kept in touch with beneficiaries and monitored their use of funds. Later, as the trustees became more proactive in their choice of projects to support, he was instrumental in establishing and managing some of those projects.

Most family members have had a strong focus on social initiatives such as education, third world development and health, but each has also had personal areas of interest: for example,

John Sainsbury, who is married to the ballerina Anya Linden and founded the Linbury Trust, is a leading patron of ballet and the arts. In 1985, he and his brothers (founders of the Headley and Monument Trusts) together announced that they would fund the Sainsbury Wing of the National Gallery in London, opened in 1991 to display the Gallery's early Renaissance collection. Apart from continuing support for his parents' bequest of their art collection, David Sainsbury has been less interested in this kind of patronage. 'David was the most interested in how society worked,' says de Quetteville. 'All of them, though David less than the others, started off too full of idealism and misguided self-confidence. As time went on, they became clearer-eyed about what it was possible to change.'

Another key figure joined the Gatsby inner circle in the late 1970s. Since its foundation, the Gatsby trustees had been Jack Lindsey, representing family and company accountants Clark Battams, and Ethel Wix, representing the family solicitors, HON&V. Judith Portrait joined that firm as a newly qualified solicitor in 1973. At the time, the senior partner on the Sainsbury's account, Willie Pybus, was looking after trusts for John and Timothy Sainsbury. 'But he was working on the public offering,' says Portrait, 'so I did all the private trust and family work as his assistant.' A few years later Ethel Wix retired, and Portrait became the representative of HON&V as Gatsby's trustee. Discreet, loyal and dedicated, she has remained a trustee ever since: from 1990, she has held the role in a personal capacity. In 1995, she established her own firm, specialising in work for family trusts. 'I'm not an interfering trustee,' she says, characterising her role as 'keeping the peace'. 'I think I would describe my position over the nearly forty years of my involvement as providing the glue which has helped to hold things together,' she says. This comment is a major understatement of the contribution she has made throughout Gatsby's history.

David Sainsbury himself has never been a Gatsby trustee,

The 1976 Notting Hill Carnival ended in a
riot – Gatsby paid off its deficit.

in contrast to his cousins who were all trustees of their own
charities. However, there has never been any doubt that the
guiding principles of the charity come from him. By 1976 the
trustees had formulated a funding policy that focused on three
themes: research in public administration, work in 'under-
developed countries' and mental health. In the following decade,
other headings came and went, such as 'medical', 'old people',
'the disabled', 'disadvantaged children' and 'the arts'. 'I would
try to squeeze various suggestions to fit the headings he and his
cousins had given me,' says de Quetteville.

In its first decade Gatsby made a regular stream of small
grants for social projects in London, often related to racial integration. The Melting Pot Foundation in Brixton, run by Jamaican
community leader René Webb, received a grant towards a hostel
for homeless adolescents. As one of a number of grants to the
North Kensington Amenity Trust (NKAT), in 1976 Gatsby
bailed out the Notting Hill Carnival to the tune of £3,000. De

Quetteville's note brought an uncharacteristic touch of humour to Gatsby's annual report:

> Although this year's carnival ended in a riot, there is no doubt that the 2¾ days which preceded were successful. ('Apart from that, Mrs Lincoln ...') Most of the £3000 will be repaid by the Carnival Committee to the NKAT so that it can be used again for the same purpose next year, when despite the present troubles there is likely to be some sort of carnival again.

De Quetteville ruefully cites another such grant as an early failure. Within a few months of his arrival, the Telegraph Hill Centre in Lewisham, founded by anti-apartheid campaigner Bishop Trevor Huddleston, asked for a couple of hundred pounds to send a young race relations volunteer to the Sixth Pan-African Congress in Tanzania. The year after his trip, Wesley Dick notoriously became one of the three 'Black Liberation Army' gunmen who mounted a botched raid on the Spaghetti House restaurant in Knightsbridge and held some of the staff hostage for six days before giving themselves up. No one was hurt, but all three received long prison sentences. 'David was very amiable, and took the line it could have happened to anyone,' says de Quetteville.

As if people mattered
Whenever developing countries were in the news, it seemed to be for the wrong reasons. War, famine, kleptocratic elites or white minority administrations entrenching racial inequality – everything seemed to be stacked against ordinary citizens wanting to improve their material well-being, to work and to educate their children. During the 1960s, however, David Sainsbury had begun to hear less despairing voices. Prominent among these was Fritz Schumacher, chief economic advisor to the Coal Board and a pioneer of development economics.

On 29 August 1965, Schumacher published a widely debated article in the *Observer* entitled 'How to help them help themselves', calling for a radical change in international aid policy. He argued that developing countries could become self-reliant, not by importing capital-intensive Western technology but by developing 'intermediate' or 'appropriate' technology that complemented their needs and resources. In 1966, with his friend George McRobie and others, he set up the Intermediate Technology Development Group (ITDG) to research and apply his ideas. It gathered support from a number of partner organisations, including the think tank Political and Economic Planning (PEP), the charities Oxfam and War on Want, the Ministry of Overseas Development, the oil company Shell, and several other businesses and NGOs. Schumacher himself carried out an exhausting international lecture programme, making high-level contacts with organisations such as the World Bank.

Despite its large constituency of influential supporters, ITDG's early days were financially precarious. Determined to launch its own programmes and professionalise its activities, in 1971 it put out an appeal to a wide range of potential donors, including the SFCT. Gatsby initially contributed £1,000. Perhaps more significantly, David Sainsbury personally loaned the group almost £40,000, interest free, to 'finance the development aspect of its operations'. Over the next two years Gatsby donated another £55,000 – a significant sum for the pre-flotation era, and representing about half of ITDG's total donation income. Successive ITDG annual reports suggest that Gatsby's contribution not only helped eliminate the deficit the group had accumulated over its first five years, but enabled it to expand its areas of research interest.

In 1973, at the height of the oil crisis, Schumacher published his critique of Western economics, *Small Is Beautiful: Economics As If People Mattered*. 'I thought it was an interesting book,' says Sainsbury. 'He said that all developing countries start in the same place – not with capital-intensive machinery, but with labour-intensive products such as textiles and electronic assembly. They have a cost advantage, because labour is cheap. Then they can upgrade and move on to higher value-added areas, as Japan has done and now China is doing.' Sainsbury saw the economic sense of this view, but he later adopted a more robust approach to innovation and growth while the ITDG, due to anxieties about the fragility of the global ecosystem, continued to champion small, low-tech industry. It was a shocking blow to his colleagues when Schumacher died suddenly in 1977, felled by a heart attack in the middle of a lecture tour in Switzerland. But by that time his personal charisma had won wide support for the organisation, and it continued to go from strength to strength.

At this point in Gatsby's history, Sainsbury took the view that because his wealth came from the purses of British shoppers, his foundation would fund only UK-based projects. Spending on ITDG's research into the problems of developing countries clearly met this criterion, while contributing at one remove to alleviating poverty overseas. In *Small Is Beautiful*, Schumacher had noted that the concept of appropriate technology was as relevant to industrialised countries as it was to the developing world. The increasingly vocal environmental movement of the 1970s took up Schumacher's ideas, demanding a new move towards sustainability in areas such as energy use and food production. In 1975, Gatsby agreed to provide start-up funds of almost £50,000 for a whole new area of ITDG's work, which came to be known as Alternative Technology in the UK, or AT-UK. To run the project, the group recruited an engineer and former executive of Shell UK, John Davis. His brief was 'To promote the formation and guide the activities of local or regional organisations whose aim is to introduce alternative small-scale technologies in their areas.'[6]

Despite his background in the oil business, Davis was a faithful adherent of Schumacher's philosophy. In 1978, he confidently wrote that 'In the next few decades ... we shall be leaving behind much of the materialistic society with its ever-increasing consumption of goods, and moving into a world of different values in which *quality of life* will be seen as of greater importance than, and quite different from, *quantity of consumption*.'[7] To this end he advocated a rebalancing of the economy through 'growth in small-scale, decentralised manufacturing, elimination of energy wastage and reduction of dependence on imports'. Through this process, he envisaged not only the creation of many new jobs, but increased job satisfaction and a sense of community pride.

AT-UK dedicated itself to promoting the development of small enterprises distributed throughout the regions, 'particularly enterprises which are widely dispersed, manpower intensive, relatively undemanding in capital requirements and economical in their use of scarce and non-renewable resources'.[8] Davis noted that, compared with European competitors such as Germany and France, Britain had very few firms employing fewer than 200 people. He cited a number of barriers to their success, including restrictive legislation, lack of credit, punitive taxation regimes, excessively favourable prices extended to big firms for materials, and the vulnerability of small firms to economic cycles.[9]

Davis advocated government action to increase the freedom of action of small businesses, and the Department of Trade and Industry (DTI) did set up incentives such as the Enterprise Initiative and Business Link in the following few years. However, these top-down ventures were expensive and bureaucratic. Davis thought there was another way. In 1977, ITDG and the short-lived but similarly motivated Foundation for Alternatives jointly proposed that non-profitmaking trusts, known as Local Enterprise Trusts (LETs), could smooth the paths of new businesses, combining 'an entrepreneurial function with social responsibility'.[10] Although Sainsbury had been attracted to ITDG because of its work on international development, its foray into local economic initiatives in the UK also chimed strongly with his own interests in that area.

In the months that followed, using Gatsby funds, Davis and Stan Windass of the Foundation for Alternatives established a unit within AT-UK to promote LETs. The prototypes were extremely diverse in their origins and structures. Some were sponsored by large industrial concerns: the glass manufacturer Pilkington established the Community of St Helen's Trust on Merseyside, while British Steel developed Clyde Workshops in Glasgow, following redundancies in their own workforces. Antur Aelhaearn on the Lleyn Peninsula in North Wales was a tiny community enterprise launched by a local doctor to create employment following the closure of a local quarry, and to save the village school. It is still in existence today. Others, such as the Hackney Business Promotion Centre, made use of government funds for inner-city regeneration.

The success of the trusts depended very much on their local management, but some were spectacular. In St Helens, the former RAF Mosquito pilot and Pilkington executive Bill Humphrey, working from a leaking former schoolroom, had stood godfather to enough new small firms to create 700 jobs in the desperately depressed area within a year. Its success came to the attention of Michael Heseltine, the President of the Board of Trade. With the support of Sir Alistair Pilkington, who acted as its first chair, business leaders got together in 1982 to form the national body Business in the Community. With their additional impetus, by 1985 there was a network of 200 LETs, from West Cornwall to Glasgow.

AT-UK played no role in the management of the LETs, but acted as a central information exchange, organising seminars, publishing regular newsletters and evaluating their operation. Davis estimated that a good LET could be associated with 200 new jobs or jobs saved per year, at a direct cost of only £300 per job.

While AT-UK raised the profile of sustainability as an issue for industrialised society, and promoted small business solutions to economic regeneration, it represented a tiny fraction of ITDG's overall activity. The group's main focus remained the relief of poverty in the developing world through the promotion of appropriate technology and community-based, sustainable economics. From 1977, the UK's Overseas Development Administration (ODA; then part of the Foreign Office, but today a separate Department for International Development) accounted for at least half of the charity's donation income each year, and from 1981 it became the major funder, with grants rising to over £1 million per year. ITDG was able to establish country offices in South America, Africa and Asia, and it greatly extended its work planning, executing and evaluating projects in the countries where it operated. It was at about this time that Gatsby itself changed its policy on funding overseas projects and decided to set up its own Africa programme (see Chapter 4).

Of the 200 LETs in operation by 1985, many have continued in some guise or other ever since. Today the National Enterprise Network, founded in 1992, represents local enterprise agencies with central government. The principle of community-based agencies to promote enterprise is now well entrenched: under Britain's coalition government in 2011, it went mainstream when the Department of Business, Innovation and Skills established thirty-nine Local Enterprise Partnerships, funded to stimulate local business development. Meanwhile the strong message on conservation of materials and energy that AT-UK disseminated has also taken root: recycling is no longer the preserve of the green fringe, but an obligation placed on local authorities, with severe fiscal penalties for underperformance. While Davis's dream of an end to consumerism remained just that, modern appliances consume a fraction of the energy of their predecessors.

ITDG, renamed Practical Action in 2005, continues to run programmes in Africa, Asia and South America, using technology to help people out of poverty, and to campaign for technology justice. Gatsby's early support played a key role in establishing the organisation on a sound financial footing, and its investment in AT-UK contributed to the growth of a movement towards local regeneration and sustainability underpinned by serious economic research. Gatsby itself learned lessons from its engagement with ITDG that it would apply in its own future programmes on small-scale economic development in Africa (Chapter 4) and on technology transfer and local economic development in the UK (Chapter 9).

Rebirth in the city

The Sainsbury's headquarters where David Sainsbury began his working life were located south of the Thames in and around Stamford Street in Southwark. The estate originally included offices, food-processing factories and distribution centres: he remembers sides of bacon being smoked, and Stilton cheeses being ripened in the basement of the combined offices and distribution depot. It was a hive of industry on the western fringes of London's Docklands, an area that had gone into catastrophic decline during the 1960s and 1970s as the Thames ceased to be a major commercial waterway in the face of competition from the huge container ports around the coast. Co-opted as a representative of local business, Sainsbury joined the Docklands Joint Committee, a body set up in 1973 between the five affected riverside boroughs and the Greater London Council to develop a strategic plan for regeneration of the area. It was his first experience of government decision-making, and it rang a number of warning bells. 'It was the only board on which I have sat that achieved nothing,' he says.

'The initial idea was to bring in new manufacturing industries to provide employment for former dockers,' he says. 'But that was precisely the moment at which manufacturing was moving out of London.' Manufacturing in the city had depended on the dominance of rail transport. But with the massive increase in motor transport in the years following the Second World War, out-of-town industrial development became more attractive. 'I realised that the local authorities that made up the Joint Committee didn't understand the economic realities,' says Sainsbury. 'We should have got roads, schools, housing and so on right, and then waited to see who would move in.' It was the start of his lifelong interest in local economic initiatives. The Joint Committee was succeeded by the more powerful London Docklands Development Corporation, but the eventual revival of Docklands initially depended as much on individual behaviour as on any grand plan. Cheap converted warehouses attracted young people into the inner city, and small businesses sprang into being to serve them, while the booming financial and services sectors provided them with jobs.

In 1975, Sainsbury picked up a Fabian Society pamphlet entitled *Inner City: Local Government and Economic Renewal*. Its authors were Nicholas Falk, at the time a senior research fellow at the London School of Economics working on community projects in Docklands, and Haris Martinos, a policy officer at the London Borough of Southwark. On meeting Falk, Sainsbury discovered that the two of them shared the experience of having done an MBA in the USA. Falk was full of enthusiasm for successful models of urban regeneration that were under way in Boston and the mill towns of Massachusetts, reusing old buildings as workshops for small businesses. He himself was engaged in several such projects in Rotherhithe, south of the Thames. One involved restoring Brunel's derelict Thames Tunnel Engine House as a museum; Falk also set up the Industrial Buildings Preservation Trust to refurbish a group of warehouses as workshops and a community arts centre. Sainsbury was interested in the idea of using small-scale creative enterprises to drive urban renewal, and through Gatsby gave a number of grants to the URBED (Urbanism, Environment and Design) Research Trust, set up by Falk to effect this.

Opened in the 1930s, J. Sainsbury's Stamford Street factory
was the first flat-slab concrete building in London.

In 1974, Covent Garden, London's historic wholesale flower
and vegetable market, had moved out to Nine Elms, south of
the Thames. An initial proposal to flatten the warehouses and
redevelop the site commercially had been averted due to a public
outcry, and the buildings had been protected by conservation
area status. But many stood empty, while the Greater London
Council and the militant Covent Garden Community Association continued to tussle over the area's future. Falk saw Covent
Garden as a testbed for his ideas, and set up the URBED office in a
converted warehouse in Earlham Street with his colleague Christopher Cadell, formerly of Boston Consulting. Other key collabo-
rators were the architect John Worthington, the planner Peter Hall,
Roger Jowell, founder of the National Centre for Social Research,
and John Cartwright MP. 'It was fantastic how easy it was to start

Former warehouse buildings in London's Covent
Garden, like this one at 48 Earlham Street, were taken
over by creative workshops in the early 1970s.

up in those days,' says Falk. Inspired by the example of David
Rock, an entrepreneurial architect who had filled a warehouse at
5 Dryden Street with small businesses, URBED organised an exhibition, 'Covent Garden Can Make It', set up a Space Exchange to
help entrepreneurs find offices and workshops, and launched the
first-ever programmes to train and support them. Their research
discovered 1,500 businesses employing 30,000 people, many
involved in creative industries. Falk persuaded investors ICFC
(Industrial and Commercial Finance Corporation, the previous
incarnation of 3i) to invest in the conversion of a warehouse
owned by the Greater London Council, which soon filled with
architects, designers, craftspeople associated with the theatre,
and other small businesses that were desperate for space.

URBED documented its work with a constant stream of reports and articles in the press. It organised a conference with IBM (International Business Machines) to share perspectives on models of economic regeneration in the USA, a meeting attended by John Davis of ITDG, whom Falk cites as an inspiration.[11] It energetically promoted ideas such as the reuse of old buildings, the redevelopment of wasteland and the 'urban village', many of which were taken up by local authorities around the country. Gatsby's relationship with URBED ended after a few years, but as a consultancy it has continued to operate ever since. Now self-funded through contracts from local authorities and developers, URBED is a cooperative of ten architects and planners, and has gone on to win awards for masterplanning and urban design in a number of British cities.[12]

David Sainsbury retained a keen interest in the economic drivers of successful cities, which eventually led him to found the Centre for Cities (see Chapter 9).

Principled ambition

The continued success of the Sainsbury's empire, the judicious management of Gatsby's investments, and further transfers of shares from David Sainsbury, meant that the amount of money available to spend continued to grow. By the mid-1980s, donations were running at between £2 million and £3 million per year. From that point on, Gatsby began to shift from responding to requests for grants of small to moderate size, to planning and funding its own projects and setting up new institutions. The time horizons of these projects could be twenty-five years or more, and their core funding tens of millions of pounds.

The change came about as David Sainsbury and his colleagues in Gatsby questioned the possibilities and limits of philanthropic activity, based on their experience so far. While the legal and tax framework within which Gatsby operates constitutes it as a charity, Sainsbury defines its activities as 'philanthropy' rather than 'charity', feeling that philanthropy is about social progress rather than simply relieving need. 'We want projects that do something, that make a significant difference, that get picked up by the system of government as the way you do it in future, and that last,' he says.

The style and scope of Gatsby's operations have evolved over the years, in parallel with developments in David Sainsbury's own career. Until 1997 he was actively interested, but employed full time as Finance Director and then Chairman of Sainsbury's, so very much dependent on the advice and management of successive SFCT directors and Gatsby trustees and advisors. From 1998 to 2006 – much longer than he had expected – he was Minister for Science and Innovation in the Labour government of Tony Blair, having been raised to the peerage as Lord Sainsbury of Turville in 1997. During this period, he was not allowed by parliamentary rules to do more than meet the chair of trustees once a year, so the SFCT director and Gatsby trustees took on almost all the responsibility for decision-making (see Chapter 7). On leaving government in 2006, Sainsbury chose to devote most of his energies to running his charity, and instituted a major shift in the type of projects funded. Since the mid-1980s, Gatsby has funded projects in seven broad areas, covered in the following chapters.

3

BALM OF HURT MINDS

Mental health and children in need

Mental health is the Cinderella of medical conditions. A recent report on medical research funding in the UK found that, while 25 per cent of the population will experience some form of mental illness each year, only 5.5 per cent of health research spending goes into the condition. That equates to less than £10 per person affected: in contrast, the UK spends over £1,500 per patient on cancer research. As for charitable contributions, 0.3p in the pound of government research spending on mental health comes from the general public, as against £2.75 for cancer.[1]

These are 2015 figures. Nevertheless, in many respects the mental-health landscape has changed for the better compared with the position even fifty years ago. The system no longer categorises people as lunatics or defectives and locks them up for life. Mental health has moved up the political agenda: there are many forms of support for people with mental illness, the training of health professionals has been transformed and, on paper at least, there is a good understanding of how areas such as employment and criminal justice might be reformed, given adequate resources, to meet the needs of mentally ill people. Much of the credit for this goes to the advocacy of charities and professional bodies such as the Mental Health Foundation, Mind and the Royal College of Psychiatrists. Alongside them, through the Sainsbury Centre for Mental Health, Gatsby has played a distinctive and influential role.

Beyond the water towers

The question of whether you could 'minister to a mind diseased' had preoccupied David Sainsbury since his days as an under-graduate studying psychology. With his classmates, he was taken to visit Fulbourn Hospital, originally founded as the 'County Pauper Lunatic Asylum for Cambridgeshire, the Isle of Ely and the Borough of Cambridge' in 1858. There the energetic Medical Superintendent, David Clark, was pioneering a model of care based on the 'therapeutic community': since his appointment in 1953 he had unlocked all the wards and instituted daily meetings between staff and patients.

At around the same time as Sainsbury's visit to Fulbourn, in 1961, the Conservative Minister of Health Enoch Powell made a powerful speech in which he declared his intention to transfer mentally ill patients out of the Victorian mental hospitals. New drug treatments meant that some did not need to be in hospital at all, while others could receive treatment in specialist wards in district general hospitals. He went on:

> Now look and see what are the implications of these bold words. They imply nothing less than the elimination of by far the greater part of this country's mental hospitals as they exist today. This is a colossal undertaking, not so much in the new physical provision which it involves, as in the sheer inertia of mind and matter which it requires to be overcome. There they stand, isolated, majestic, imperious, brooded over by the gigantic water-tower and chimney combined, rising unmis-takable and daunting out of the countryside ... Do not for a moment underestimate their powers of resistance to our assault.[2]

As a student, David Sainsbury visited Fulbourn Hospital,
built as the county asylum for Cambridgeshire in 1858.

By 1976, the fifteen-year horizon Powell set in his speech,
not a single mental hospital had closed. Numbers of acute beds
had fallen, but admissions were still rising as 'revolving door'
patients made more frequent but shorter stays. The hospitals were
expensive to run: one estimate suggests they absorbed 80 per
cent of mental health resources while caring for only 20 per cent
of people with mental health needs.[3] Community mental health
teams, where they existed, struggled to help former patients to
make the transition into the community. Rare but distressing
instances of disturbed individuals causing harm to themselves
or others always received disproportionate coverage and engen-
dered public anxiety. Meanwhile writers such as Thomas Szasz
and survivors such as Judi Chamberlin challenged the very
basis of psychiatry, arguing that conventional diagnosis and

physical treatments, especially when coercive, constituted unacceptable oppression and inequality in the relationship between patient and doctor. A series of scandals highlighted examples of inhumane and abusive treatment in long-stay institutions.

David Sainsbury had imagined that, one day, neuroscience might provide some of the answers to the distress caused by mental illness, but he understood that such a day was very far off. The treatments in use at the time still included so-called 'psychosurgery', electroconvulsive therapy and a variety of strong drugs. None was based on a scientific understanding of the physical basis of the illness. So he concluded that the best way to contribute was to carry out research to evaluate new models of care that were both humane and cost-effective, and to try to influence policy by disseminating the results.

Toe in the water

By the mid-1970s, piecemeal initiatives were under way around the country to develop new models of caring in the community for people whose mental health was fragile. David Sainsbury's mother Lisa was a supporter of the Richmond Fellowship, a charity founded in the 1960s by a young Dutch theology student, Elly Jansen, to support people with mental illnesses outside psychiatric hospitals through providing halfway houses. In its annual report of 1975, Gatsby listed 'Mental Health' for the first time as one of three key areas of interest, and gave £20,000 to the Robert & Lisa Sainsbury Charitable Fund to be spent on the Richmond Fellowship. Also in 1975, grants went to: the Cherchefelle Housing Association, which provided similar services in Surrey; the Psychiatric Rehabilitation Association, to help it open a restaurant and day centre; and One-to-One, a charity that trained volunteers to go into psychiatric hospitals and talk to the patients.

Such grant-making, however, did not meet the ambition of David Sainsbury and the Gatsby trustees to change the landscape of mental health care provision. The chance to do that came from London health authorities, notably Lewisham and Hackney, who asked for grants to enable them to evaluate the effectiveness of their developing community-based projects. Gatsby funded a full-time research worker within Lewisham's Multi-professional Psychiatric Research Unit, headed by consultant psychiatrist Douglas Brough. The unit was based in the Mental Health Advice Centre, an innovative walk-in clinic established by a multidisciplinary team, which later incorporated a crisis intervention team to visit people whose difficulties made it unlikely that they would present themselves at the Centre. An evaluation of the centre after four years suggested that it was reaching a group of clients whose needs were previously unmet.[4] Gatsby also supported St Bartholomew's Hospital to set up a Community Psychiatric Research and Support Unit at Hackney Hospital to assess the needs of discharged patients, and to work with them to try to prevent readmission.

The work supported by Gatsby up till this point met David Sainsbury's description of 'splashing about in the shallows' – getting involved in the field, getting to know the right people and becoming known in turn. In 1985, the Gatsby trustees began to adopt a more proactive approach. Brough and his colleague Jim Watson, Professor of Psychiatry at Guy's Hospital Medical School, requested funds to set up a research unit to explore models of psychiatric care. Gatsby gave a grant of £200,000 to the recently merged United Medical and Dental Schools of Guy's and St Thomas' Hospitals (UMDS) to set up the National Unit for Psychiatric Research and Development (NUPRD). Appointed as Research Director was psychiatrist Thomas Craig, now Professor of Community and Social Psychiatry at the Institute of Psychiatry, Psychology & Neuroscience, King's College London. 'At first there was just me, another young psychiatrist [Jed Boardman], a psychologist [Paul Clifford] and a social worker [Liz Sayce], working out of the third floor of the nurses' home at Lewisham

Hospital,' he says. The group began to write about the case-management approach – looking at the whole individual, not just a set of symptoms, and paying attention to issues such as employment and housing. With advice from David Goldberg at the University of Manchester, they also did work on improving the skills of general practitioners in managing patients with mental health problems. With Sayce, Craig carried out studies of the early community mental health centres, and ran the first conference, held in Cirencester, on community mental health. Sayce, who is now Chief Executive of Disability Rights UK, initiated work on patients' rights and the survivor movement.

NUPRD also supported work elsewhere, including an evaluation of the Archer Centre in Birmingham, where Max Birchwood was working with young men who had had a first episode of psychosis. 'It was the first example of early intervention in psychosis,' says Craig, 'which became the thing we should all do. Birmingham produced very influential research, which later became part of the implementation plan for crisis intervention, early intervention and assertive outreach.'

In 1989, there was a change of gear. NUPRD changed its name to the less unwieldy Research and Development in Psychiatry (RDP), and moved to more salubrious offices in Borough High Street. It was governed as a separate charity with its own trustees (Judith Portrait and Christopher Stone, the Gatsby trustees), while its staff continued to be notionally employed by UMDS.* 'We moved into a different league,' says Craig. 'We went from seven or eight enthusiastic researchers to something much more public-facing.'

The previous year the energetic deputy chairman of Sainsbury's, Sir Roy Griffiths, had produced a report for Margaret

---

*Around 2000, UMDS merged with King's College London, which by then included the Institute of Psychiatry, bringing the unit administratively under the remit of King's.

Thatcher's government entitled *Community Care: Agenda for Action*. This became the basis for the 1989 White Paper *Caring for People*, enacted in 1990 as the National Health Service and Community Care Act. The Act introduced a more market-based approach to health and social care. Regional health authorities, and to some extent fundholding GPs, became 'purchasers' of care from 'providers', the hospitals and other services that were reorganised into NHS Trusts. Mental health care had always straddled an uncomfortable divide between health services and social services departments funded by local government. With a radical shake-up of services in prospect, the need for informed advocacy was even more pressing.

While RDP was producing excellent research, it remained effectively an academic organisation and its profile was not high. 'We produced two policy documents,' says Craig; 'one on case management, and one on training GPs. But we were much more formative and academic in those days. I remember a discussion with David Sainsbury, when he said, "Publications gather dust on the shelves. How are you actually getting your messages out there?" I learned a lot from that.' Craig had by this time been appointed to his current chair at the Institute of Psychiatry. He was still directing RDP and had become involved in the government-funded Homeless Mentally Ill Initiative in London. A small project that RDP had funded to work with the homelessness charity St Mungo's had mushroomed into a £25 million, multi-agency, London-wide project, which ran alongside the even larger Rough Sleepers Initiative. 'We got involved in leading that programme,' says Craig, 'though it wasn't funded by Gatsby. There was a tension between the independence of RDP and the aspirations of the medical school.' Something had to give, and in 1991 Craig stepped down as Director of RDP to focus on his clinical work and the homelessness programme.[5]

A new face, a new name

One of those who applied for his post was a young Dutch psychiatrist, Matthijs (Matt) Muijen, then a senior registrar at the Institute of Psychiatry. He had just completed a PhD comparing community-based crisis intervention and outreach in severely mentally ill patients with conventional inpatient care. The Daily Living Programme had been launched at the Maudsley Hospital in 1987, under the direction of the Professor of Experimental Psychopathology, Isaac Marks. It was the first attempt in the UK to replicate controlled studies in Madison in the USA, Montreal in Canada and Sydney in Australia that had reported lower costs and somewhat better outcomes in patients cared for out of hospital than those admitted to long-stay wards. These programmes deployed 'assertive outreach', a concept developed in the USA and designed to cut acute hospital stays through frequent visits to patients at home by well-trained multidisciplinary teams.

The Maudsley study showed that home care could reduce the duration of inpatient admissions by 80 per cent, even in severely mentally ill patients. Muijen was the principal research worker on the study, and keen to find a way to spread its message further. Today he is head of mental health for the World Health Organization's European region. 'I recall thinking in those days that what I was really interested in was dissemination,' he says. He had been heavily influenced by the work of Everett Rogers, whose 1962 book *Diffusion of Innovations* charts the way new ideas spread through social systems. 'I was interested in translation between basic research and practice. And I saw [the job at RDP] as a wonderful opportunity.' Before his interview with the Professor of Psychiatry at Guy's he was subjected to a grilling by de Quetteville, something of a culture shock for the young Dutchman, who had previously had little to do with what he perceived as 'the English aristocracy'. To his surprise he got the job, over the heads of more senior candidates. De Quetteville summoned him again a few days after starting, and told him in no uncertain terms to cut the unit's costs: it was funding its support staff by adding large overheads to its applications for project grants. 'The projects were almost an add-on to these large internal costs,' says Muijen. 'That was something Hugh de Quetteville had identified as needing to change.'

De Quetteville also told him that a measure of his success would be 'how well known *you* will be'. Muijen set about raising the profile of the unit – as well as his own. As he wrote in the *Journal of Mental Health*, there was a lot to do: 'So much psychiatric practice is based on tradition, and so many new ways of practice are evolving at the moment that the challenge for a unit such as RDP is not to find areas to evaluate, but rather to prioritise.'[6]

Muijen quickly found a mentor in Trevor Hadley, founder of the Center for Mental Health Policy and Services Research at the University of Pennsylvania, who had previously been a commissioner for state mental health agencies in the USA. 'Matt was really smart and engaging but also pretty green,' says Hadley. 'His PhD was an impressive piece of work, but the policy stuff was staggering for him.' Hadley spent time in the unit on several sabbatical visits, and wrote a 'white paper' as an agenda to guide its strategy. 'It was never adopted as such, but it probably guided some of his thinking,' he says.

In the first few years after Muijen's appointment the unit underwent rapid changes in its profile and administration. Conscious of the importance of branding, he proposed changing the name from the unmemorable RDP to the Sainsbury Centre for Mental Health (SCMH). The Sainsbury family approved the use of the name, and it came into effect in February 1992. 'That was very significant,' says Muijen, 'because it meant the Sainsbury family supported mental health, even though the funding came from Gatsby only.' With an overall budget of £1.2 million in 1993/4, the Centre was in a good position to expand, using its resources to leverage further grants from the Department of Health, health authorities, social services departments and other voluntary and charitable trusts.

In 1994, Gatsby put up a further £3 million to establish the Mental Health Development Initiative (sometimes known as the Sainsbury Initiative), a joint project with the Department of Health to develop and evaluate innovative models of care in the community for people with severe mental illness and their families. Launched in February 1994 with great fanfare at the Whitbread Brewery by the Secretary of State for Health, Virginia Bottomley, and David Sainsbury, it received almost 300 applications from regional mental health services. Eight (six in England and two in Wales) were funded for three years. 'Up till then we had been one of several charities working with the Conservative government,' says Muijen. 'Now we had found a role.'

Roy Griffiths was invited to chair the steering group for the Initiative, but after he died suddenly in March 1994, David Sainsbury attended many of the meetings and chaired them himself. Also on the steering group was Lionel Joyce, then chief executive of Newcastle's mental health services and chair of the National Association of Health Authorities and Trusts. Joyce had unique insight into the needs of mental health service users: as well as running mental hospitals, he had himself been hospitalised after a crisis as a young man, and periodically received further treatment. Having introduced a number of innovations in Newcastle, he had become an influential voice in both government and academic circles, and he became a friend and ally to Matt Muijen. Now retired from the NHS, he chairs the Newcastle charity the Road to Recovery Trust. 'The Sainsbury Initiative started over a lunch with David and Susie Sainsbury and [Rabbi] Julia Neuberger', says Joyce, 'in a suite at the Sainsbury offices. I had been advancing the argument that to win £1 million people would make an effort, and enough people making an effort to win it would in itself change their thinking.' In the event the 'pump-priming' grants to health authorities were each worth £500,000, but Joyce's point still stood.

One of the successful applicants to the scheme was the mental health service in the Yardley/Hodge Hill area of north Birmingham. Like south London, where SCMH was based, this is an inner-city area with a mainly working-class population and a higher than average level of need. The health authority recruited John Hoult, who had introduced the pioneering reforms of community mental health in Sydney, Australia, to lead its programme. The aim of the Psychiatric Emergency Team (PET – later known as the Home Treatment Team) was to provide a safe, effective and economically viable alternative to inpatient care for people with severe mental illness, enable more people to receive care, and so free up resources from inpatient care for longer-term, home-based care for those with severe needs. The multidisciplinary team included mental health nurses, social workers, community support workers, a psychologist and cover from consultant psychiatrists. Critically, the service was available twenty-four hours a day. During the first three years of the programme, the number of acute beds in the area was reduced by half.

The evaluation of the PET initiative[7] concluded that costs were significantly lower for the patients recruited into the home care programme relative to those admitted to hospital in a neighbouring area, once start-up costs had been absorbed and the benefits of cutting the number of acute beds had been realised. The level of staff satisfaction on the PET team was high relative to community mental health nurses or ward staff generally, and the patients liked being cared for at home. There was no increase in the number of incidents, such as suicide, violent assaults or self-harm, all of which remained at a low level. As a model of service provision, it had many advantages over a conventional nine-till-five service that left casualty departments to pick up out-of-hours emergencies. At the same time, it was well integrated into a comprehensive service that was oriented towards community provision, including an assertive outreach team and a community care team, funded with the savings from the closure of acute beds.

The Birmingham model helped to accelerate a movement away from hospital-based care wherever possible. 'Getting people to switch their thinking was really hard,' says Joyce. 'What the Initiative did was to give a shift to the system to move it in another direction. Not instantly, but there's no doubt it contributed significantly to a different attitude to patients and staff.' Not all the Initiative's projects were equally successful, but overall they demonstrated that it was possible to develop integrated services at a local level that met the needs of people in crisis (largely due to the Birmingham experience); and that assertive outreach was a cost-effective alternative to hospitalisation for severely mentally ill people with chaotic lives. It also identified blocks to reform: lack of 'ownership' of the reform agenda at a strategic level, and 'territorial intransigence'.[8]

The impact of the initiative can still be seen today, but the overall picture is patchy. 'The authorities that did well at the time of the initiative, such as Birmingham, are still good,' says Matthew Williams, who joined Gatsby in 1997 as grants executive on the mental health programme. 'But those that were bad are still bad. This type of structure works only if the savings from acute hospitals are transferred to community care. And it's very difficult to get money out of hospitals – they're like black holes.'

Unlike in the USA, where there are dedicated multiprofessional mental health agencies, money for mental health in the UK comes from both health and social services budgets. A year after the bonhomie of the Sainsbury Initiative launch, Trevor Hadley and Matt Muijen published an article in the *Health Service Journal* entitled 'The Initiatives War', asking whether 'overlapping responsibilities and conflicts of interest are putting mental health services at risk'.[9] The journal put a photo of Virginia Bottomley

Director of the SCMH Matt Muijen's cover story in the *Health Service Journal* in 1995 challenged health secretary Virginia Bottomley to integrate funding for mental health and social services.

on the cover, apparently in the dock to face charges. 'It created quite a stir,' says Hadley. 'I didn't even know who Bottomley was. A week later I flew in, having been on a plane all night, and Matt said, "We're going to this dinner." Bottomley was speaking at the dinner, and someone was primed to ask a question about this paper. And they dragged me up to defend our paper in front of her.'

SCMH was no more successful than any other agency at winning the battle over integrated funding, but in other areas its work on policy and practice had a major impact.

First service
The commitment to disseminate the results of its research

findings led SCMH inexorably towards service development and implementation, which began to take priority over pure research. As Muijen admits, 'The academic side was a bit of a blind spot. I never really tried to integrate with academic circles: it wasn't a world I felt comfortable with.' The Sainsbury Initiative, for example, he frankly admits was 'lousy research': each funded agency designed its own project, so the findings overall were not necessarily comparable. Yet the Initiative was effective in changing the way services were delivered: 'The priority was implementation,' says Muijen.

The Gatsby trustees were certainly satisfied with the way things were going. Five years after Muijen's appointment they invited Professor Howard Goldman, a world leader in evaluating mental health services from the University of Maryland, to conduct a review of its performance so far. Goldman's report led to another major restructuring. 'I thought the funding was too project-based, and too diverse,' he says. 'I thought Gatsby should provide infrastructure funding for five years, so that Matt and his advisors could make more strategic decisions.' The trustees agreed, and from 1997 Gatsby provided a rolling programme of substantial grants that covered both core costs and the costs of activities under the headings of research, service development, policy, training and communications.

Given the freedom to plan strategically, Muijen appointed directors in each of these areas. As director of policy he recruited Andrew McCulloch, who was previously a senior civil servant in the Department of Health in charge of mental health policy; he had commissioned Tom Craig to evaluate the Homeless Mentally Ill Initiative, and overseen the Department of Health's contribution to the Sainsbury Initiative, so he knew the Centre well. After leaving SCMH, McCulloch became Chief Executive of the Mental Health Foundation; he is now the Chief Executive of Picker Institute Europe, which provides research and consultancy on patient-centred care. 'I saw the Sainsbury Initiative as an opportunity for practice to be developed in an evidence-based way,' he says. 'That's where Matt and I saw eye to eye – we like evidence. We also don't have much time for the full panoply of academic rigour, because by that time it's too late.'

Geraldine Strathdee, who was Director of Service Development at SCMH from 1995 to 1998, was National Clinical Director of Mental Health for NHS England from 2013 to 2016. Paul O'Halloran, Head of Training and Practice Development, went on to be a leader in service development for the National Institute for Mental Health in England (NIMHE). Richard Ford, Head of Service Evaluation, also went to a senior position in NIMHE. 'Our best strength was in appointing the right people,' says Muijen.

Professional development became an increasingly important plank of SCMH's position. It ran courses and conferences for nurses, general practitioners, clinical psychologists, social workers and psychiatrists, increasing their confidence in their roles and spreading a consistent message on policy and practice. Fees did not cover the costs of developing and delivering their own courses, but the Centre was turning over £4–5 million a year, with core funding accounting for half that figure. 'We could use the core grant to subsidise courses,' says Muijen. Working with Middlesex University, SCMH also developed an innovative and flexible postgraduate diploma in mental health studies, still available today as an MSc.

'We had great conferences', says McCulloch, 'which really energised staff in all specialisms. They realised that they could have a valued, evidence-based role. That has had lasting benefits.'

Policy priorities

Soon after the election of the Labour government in May 1997, David Sainsbury (who had just entered the House of Lords) took Muijen and McCulloch to 10 Downing Street to meet Robert Hill, Prime Minister Tony Blair's policy advisor on health. They briefed Hill on assertive outreach and how it could be incorporated into community-based mental health policy. 'It was probably the right message at the right time,' says Muijen. The following year, Sainsbury took up the post of Minister for Science and Innovation and 'became invisible' to Matt, under the strict conditions that prevented him from having any decision-making role in his charity while holding office (see Chapter 7).

SCMH had had good relationships with the Department of Health under the previous administration: it was part of a policy group pushing for change along with Mind, the National Schizo-phrenia Fellowship and the Royal College of Psychiatrists, as well as having good contacts with the heads of regional mental health services. 'The election of Labour was a transformative change,' says Muijen. 'There were people at the Department of Health who had the same agenda.' As well as having Andrew McCulloch on his team, he benefited from the advice of Philip Hunt, the former CEO of the National Association of Health Authorities and Trusts (NAHAT; later the NHS Confederation), who had also been made a life peer in 1997. For several months, before he became a Labour whip, Hunt spent a couple of days a week in the SCMH office advising on policy. 'I gave them advice on how to be more influential,' he says. 'Because of my knowledge of the NHS, I was able to advise them about how key policy papers could be got across to key senior people. They were doing really good-quality, excellent research. You could always have confidence in the quality of the stuff, and you wanted to make sure that what they produced had an impact.'

An enduring difficulty with planning mental health services is how you define mental health. Some studies of the prevalence of mental illness come up with a figure of 37 per cent of the popu-lation per year. 'That includes everything from mild distress to schizophrenia,' says Muijen. 'Policymakers cannot handle that. A more realistic figure is that 8 per cent per year suffer from mental disorders. That's manageable.' Even within that group, however, there is a wide range of severity and symptoms. Those that demand most in terms of resources are, not surprisingly, the most severely ill, and it is this group that presents the greatest challenge for community-based care. The isolated but distressing case of Christopher Clunis, a patient diagnosed with schizophrenia who had 'fallen through the net' of community care and stabbed a stranger to death in 1992, gained disproportionate publicity, and policymakers were motivated as much by public safety as by the needs of service users.

Armed with the experience of his PhD research, and some of the findings from the Sainsbury Initiative, Muijen and his colleagues had carried out a review of ways of approaching severely mentally ill patients who were not voluntarily engaging with services and so at risk of social exclusion. *Keys to Engagement* emphatically restated that assertive outreach in the context of a well-managed community mental health service could be a safe, appropriate and cost-effective approach to severely mentally ill patients.[10] It was exactly the message the new government was looking for, and SCMH was perfectly positioned to get that message across. 'It was everyone's fantasy of a public affairs model,' says McCulloch, who had contributed to the research. 'Influential people in their field take a report that they have generated, inject it at the top of the policy tree, and the department is told to implement it. Of course, the buy-in was already there, so the report was in effect implemented, as far as any voluntary sector report would ever be implemented by government.'

Along with other voluntary sector organisations such as Mind and the Mental Health Foundation, the Centre provided expert advice to the Department of Health as it developed the policy document *Modernising Mental Health Services: Safe, Sound and Supportive*, published in January 1998. This introduced a National Service Framework (NSF) for Mental Health, which included crisis teams, assertive outreach teams and early intervention teams in addition to the existing network of community care teams. Muijen supported the NSF, but was anxious to retain an independent stance, and did not hesitate to publish his view that its implementation was too prescriptive, and that it worked well only in cities such as London and Birmingham.

In 2001, SCMH delivered a report commissioned by the NSF Workforce Action Team entitled *The Capable Practitioner*, recommending flexibility across the specialisms that made up the various teams.[11] 'Capability extends the concept of competence to include the ability to apply the necessary knowledge, skills and attitudes to a range of complex and changing settings,' wrote the authors. 'The Capability Framework combines the notions of the effective practitioner with that of the reflective practitioner.' Andrew McCulloch (who was not an author of the report) says that he is still using this capability framework in his work on person-centred care, 'because I can't find anything better'.

The Centre also developed policy on issues such as workforce, acute care and the needs of poorly served communities such as ethnic minorities. Another landmark publication was *Breaking the Circles of Fear,* which exposed the inequities of mental health provision as experienced by African and Caribbean communities.[12] The review panel, chaired by sociologist Shirley Tate, documented what it called the 'circles of fear'. 'When prejudice and the fear of violence influence risk assessments and decisions on treatment,' wrote the authors, 'responses are likely to be dominated by a heavy reliance on medication and restriction. Service users become reluctant to ask for help or to comply with treatment ... resulting in a downward spiral ... in which staff see service users as potentially dangerous and service users perceive services as harmful.' Until that point, the issue had been barely addressed, but Gatsby funded further follow-up work that eventually led to changes in policy.

As part of its policy discussions with the Department of Health, Muijen and his colleagues had urged the establishment of a regional development and training network, coordinated by

SCMH, to take best practice into local services. The Department of Health liked the idea, but preferred to take it in house. In 2001, it set up the NIMHE under 'mental health tsar' Professor Louis Appleby. This was a disappointment to Muijen, as it would operate in a similar space to SCMH (and indeed hired several senior SCMH staff), though without the impartiality of a non-governmental body. He felt that it was the beginning of the end of his time as chief executive. 'I had reinvented the Sainsbury Centre more than once,' he says. 'I did not know what else to do.' By 2003, Christopher Stone, the Gatsby chair of trustees who was also a trustee of SCMH, was gently suggesting it was time he moved on. 'I always felt fairly treated by Gatsby,' says Muijen. 'It was a very constructive partnership. David Sainsbury was the voice of reason. I felt he really looked for value in the projects he funded, and really wanted to do something good.'

With so many voices feeding into the process, and so many changes since, it is difficult to quantify the impact SCMH had on the transformation of mental health services that took place in the late 1990s and early 2000s. But Philip Hunt believes it was significant. 'In a difficult area SCMH had this very energised, innovative organisation that was strongly evidence based,' he says. 'I believe it had a real impact on the development of policy both at government level and out in the field.' Trevor Hadley is equally positive. 'I was always impressed with the place,' he says. 'There were a lot of smart people around. I think they were always focused on the right thing – not necessarily the right answers, but the right questions.'

Where need is greatest
Angela Greatley, who had come from the King's Fund to succeed Andrew McCulloch as director of policy at SCMH in 2002, took over as director when Muijen left in 2004. The trustees felt that SCMH had become overextended and lacking in research focus, while its excellent initiatives in service development had largely

been taken up by other bodies (a success, in Gatsby's terms). Greatley oversaw a major restructuring, cutting the number of staff from seventy to twenty by 2006. 'The Centre had grown, because the generosity of the funding and the ability to match that with Department of Health funding meant there were lots of areas that could be explored,' she says, 'but it had become unwieldy, and we were living beyond our means. One of the things that I became engaged in was making it a tighter ship.'

Meanwhile she reoriented the work of SCMH from service development to research in the area of social inequality. As head of research as well as policy, she had taken over the team that was disseminating the findings of the *Breaking the Circles of Fear* report. 'We'd all say it didn't go as far as we wanted,' she says, 'but it really influenced the DoH about the need to address equality issues in the delivery of services. I took that through into my time as chief executive.' It was clear that, despite the reforms of the late 1990s, mental health services were still failing to meet the needs of many vulnerable people. 'Mental health and well-being are rarely a matter for individual lifestyle choice and are closely connected to social and family environments,' Greatley argued at the time. 'Discrimination and stigma have to be tackled head on.'[13] She and her colleagues promoted the concept of 'recovery', defined as a personal route to overcoming challenges rather than a 'cure' in a medical sense.

Following the advice of a second peer review by Howard Goldman, the Gatsby trustees urged the Centre to concentrate on two obstacles that blight the lives of mental health service users: the criminal justice system, and unemployment. 'Employment was sitting there as an issue,' says Greatley. 'Work is what most of the rest of us do. If you are able to work, you are participating in your local community, following a professional career, earning money – not being consigned to a scrapheap. It was a huge topic for us.'

Bob Grove led research into the practice of 'individual

placement and support', developed in the USA, as a route to paid employment for people with mental health problems. 'A lot of people in the mental health field thought that employment was a bad thing if people are ill,' says Andy Bell, former head of communications at the Centre and now co-director. 'Actually, work is part of the recovery journey.' To date, numerous randomised controlled trials have shown that putting people into jobs and supporting them there leads to higher rates of employment and lower costs than giving them training and then launching them on to the jobs market.[14] Half of mental health providers in the UK now offer some form of employment support, and in 2015 the government announced further funding for its implementation across the country.

It had also been apparent for years that the prisons were full of people with mental health problems. 'We asked what it would take to treat people in prison more effectively, or to divert them from ever going to prison in the first place,' says Greatley. She recruited former mental health nurse Sean Duggan from the Department of Health, where he had been leading a programme in the same area, to direct the new programme on criminal justice. A hard-hitting report examined the experience of almost 100 prisoners incarcerated in the West Midlands, finding that 'mental illness was not the exception but the rule', and that even where mental health teams were available, boredom and isolation exacerbated mental health problems while provision for rehabilitation on release was inadequate.[15]

SCMH also carried out a study of diversion and liaison services, which attempt to divert people with mental health difficulties who are up before the courts into the care of mental health services rather than the criminal justice system. It found that such services were available to only one in five of people who might benefit, but that, where they were, they cut costs and reduced the risk of reoffending.[16] These and other SCMH reports were extensively quoted in Lord Bradley's 2009 report[17] into people with mental health problems or learning difficulties in the criminal justice system; the strong business case has led to funding being allocated specifically to liaison and diversion services, which should extend to the whole country by 2020.

At the same time, SCMH researchers continued with analyses of the economic costs to the country of not dealing well with mental health problems, something that had begun under Muijen's leadership and one of the Centre's key contributions to the sector. 'Gatsby did not shy away from unpopular areas,' says Sean Duggan. 'It takes time to get interventions to the point where government will invest – which they have in both criminal justice and employment.' SCMH members also played a prominent role in the Mental Health Alliance, a group of some dozens of organisations that came together in 1999 to campaign for improvements to the Mental Health Act of 1983. Andy Bell served as its chair. After years of battling and the scrapping of the first draft bill, the amended Mental Health Act was passed in 2007, including provision for independent advocacy for people subjected to coercive treatment either in inpatient wards or in the community, and deprivation of liberty safeguards to protect the interests of people who lack mental capacity.[18]

On its own two feet
On leaving his post as science minister in 2006, David Sainsbury reviewed all the Gatsby projects, and decided that the policy environment no longer provided an opportunity for SCMH to contribute to really transformative change. Greatley and her colleagues were told that Gatsby would no longer provide core funding to SCMH after 2009. 'That was a difficult moment,' says Greatley, who decided to time her retirement to coincide with the inevitable reorganisation. She continues:

Although personally I learned a great deal from working with Gatsby about philanthropy and its incredible value to communities. It's an important motivation to say, 'What's the next thing we should do?' so that they don't create dependence. Once an organisation is able to engage other grant givers, Gatsby can move on and think about what else to do with their money. I understood that, but it was hard for the staff.

Duggan and Grove became joint chief executives, and since 2011 Duggan has headed the Centre, with Andy Bell as his deputy. 'It was hard,' says Duggan, 'but I'd come from working in the NHS, where changes happen all the time. We had to come up with a solution. One was to wind down, and migrate the programmes to other charities. But I thought we could continue.' After considering various name changes, they decided simply to drop 'Sainsbury' from the title and become the Centre for Mental Health. It had become such an integral part of the landscape that many of its previous partners – the charities Mind, Rethink and the Mental Health Foundation, together with the NHS Confederation and the Royal College of Psychiatrists (RCPsych) – stepped in and offered support. Instead of taking Gatsby's farewell grant of £6 million all at once, Duggan and his colleagues worked to develop alternative sources of income, and did not need to take the final instalment until 2016. The Centre is now sustained by a mixture of consultancy fees, grants from trusts and foundations, government grants and fundraising. It has a new board, chaired by Lady Vallance, and including Lord Bradley and representatives of other mental health agencies.

The Centre remains as active as ever, and has begun to develop new interests, such as services for children and young people. 'Over the past five years, the world has not stood still,' says Andy Bell. 'While we retain our focus on employment and criminal justice, it was pushing us to think about mental health problems in children, and in perinatal mental health. The sooner you can intervene, the more effective you can be.' A report giving a cost–benefit analysis of various interventions in children's mental health has been extremely influential in gaining increased investment in this area,[19] cited by the Department of Health's Child and Adolescent Mental Health Services Taskforce that recommended improvements to services in 2015.[20]

After the 2015 election, the Centre went back into the policy fray, in partnership with five other mental health charities, to challenge the Conservative government to value mental health and physical health equally.[21] That year the Chancellor's autumn spending review announced further funding for mental health services: however, as Andy Bell pointed out in the policy group's response, there were 'sizeable question marks' about the impact of cuts in local government and public health on people with mental illness. 'We are simply not investing enough in preventing mental health problems in the first place,' he said, 'leaving people to become more unwell and in need of more long-term and costly treatment.'[22]

Over twenty-five years, Gatsby made grants totalling almost £50 million for research in mental health, mostly to or through the SCMH. The vagaries of funding in an age of austerity aside, a huge transformation has taken place in how health and social services in the UK respond to the needs of users. In 2014, a study by the Economist Intelligence Unit judged the UK to be the second-most effective country in Europe at integrating people with mental illness into society.[23] To quote Philip Hunt once more, 'The Centre is a classic example of how charitable moneys can be used to make big change. The ultimate test must be: has it helped to change the way people with mental health issues are looked after? Has it helped to improve the quality? I'm convinced that it has.'

There is still work to be done, and the Centre for Mental Health continues to play a key role in highlighting areas of need. In 2016, it produced another report, commissioned by the NHS England Mental Health Taskforce as it grappled with the

Treasury's demands for 'improved productivity', setting out nine priorities for service improvement where there is good evidence that interventions are cost-effective.[24] Meanwhile, Gatsby has come full circle: its neuroscience programme is now supporting a project to educate psychiatrists in the latest neuroscience research, which may have implications for the diagnosis and treatment of mental disorders (see Chapter 8).

A voice for children

David and Susie Sainsbury married in 1973, and had three daughters. Susie gave up her career in publishing to become a full-time mother, but her tireless energy soon saw her becoming involved with her husband's philanthropic activities. The areas closest to her heart were children's charities and the arts, neither of them a priority for David Sainsbury (except in his continuing support for the Sainsbury Centre for Visual Arts, his parents' legacy – see Chapter 9). But from around 1980 he and the trustees spent up to £1 million per year (later rising to over £5 million) on projects for 'disadvantaged children' and Susie became their lead advisor in these areas.

Initially the trustees made multiple small grants to organisations delivering services to children with special needs, such as the Polka Theatre, which mounted productions that could be enjoyed by children with visual impairments, and a wide range of voluntary and public sector bodies supporting children in and out of school. School-Home Support Services (now School-Home Support) was one of these early beneficiaries, receiving a £10,000 grant in 1984. At the time, the charity operated in East London, providing trained support workers to help children who were truanting, at risk of exclusion or in difficulties at home. With steadily increasing support from Gatsby and other sources of funds, School-Home Support Services had extended its reach to 100 schools in ten London boroughs by 2005, and is now a national agency.[25]

Gatsby never mounted its own programmes in this area, as it came to do in its other areas of interest. However, from the mid-1990s the trustees increasingly made larger grants to organisations that combined research with delivering services. In 1991, the retired Head of Children's Services for Oxfordshire, Barbara Kahan, had co-authored the report of an inquiry on 'pindown', a form of solitary confinement used as punishment in Staffordshire children's homes. During the 1990s the scandal of the abuse that had routinely occurred in children's residential homes in North Wales began to emerge into the public eye. Kahan, by then Chair of the charity the National Children's Bureau (NCB), began to research the experience of children in residential care, collecting evidence of good practice, which she published as *Growing Up in Groups* (1994).

From 1992, Gatsby made a series of grants, totalling £14 million by 2006, for the work of the residential care unit and other projects at the NCB. Gatsby funds enabled NCB to set up a pupil inclusion unit, addressing the poor school attainment of looked-after children. Its research and service development project, Taking Care of Education, worked with three local authorities – Derby, Harrow and Portsmouth – to provide them with the staff and funding to help strengthen their existing policy and practice, and then to disseminate their findings.[26] It was the first attempt to develop an evidence base for the extra support needed by children in care within the school system. 'The value of the work done by the NCB is not transparent unless you know a lot about it,' says Matthew Williams, who oversaw the disadvantaged children programme at Gatsby along with mental health, 'but it had a real and lasting impact on how things were done. Many points of policy and practice today come from that work.'

When David Sainsbury went into government in 1998, the disadvantaged children programme commanded a budget that was a fixed fraction of the funds available to be distributed, a figure that rose every year. At the same time it had reduced the number of recipients, leaving a few beneficiaries receiving generous support. Unable to consult the settlor's wishes, the trustees continued to fund the kinds of causes they had funded previously. Following Susie Sainsbury's interests, they paid particular attention to the needs of children with speech and language difficulties. A succession of substantial grants went to two charities working in this area. I CAN, which develops programmes for children at all stages of schooling and runs residential schools, received grants to support its continuing professional development and accreditation programmes for teachers.[27] The ACE Centre in Oxfordshire (and to a lesser extent its sister organisation in Lancashire) received grants to support its work for children that need technology, such as electronic speaking aids, to help them communicate.[28] And in 2000, Gatsby initiated an adventurous ten-year project, Big Wide Talk, that brought children, practitioners and parents together in region-ally organised 'theatres of learning' to give all three groups an equal voice.[29]

While thousands of individual children benefited from Gatsby support to children's charities over more than twenty-five years, David Sainsbury did not feel that the projects met his ambition to achieve 'real, systemic change'. On his re-engagement with Gatsby after 2006, he decided to discontinue funding for disad-vantaged children, and Gatsby grants were wound down over the following three years. Since 2012, Gatsby has provided annual funding to Susie Sainsbury's charity the Backstage Trust, which funds engagement with disadvantaged children through live performance (see Chapter 10).

Case study: Making use of service users

The SCMH was a pioneer in making the experience of users of mental health services central to its research programme. The Centre itself employed a number of people with a history of interaction with such services. 'At one point as many as 10 per cent of our staff were service users,' says Muijen. 'I believe that the people best able to judge the quality of care are the users.' One of these was Diana Rose, who Muijen recruited part-time to run a short-term research project after hearing her speak about her voluntary work with a service users' group. Rose, who has bipolar disorder, had been medically retired from an academic post almost a decade before.

'While I was there [at SCMH],' she says, 'Sally Hargreaves of Kensington & Chelsea and Westminster Health Authority approached Matt, wanting to know how people who had come out of the old hospitals were faring on tier 3 of the care programme approach. Her idea was to get them interviewed by other service users. I got the job and was amazed. I thought I was on the scrapheap.'

She began by recruiting a user group of twelve to fifteen people who were or had been in the care of the Authority, explaining the project at local user group meetings, work projects and day centres and asking for volunteers. The group then met monthly at the SCMH offices. 'The first thing we did was make a questionnaire,' she says. 'That took about five meetings. Then we did some training, getting them used to asking and being asked the questions.' Meanwhile she was encountering some opposition to the idea that service users could report reliably on the care they were receiving. 'I had the database of people we wanted to interview,' she says. 'I randomly sampled a hundred of them and sent letters via their key workers. They [the key workers] were really resistant. In the end we interviewed thirty-nine people.' She herself never doubted the value of the exercise. 'We took as our starting point the view that interviews with people with serious and enduring mental health problems can give rise to fruitful and valid findings which have implications for policy,' she later wrote.

The results were highly illuminating.[30] The interviewees proved well able to answer questions about the care that they were receiving, and many were satisfied with it, expressing particular gratitude to the community psychiatric nurses who visited them. But a high proportion were either confused about or unaware of the way that provision was structured: only just over half knew who their keyworker was, fewer than half knew what their care plan was, and only half knew who to contact in an emergency. Very few knew that they were regularly reviewed, and none knew that they could invite an advocate to their reviews. Many felt they had insufficient information about the side effects of the drugs they were prescribed and 30 per cent said they were 'overmedicated'. Over 70 per cent had had encounters with the police, and most complained of rough handling: one of the interviewers recorded with distress that three of her interviewees were slightly built women who had been pushed to the ground and handcuffed.

The interviewers, although apprehensive at first, found the process rewarding, worthwhile and confidence-building. The interviewees were happy to talk, and were able to relax, knowing that they were speaking to people who had shared some of their experiences. 'Mostly people were very lonely,' says Rose. 'They had spent years in hospital, now they were alone in the community. A lot of them would keep the interviewer there just to talk.' Rose, together with representatives of the user group, presented the results of the survey to health authority managers and mental health staff, who were able to incorporate the findings into their planning and training. Rose later extended the research to a further five projects with similar findings.

Today she is Professor of User-Led Research at King's College London, where she co-directs the Service User Research Enterprise (SURE). The concept of user-focused monitoring has been widely adopted, and is an integral part of evaluation and improvement of the delivery of service. 'It was very democratic,' says Rose. 'Where I work now many of the people in my team have PhDs, as well as being service users, but the ones who started it mostly hadn't finished school. Some went on to be researchers in mental health trusts. People are open with others that they know can understand.'

4

GROWING AFRICA

Economic development south of the Sahara

In 2014 sub-Saharan African countries received $44.3 billion in overseas aid from donor countries in the Organisation for Economic Cooperation and Development (OECD).[1] A wide range of charities, from the Bill and Melinda Gates Foundation to Send A Cow, focus much if not all of their spending on the same region. Yet, after decades of aid at similar levels, 80 per cent of the population still depends on subsistence agriculture, and the statistics on the well-being of poor farmers throughout the region have barely improved. In the decade following 1990, levels of poverty plummeted in South and East Asia, but in sub-Saharan Africa they remained stubbornly high.[2]

While in 2015 the UN was able to report progress towards its Millennium Development Goals on poverty, primary education, gender equality, infant mortality and other indices, most sub-Saharan countries fell far short of achieving them.[3] Infant mortality remains high, nutrition is poor, a third of children fail to complete primary education, and resilience against shocks such as drought and HIV/AIDS is minimal. In some countries tribalism, or a lack of transparent relationships between business and government, can sometimes undermine attempts to establish good governance and stable civil institutions. Meanwhile donors have to contend with critics of the whole aid business, who argue that it entrenches dependence while companies from donor countries extract more in contracts from the region than the total aid budget.[4]

Any private donor wishing to support change in these countries needs to have generous reserves, not only of money, but of optimism and patience. Gatsby has done so, with its eyes wide open and with a commitment to take risks, learn from its mistakes, and be prepared to adapt its programmes in pursuit of long-term objectives. From the late 1980s the trustees defined Gatsby's mission in Africa as supporting 'small-scale wealth creation in agriculture and manufacturing' in a limited number of countries, also deciding to 'work through local people to develop sustainable projects and ensure any effort was genuinely responsive to local needs'. Since 2007, Gatsby's Africa programme has brought its focus to bear on the transformation of whole market sectors – cotton, textiles, tea, forestry – in East Africa. This strategy has the potential to generate investment, boost national as well as local economies, and raise the living standards of people from many walks of life, including the poorest.

By comparison with national aid agencies such as the United States Agency for International Development (USAID) or the UK's Department for International Development (DFID), development finance institutions such as the World Bank, or major charities and NGOs such as the Gates Foundation or Comic Relief, Gatsby's spending in Africa (£5–7 million per year in the mid-2010s) is small change. It is well positioned, however, through its network of contacts both in Africa and in the donor community, to build partnerships and influence policies well beyond its own programmes.

Why Africa?
Sustainable development had been an interest of David

Sainsbury's since his undergraduate days: Gatsby began to fund work on appropriate technology and development studies in the 1970s (Chapter 2). By the mid-1980s, with serious money to spend, Sainsbury and his trustees were ready to be more ambitious and fund work in developing countries themselves. 'I decided we should focus on Africa, because it was the place with the greatest problems,' says Sainsbury, 'though I had a startling lack of knowledge of how big Africa was.'

For advice he turned to an old family friend, Robert Cassen, a former senior economist at the World Bank and author of several reports on development economics and aid. Cassen subsequently became Director of the Department for International Development at the University of Oxford, and Gatsby helped to support its work. But Cassen's expertise was in India, not Africa. So he invited his fellow development economist Laurence Cockcroft to co-author a paper setting out options for Gatsby support in Africa, and Cockcroft readily agreed.

With twenty years' experience advising governments in Zambia, Tanzania, Cameroon and elsewhere in Africa, Cockcroft felt he had a book in him. Finding himself within the Gatsby circle, he applied for funds to support him while he wrote it. Hugh de Quetteville rejected his application – 'We don't do that kind of thing.' Instead, he invited Cockcroft to become Gatsby's full-time advisor on setting up its own Africa programme, a role he held for more than twenty-five years. Deploying his intimate knowledge of African political and social structures, Cockcroft oversaw a gradual build-up of Gatsby's engagement within Africa, amounting to around £50 million in grants, loans and investments for agricultural technology and small business development by 2010. The book, too, got written.[5]

Raising yields, creating partnerships
Agriculture is vital to the prosperity of many Africans. Yet the spectacular gains in yield experienced in the 'green revolution'

countries such as India, Mexico and Brazil had somehow passed Africa by. Farmers were growing the same crops, using the same methods, battling the same pests, unable to access new varieties or adopt new technologies. 'I saw agriculture as a means to an end,' says Cockcroft. 'I never lost interest in political economy. But raising the incomes of small farmers is fundamental to development in many African countries.'

The first major theme of Gatsby's work in Africa was the dissemination of new agricultural technologies developed in African research institutes in order to increase the yields produced by small-scale farming. Even good-quality science with commercial potential tended to stay on the shelf, as there was no mechanism for encouraging farmers to adopt new seed varieties or other technologies. One of the crops that were causing concern was cassava, widely grown as a staple in East and West Africa, but prey to pests and diseases. Gatsby funded the International Institute of Tropical Agriculture (IITA) in Nigeria to set up a network of farmers in Cameroon who could participate in propagating disease-resistant varieties of cassava. After one false start, they discovered that the most effective way of doing this was through women's groups, selected women being trained as 'farmer teachers' to grow the new varieties in their own plots and educate their fellow group members in their benefits.

Within five years, 100,000 hectares of improved varieties had been planted. 'As researchers, we were trained to evaluate impact, not create it,' said IITA researcher James Whyte at the time, 'but now we see dissemination as part of an integrated R&D process.' Gatsby went on to work with the Rockefeller Foundation to fund the IITA and the Kenya Agricultural Research Institute to develop the same model of dissemination, led by researchers and implemented by 'farmer teachers', in other African countries.

In Uganda, Joseph Mukiibi, a plant pathologist who had revived the Ugandan National Agricultural Research Organisation (NARO) after the fall of Idi Amin, approached Gatsby

Susan Elango (facing camera, centre right), director
of the Cameroon Gatsby Foundation, with members
of a women's group the CGF has supported.

for research funds. Mutation had led to an epidemic of a more
virulent form of the cassava mosaic virus, but within a short time
crossbreeding produced high-yielding, virus-resistant strains of
cassava. However, many farmers reverted to traditional varieties
once the epidemic died down, largely because they tasted better.
Some of the resistant strains remained susceptible to an equally
devastating disease, cassava brown streak disease. NARO
continues its research to develop varieties that are resistant to
both diseases and also have the taste and nutritional qualities
that people expect.

Gatsby's staff soon saw that there might be opportunities
for the plant pathologists funded by Gatsby in Norwich (see
Chapter 5) to collaborate with African colleagues on developing
pest- and disease-resistant varieties. Accordingly Dick Flavell,

Director of the John Innes Centre (JIC) and a key advisor to the Gatsby plant science programme, travelled with Cockcroft to visit flagship research institutes in Africa and set up joint projects. One successful example focused on banana streak virus disease in Uganda and elsewhere. The JIC scientists worked with IITA, which had outreach in Uganda, to identify the genetic sequence of the virus, making it possible to detect the disease in plant tissue. IITA then rapidly propagated virus-free varieties and distributed them to farmers, who evaluated the new varieties. Gatsby later supported the International Network for the Improvement of Banana and Plantain (INIBAP) in developing its collection of disease-free genetic resources for hundreds of varieties of banana and plantain, cryopreserved at the University of Leuven in Belgium and issued as needed to re-establish plantations on small farms hit by pests and disease.

The partnership Flavell brokered between Rothamsted Research, a UK-based agricultural research institute with a strong record in pest management, and the Kenya-based International Centre of Insect Physiology and Ecology (*icipe*) led to one of the most dramatic instances of research translated into improved agricultural practice. *icipe* had been founded in 1970 by the entomologist T. R. Odhiambo, with a mission to develop indigenous methods of pest control. The target of the new partnership was the stem borer moth, a pernicious pest of maize and sorghum, both staples for millions of East African farmers. By studying the way the stem borer interacted with maize and other wild host plants, the researchers, led by Zeyaur Khan of *icipe*, identified wild grasses – Napier grass and Sudan grass – that attracted the females to lay their eggs.

A border of these grasses planted around the maize patch 'pulls' the stem borers away from the crop. Meanwhile a 'push' crop, the legume *Desmodium*, planted among the maize, emits chemicals that deter the moths. As a nitrogen-fixing plant, *Desmodium* improves soil fertility: it also provides forage for

Flourishing push-pull maize plot, underplanted with
Desmodium and with a border of Napier grass.

animals, and unexpectedly proved able to eliminate a pernicious weed called *Striga*, which undermined the early growth of
maize. From 1998, the researchers began encouraging farmers to
adopt this 'push-pull' technology in Kenya and Uganda. Initial
trials were spectacularly successful. By 2014, more than 70,000
farmers were using push-pull methods. An independent study
published in 2010 found that push-pull was 'probably the single
most effective and efficient low-cost technology for removing
major constraints faced by the majority of smallholder farmers
in the region, resulting in an overall and significant improvement of their food security and livelihoods'. Maize yields had
more than tripled. In addition, the extra forage plants meant
that farmers could keep more goats and cows and increase milk
production.[6]

Former Gatsby Chair of Trustees Christopher Stone remembers this project as one of the highlights of his tenure. He says:

> I went to visit a farmer who was participating in the project. The previous year he had had no yield from his maize. This year he was going to harvest a significant crop. As I approached he ran out of his hut, then turned and went back inside and returned wearing a 'Gatsby Stem Borer Project' T-shirt. He grasped my hand and said, 'It is the most wonderful thing I have ever seen in my life.'

A few years later, Stone witnessed the wider impact on the community: children going to school, brick houses instead of tin shacks, new sheds for animals. The project has been cited as an exemplary case study of the sustainable intensification of agriculture based on appropriate scientific research.[7] 'It deserved to be promoted,' says Cockcroft. 'I've never seen a project that so combined novel science and development benefit.'

The African Gatsby Trusts
Side by side with the agricultural projects, Laurence Cockcroft wanted to see independent entities established in African countries that could support small-scale businesses in towns and villages. As he points out, the idea that philanthropy is a purely Western concept is quite mistaken. 'Middle- and upper-class Africans give generously of their time and money,' he says. 'For instance, I've been amazed at how many families have taken AIDS orphans into their households. We in the West have such a structured view of charity – in Africa it's very different.' Between 1991 and 1995, Gatsby provided the funds to establish trusts devoted to supporting small-scale enterprise in Kenya, Cameroon, Tanzania and Uganda. The critical feature of these trusts is that the trustees, including the chairs, are influential people drawn from the local community. Cockcroft himself

was the only exception, having a seat on all the Trust boards as Gatsby's representative. 'Laurence was brilliant,' says David Sainsbury. 'It was very imaginative to set up these trusts, filled with people on the ground who could advise us.'

The Kenya Gatsby Trust (KGT), the first to be established, was developed by Harris Mule, formerly a Permanent Secretary in the Ministry of Finance, and Joe Githongo, head of a successful accountancy business. In Tanzania, where commercial activity was newly permitted after decades of centralised state socialism, Ibrahim Seushi, formerly of the Tanzania Rural Development Bank and a partner in Price Waterhouse, helped Cockcroft to develop a model that would work for the country and chaired the Tanzania Gatsby Trust (TGT) for many years. Seushi continued as an invaluable advisor to other Gatsby Africa projects until his death in 2015. The same approach, working with leading figures from both public and private sectors, proved successful in Cameroon, and in Uganda, where the Uganda Gatsby Trust (UGT) was set up in partnership with Makerere University's Faculty of Technology to promote technology transfer to small and medium-sized enterprises (SMEs). Day-to-day administration has been in the hands of dynamic local general managers, many of them women: Susan Elango in Cameroon, Thithi Watene in Kenya and Olive Luena in Tanzania.

Luena first heard of Gatsby when she was on an Eisenhower Fellowship in 1994, studying enterprise development at Cranfield School of Management in the UK. There she befriended Thithi Watene, who had just become the executive secretary of the Kenya Gatsby Trust. On her return to her job in human resources at a government-owned plastics factory in Dar es Salaam, Luena saw an advertisement for the equivalent post in Tanzania. Applying almost out of curiosity – she had just been made acting general manager of her company, and was already secretary general of an umbrella organisation for Tanzanian NGOs involved in poverty alleviation – she was immediately offered the job. With some trepidation, she accepted. 'I had no office, no employees, no furniture,' she says. 'My daughters, who were doing their A levels, worked as my secretaries in their free time, and even cleaned the office that we rented.'

With an initial budget of £80,000 she set up projects in three areas of Tanzania – Mwanga, Mtwara and Zanzibar – sponsoring existing or newly created artisans' associations to organise trade fairs, provide training and help with credit. The philosophy was to help thousands of individuals by working with the grain of a strong tradition of community collaboration. A street cobbler trained in tanning technology, for example, was able in turn to train and employ four workers and reach markets for leather goods across the country.

Much of the work of the Trusts has been delivered through microcredit schemes. Learning of the 'tontines' or women's savings groups that were being supported by the Cameroon Gatsby Foundation (CGF), Luena researched the possibility of a similar microcredit scheme specifically targeted at women. Finding that 'upatu' savings groups were sufficiently well established in the contrasting districts of Mwanga and Rukwa, she set up microcredit programmes in 1998, with additional help for Zanzibar from the Ford Foundation, and later extended it more widely. Women who saved small amounts over a few months were able to take out not only their own savings but also a small loan to increase their working capital. For example, one used her loan to buy fishing boats that she leased out to fishermen, eventually building up a fleet of six boats.[8]

With increasing budgets year on year, TGT expanded into other areas, such as working with technical education institutions to encourage entrepreneurship in their graduates. Seushi was insistent that TGT should be seen as a catalyst for growth, not a source of handouts. 'One of our strategies was to keep a lean but highly motivated staff to cut down the costs but have greater impact,' says Luena. She is also highly committed to building capacity, training several of her own office staff to go on to more senior jobs in areas such as finance. In 2005, TGT founded the Community Banks Association of Tanzania, which supports existing community banks and fosters the development of new ones, several of which have gone on to be commercially successful.

Every two years since 1996 the four Trusts would meet for an Inter-Trust Seminar to share experience, successes and failures. The idea was always that they would not merely funnel funds from Gatsby to deserving beneficiaries, but would also earn income from loan interest and fees for services.

Locally managed investment

In 1998, Yvonne Pinto, who had been researching diseases of rice at The Sainsbury Laboratory in Norwich (see Chapter 5), joined the small team of executives working at the SFCT. Born in Kenya and brought up in Ethiopia, of Goanese heritage and with dual Kenyan and British citizenship, after 2000 she became the executive responsible for Gatsby's Africa programmes, working alongside Cockcroft. 'The contributions Gatsby made in the science it funded were exceptional,' she says.

At about the same time, Cockcroft began to change Gatsby's focus from directly funding agricultural projects to investing in locally managed financial institutions that could respond to local needs. In 2002, he and Pinto negotiated a partnership with the Rockefeller Foundation to create the Maendeleo Agricultural Technology Fund, managed by the charity FARM Africa. Over eight years this fund gave grants for sixty-seven technology transfer projects to benefit small-scale farmers, raising household incomes by between 60 and 400 per cent.[9] One such grant to the non-profit consultancy Technoserve raised the quality of coffee produced by smallholders in Tanzania through supporting coffee cooperatives and providing training and business support. Subsequently the Gates Foundation invested another

$47 million with Technoserve to extend the approach to five further countries, reaching a quarter of a million coffee farmers.

In 2005, Gatsby Africa established a new body, the Kilimo Trust, a locally managed grant-making organisation that aimed to help small farmers identify and overcome the market constraints that prevented them from raising their income. The deputy chair of the Kilimo Trust was Hatim Karimjee, a prominent Tanzanian businessman and long-standing advisor to Gatsby. 'We would do a study on cotton, maize or other crops,' he says, 'and then figure out how the constraints could be unblocked. We also gave grants in response to emergencies, such as outbreaks of diseases in crops. It was very effective.' The Kilimo Trust now operates independently and is managed by a local team (although Laurence Cockcroft and Yvonne Pinto remain trustees in their personal capacities).

One of the lessons from the Maendeleo project was that between the farmers and their markets there was a range of 'first mile' small businesses – wholesalers, transport and delivery enterprises, seed suppliers and so on – that themselves needed access to short-term finance to manage their cash flow. They constituted what came to be known as the 'missing middle' of small and medium-sized businesses that were too small to access finance from banks or big development finance institutions, but too large for microfinance to meet their needs. Approached by Joseph de Vries, a plant scientist and development executive for the Rockefeller Foundation, Cockcroft brought Gatsby into a partnership that also included the Belgian investment company Volksvermogen to set up an $8 million venture capital fund, African Agricultural Capital (AAC), chaired by Hatim Karimjee. AAC amassed a portfolio of medium-sized loans for which it charged near-commercial rates of interest.

AAC was sufficiently successful to attract other investors, including the Gates Foundation and J.P.Morgan. As a result, AAC's fund management team were spun out as Pearl Capital

Partners; they currently oversee a new $25 million African Agricultural Capital Fund (AACF), as well as other funds that they have under management. The aim, not always easy to achieve in the agricultural sector, which is difficult and high-risk, is to deliver both a return for investors and a social impact through increasing the well-being of farmers. The long-term sustainability of this approach will depend on being able to juggle the sometimes inflated expectations of purely commercial investors with those who are more interested in seeing a return in terms of measurable social impact. Gatsby itself is now a 'limited partner' investor in AACF, but continues to monitor and evaluate Pearl's performance.

Having helped to shepherd these projects into being, Pinto joined the Gates Foundation as a programme manager, working on projects funded by the $400 million Alliance for a Green Revolution in Africa (AGRA). She now runs a consulting practice, the Agricultural Learning and Impacts Network (ALINe), focused on evaluating agricultural projects in the developing world. She regards her years with Gatsby as formative. 'It was the best education ever,' she says. 'I learned a huge amount about management, governance, organisational reform and so on.' Pinto was the lead author of a 2014 report for the African Union that became the basis of the Malabo Declaration later that year.[10] The Declaration, among many other commitments, identified 'the pursuit of agriculture-led growth as a main strategy to achieve targets on food and nutrition security and shared prosperity'.[11] 'All the things that we had experimented on at Gatsby', says Pinto, 'I feel are really fundamental to enabling Africa to produce enough to feed itself and to be able to develop a consumer class.'

Education and land reform in South Africa

With the ending of apartheid and the adoption of black majority rule under Nelson Mandela's African National Congress (ANC) in 1994, David Sainsbury was keen for Gatsby to help the black community develop after years of oppression. Laurence Cockcroft visited the country with Roger Baker, Assistant Director of SFCT and with responsibility for Gatsby's education programme. 'People were pessimistic that we could do anything,' says Baker. However, the Gatsby trustees decided to set up a locally managed trust, the Scientific and Industrial Leadership Initiative (SAILI). The aim was to support science and maths students in the Western Cape, from primary school onwards, to gain places in engineering and science at one of the Western Cape's five universities, including the University of Cape Town. They also provided a small number of Sainsbury Management Fellowships (see page 141) so that successful students could go on to MBA study jointly at Cape Town and Cambridge, producing the next generation of leaders for industry.

By the late 1990s, Gatsby was putting £400,000 per year into eight primary and six secondary schools to support in-service training, classroom materials, after-school clubs and other initiatives to support science and maths teaching, and giving scholarships to university candidates, top undergraduates, and MBA students. The strategy was modelled closely on the Engineering Education Continuum funded by Gatsby in the UK (see Chapter 6).

However, the inclusive approach proved relatively ineffective in schools that were otherwise poorly resourced, and gradually evolved into a model in which selected students were provided with the opportunity to attend selected schools. By the mid-2000s other opportunities were open to such able students within the South African system; at the same time Gatsby decided to withdraw from the region and focus on its interests in East Africa. SAILI remains in operation today, offering bursaries to students to attend schools that meet stringent criteria for effective education.[12] Meanwhile the South African Sainsbury Management Fellows, who hold senior positions throughout South African industry, have set up the Sainsbury Management

Fellows Society with a view to raise funding in the country to continue to support the scholarship scheme.[13]

Gatsby also made a brief foray into land reform in South Africa, helping to support social justice organisations the Legal Resources Centre and the Surplus People's Project.

The business of development

It is taken as read by donor agencies that economic growth is the best way of combating poverty in Africa, but the former does not always entail the latter. The economies of countries such as Kenya and Tanzania have seen impressive growth since 2000, to the extent that since 2014 Kenya has been defined as a middle-income country by the World Bank. However, as DFID reported in 2008, 'The extent to which growth reduces poverty depends on the degree to which the poor participate in the growth process and share in its proceeds.'[14] In East Africa raw materials, construction, and services such as telecoms and finance, have begun to build up an urban middle class; but they have so far provided little in the way of 'trickle-down' benefits to the largely rural population, and there are still too few opportunities for people to engage in profitable business for themselves.

When David Sainsbury stood down as science minister in 2006, he called for a review of Gatsby's work in Africa. At DFID, the private sector development expert Justin Highstead had led on the design of the African Enterprise Challenge Fund, which provided grants to companies to alleviate poverty through business innovation. In that capacity, he had met Yvonne Pinto, who was on the point of leaving Gatsby and whose job was about to be advertised. 'I saw an incredible degree of potential for an organisation like Gatsby, with the freedoms that it has, to have a significant impact in the international development world,' says Highstead. His commitment to working through private industry resonated with David Sainsbury, who took him on to lead the Gatsby Africa programme. 'It's about getting economic growth going,' says Sainsbury. 'It's not about handouts or seeing people through the next crisis. You have to make a long-term commitment of time and effort. You have to experiment and take risks. You have to empower people so that long after we've gone they can go on progressing.'

Reviewing the agriculture programmes, Highstead concluded that, while there had been some successes, their impact had been limited. Even push-pull had failed to maintain its momentum. It was difficult to persuade farmers to put in the enormous effort required to establish push-pull plots, and there were problems in the supply of *Desmodium* seeds. The technology failed to take root in Tanzania and Uganda. 'Push-pull won awards, but it was in the fields because we subsidised the dissemination into fields,' says Highstead. 'We were funding something that was unsustainable for a long period of time, irrespective of the compelling nature of the science.' *icipe* would continue to promote the technology with support from other funders, but Gatsby had learned the hard lesson that technology alone could not solve the African farmers' problems. 'A significant number of agricultural technologies never reach the fields,' says Highstead. 'Why? We need to ask, do the farmers have credit, do they have access to markets, do the markets work?'

At the same time, Highstead and Sainsbury came to the conclusion that, while the country trusts had benefited some thousands of people, Gatsby could reach even greater numbers by taking a different approach. Since 2009, core support for the Trusts has gradually been withdrawn, while they have been encouraged to define their individual missions and plan for independent futures. UGT spun out a commercial company, Gatsby Microfinance Ltd (GMFL), in 2005. TGT followed suit with Fanikiwa Microfinance Company Limited in 2010. Both microfinance institutions have had problems: to her anguish, the endowment Luena had carefully built up to help TGT to be sustainable in the long term was invested in Fanikiwa, whose

Gatsby Microfinance Ltd (GMFL) supports
small businesses in Uganda.

managers then lost the money through making too many loans too quickly and being overoptimistic about their ability to raise more capital.

Gatsby helped to get Fanikiwa back on its feet, with a fresh loan and new management, and it has now been sold to a larger microcredit firm operating across East Africa. A similar package of emergency finance and company restructuring has been applied to GMFL, though the results are still uncertain. Meanwhile, TGT has continued with poverty alleviation projects in support of women, young people and small businesses, funded by organisations such as the United Nations Industrial Development Organisation (UNIDO), the Ford Foundation, the Cherie Blair Foundation, Comic Relief and the Danish International Development Agency (DANIDA). Now nearing retirement, Olive Luena is aiming to leave the organisation able to operate independently before she goes in 2017.

'Olive is brilliant,' says Highstead:

Her life is one of sacrifice and service to others: if anything needs doing in the national interest she gets a call, she has chaired the parish council of St Joseph's Cathedral in Dar es Salaam for many years, she was on the Vatican's Council of the Laity appointed by Pope John Paul II, and is a member of the International Bretton Woods Committee. A large part of the success of TGT is Olive's passion and commitment.

Speaking in her personal capacity, Luena observes that the landscape has changed. 'All through my life in TGT I have had Gatsby UK as a family,' she says.

In the 1990s and early 2000s funding was available for local organisations; now it's very difficult. I sit as a board member on other NGOs, and what TGT is going through is the same for the others. They are all struggling with sustainability issues. Most Northern NGOs that were partnering with local organisations are now setting up their own structures, bringing their own people, changing from funding to implementing. That brings a challenge.

KGT spun out a successful professional factoring business, Biashara Factors, helping small businesses with cash flow through buying their invoices. KGT was renamed the Kenya Markets Trust (KMT) in 2011, in a joint project between Gatsby and DFID, and now focuses on developing markets for agricultural products: dairy, livestock, water, seeds and agrochemicals. The dairy programme, for example, has the potential to increase income directly for up to 100,000 households, while contributing to food security through increasing the quality and productivity of the industry. KMT is also aiming to help nomadic pastoralists in northern Kenya to raise healthier animals and access markets for meat. As Gatsby has concentrated its activities in East Africa, it has withdrawn from Cameroon, assisting the merger of the Cameroon Gatsby Foundation's microfinance portfolio with that of MUFFA (Mutuelle Financière des Femmes Africaines), a very successful microfinance company specialising in women's credit.

For Gatsby, the experience of working with the Trusts and agricultural projects has been of inestimable value. The trustees and board members represent a network of senior East Africans who have continued to help Gatsby Africa staff to negotiate the often complex political and social environment in which they work. Decades of work with farmers in their fields, local agricultural suppliers, processors and financial institutions have built up a picture of agricultural markets and why they often don't benefit small producers. And it has given Gatsby Africa an unrivalled awareness of the need for local ownership, and of the political and economic relationships that can make the difference between success and failure.

To market

Looking at the aid industry as a whole, it had become apparent that few initiatives that targeted small and medium-sized businesses were able to become financially self-sustaining without subsidies from donors. Reviewing their options, the team decided to make a substantial, focused commitment to the development of market sectors. Research and dissemination of improved agricultural technologies remains an important part of the process, but with new attention to partnerships between the private and public sectors, effective local institutions, appropriate incentives and supportive regulation. The approach is strongly research-based, looking across whole sectors and identifying all the reasons that might be holding them back.

Many of these constraints could be traced to weak or counterproductive government regulation. 'In most countries in East Africa, governments have struggled to take on the responsibility of ensuring that key sectors are really working for their populations,' says Highstead. 'This has often left these sectors serving only the interests of a narrow minority.' Gatsby is trying to pick sectors where it can make a difference to large numbers of people by engaging with government and the private sector: cotton, textiles, tea (see Case study, page 102) and forestry. Its goals are to improve: competitiveness; inclusiveness, the extent to which a sector's growth benefits as many people as possible; and resilience, the ability of the industry to implement effective governance, manage risks and adapt to changes in the future without external support.

While this programme is ambitious, Highstead argues that by choosing sectors where the incentives of stakeholders can be aligned, finding and working with 'good people who want to do the right thing', setting up transparent information systems and strengthening representative bodies such as trade associations, it is possible to effect change. 'We try to be pragmatic,' he says. 'You are making transparent information available and building up the voice of all the stakeholders in that industry, making it more and more difficult for any minority to capture the benefits or to put pressure on those in power to misuse their public roles.'

This approach entails engaging politically at the highest level, and David Sainsbury, with his own record of ministerial office, is well placed to help with that process. 'He's engaging with ministers, he's been in their seat,' says Highstead. 'In the development industry you often see the big international donor institutions focusing their finance and support on things the donor finds important rather than listening to the government's own priorities. David is entirely different. He goes in and says, "How can I help you?" That's quite rare for an African minister to hear.'

Cotton

In January 2007, David Sainsbury visited Tanzania in the company of the President of Columbia University, Lee Bollinger, and the Director of the Earth Institute, Jeffrey Sachs. 'Jeffrey and I agreed that Tanzania was interesting,' he says. Ruled as a one-party socialist state since independence by the charismatic Julius Nyerere, Tanzania had made some progress in health and education, but entrepreneurship had been stifled and the economy was stagnant. Nyerere stood down as President in 1985, after which the country moved to multi-party democracy, but economic development was painfully slow.

Challenged at a meeting with the (then) recently elected President of Tanzania, Jakaya Mrisho Kikwete, to propose a project to improve the country's economy, Sainsbury had to think on his feet. 'I said that developing countries always start in the same place,' he says. 'Cheap clothing, plastics, toys – products where low wage costs allow you to compete. I offered to fund a study of what could be done to develop the clothing and textile industries.' When he put the idea to the TGT Chair, Ibrahim Seushi, Seushi advised that it would be best to start with the cotton industry – 'get that right first, and textiles will follow'.

Cotton supports 400,000 families in the Lake Zone of Tanzania, one of Tanzania's poorest regions, but by 2007 yields were a fraction of those in other countries: the seed was low-quality, traditional ploughing destroyed the soil structure, and farmers could not access credit to buy fertiliser and other inputs. The quality of the product was poor, and attracted a low price on world markets. 'Smallholders, at the time they need to do planting and spraying, don't have the cash to buy inputs,' TGT chair Ibrahim Seushi told Sainsbury. 'So availability of credit is paramount.'

He felt that yields could be tripled by giving farmers access to credit, and to advice and support to improve their farming practices. Through the TGT, Laurence Cockcroft recruited a team of six to carry out an initial study. They produced a report on the possibilities for intervention, from the commercial production of cotton seed to setting up contractual relationships between farmers and 'ginners' who process the raw cotton heads.

TGT then organised a high-profile stakeholders' meeting, jointly chaired by David Sainsbury and the Tanzanian minister of agriculture, bringing together farmers, ginners and textile companies to present the report and agree a programme that Gatsby would fund. The Tanzania cotton programme has advanced on three fronts. First, it has trained 1,700 lead farmers to practise conservation agriculture to improve soil quality. Second, it set up a public–private partnership between local research institutes and a successful Zimbabwean seed company to produce improved seed. Finally, and most significantly, Gatsby Africa has worked with the Tanzania Cotton Board (TCB) to establish a new relationship between groups of farmers and the 'ginners' who process the cotton ready to be turned into textiles. Contract farming commits the ginners to supply inputs to the farmers on credit, while the farmers undertake to sell their crop only to those ginners, repaying their loans from the proceeds. If both sides honour the agreement, both benefit from the increased yield and quality.

Promising trials led to a modified form of contract farming being extended, by law, to 290,000 farmers in the 2011/12 season, leading to a record harvest. However, the level of governance was frail. 'Many of the key players in the industry are involved in varying degrees of politics,' says Highstead, 'making sector governance very challenging.' The following year the TCB abandoned the scheme. Highstead recognises that the programme tried to move ahead too quickly in the first instance. However, Gatsby had seen enough to believe that it was still the best way forward. With an additional £7 million from DFID, it is now working with central and local government to pilot and roll out contract farming where the necessary political support is available. In 2014/15, 95,000 farmers received training and inputs through nine ginners, who had recognised that investment helped them to secure a good-quality supply. Their productivity was significantly better than that in areas not practising contract farming.

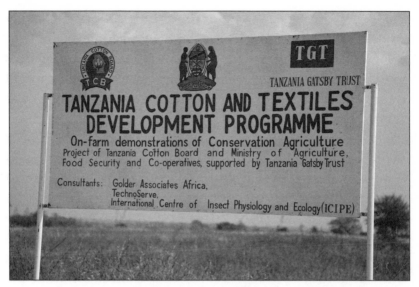

Since 2008, Gatsby has been running sector-wide projects
in Tanzania to develop the cotton and textile industries,
beginning with improvements to farming practice.

Meanwhile farmers are being selected and trained to become
bulk purchasers and distributors of inputs, an alternative route
to increasing productivity that does not depend on government
regulation. And Gatsby Africa continues to work on the governance issues, encouraged that a new president, John Magufuli,
was elected in October 2015 on a largely pro-development and
anti-corruption platform. 'If you can strengthen the governance
of the sector and the role of the TCB,' says Highstead, 'even if
the president leaves office you would have checks and balances
in place that would help the industry to survive.'

Despite the political ups and downs, thousands of farmers
and ginners have seen their incomes increase, enabling them
to build homes, pay for health care and educate their children.
'We haven't advocated contract farming as an ideological
solution,' says Highstead. 'Contract farming has arisen because

it addresses the constraints that are holding back the cotton industry at the moment, and it's probably the best way of trying to address those.' The transformation of the cotton industry has the potential to leave lessons both for governments and for other aid agencies as to how other cash crops, such as sugar, could also be regulated.

Textiles

With the expectation that Tanzania would soon be producing more and higher-quality cotton, in 2012 Gatsby set up a Textile Development Unit (TDU), housed within the Tanzanian Ministry of Industry and Trade.[15] In the 1970s, a state-owned textile and garment industry had flourished, but since privatisation Tanzania had failed to compete in the sector with countries in Asia and even other parts of East Africa. Many garment factories and spinning and weaving mills had closed. With just eight staff, the TDU has identified and begun to address many issues that were holding back Tanzanian textile producers, from large mill and factory owners to sole traders with a single sewing machine.

They ensured that customs officials assessed imported cloth at its true value – in one year raising the value of imported products by 782 per cent – so that the right tariffs would be paid and local producers were able to compete. They helped to set up a trade organisation, the Textile and Garment Manufacturers Association of Tanzania, to build a stronger voice for the industry in lobbying for government action. They have set up training programmes, and supported the installation of improved equipment so that mills can be reopened. And they are delivering a message to potential foreign and domestic investors that Tanzania is well placed, as costs rise in countries such as China, to offer cheap labour, high employment and environmental standards, and good-quality, locally sourced raw materials.

A trained workforce is critical to this endeavour and Gatsby worked with the University of Dar es Salaam in 2008 to foster a joint programme with the University of Manchester that enabled ten engineering and design graduates from Dar to enrol in MA and PhD programmes at Manchester. By 2014, these students had returned to Dar to establish courses at the university in textile engineering and design, with a very successful uptake of graduates by the industry. Gatsby envisages that 5,000 new jobs will have been created by 2018, with the potential to increase this number to 150,000 by 2030. All this depends, however, on the government prioritising the textile industry's development, though major investments in textile manufacturing by China and Japan are under way.

Forestry

The forestry programmes grew out of Gatsby's long-standing interest in promoting agricultural innovation through disseminating new and more productive plant varieties. Laurence Cockcroft had been approached by the 'force of nature', Kenyan plant pathologist Florence Wambugu, in 1995 to support a venture propagating improved *Eucalyptus* hybrids from cuttings, so that they would retain their genetic advantages. Originating in Australia, the species is fast-growing and thrives in tropical and subtropical regions, providing wood and oil. From 1997, Gatsby established nurseries in Uganda, Kenya and Tanzania, growing for distribution to small farmers. The Kenyan and Ugandan nurseries, run by local boards as social enterprises, are now self-financing.

Building on this, and working in partnership with DFID, in 2014 Gatsby provided five years of funding to set up the Forestry Development Trust (FDT) in Tanzania. FDT works with both public and private sectors to support small growers. It begins with technology transfer, improving genetic resources in both native and non-native species and developing better-quality material for planting; and works through all the way to ensure that growers have markets for their produce and can reach them through more efficient harvesting, transport and processing.

The project aims to turn the country into a net exporter of timber rather than a net importer, while raising the incomes of around 60,000 tree growers. At the same time, Gatsby has established the Kenya Commercial Forestry Programme, using similar methods to support private sector growers in Kenya while relieving pressure on natural forests.

Msingi: technology transfer for development

Soon after he came out of government, David Sainsbury read an article about Fundación Chile, a foundation set up in 1976 with $50 million waived by the US telecommunications conglomerate ITT (International Telephone & Telegraph) as compensation for the earlier nationalisation of its Chilean businesses. He was sufficiently interested to pay a visit to Chile and see the foundation at work. Salmon farming and wine producing were among its major successes: Chilean wines were on every supermarket shelf, and Chile had joined Norway and Scotland among the top three world exporters of salmon. To date, Fundación Chile has contributed more than $1.3 billion to Chile's GDP and encouraged the commercialisation of more than fifteen areas of industry.[16] 'I thought, "That's what you need in Africa",' says Sainsbury.

In 2015, in partnership with DFID, Gatsby set up Msingi on the same model – commercially focused, locally managed and staffed, independent of government, and with the resources to create or transform industries in East Africa predicted to have high potential. Between them Gatsby and DFID have committed at least £30 million for the first five years. Still in its early stages, Msingi is an ambitious experiment, in which Gatsby is taking a highly engaged role, as it works to pass on the benefits of its experience and research to locally recruited board members. 'Msingi seeks to build East Africa's industries of the future – dynamic industries that can drive growth and the structural transformation of the region,' says Ali Mufuruki, the first chair of Msingi's board of directors. A Tanzanian entrepreneur and philanthropist, Mufuruki is the co-founder and chairman of Infotech Investment Group: he also co-founded the Africa Leadership Initiative and the CEO Roundtable of Tanzania. Says Highstead:

> Ali Mafuruki is one of the most prominent businesspeople in East Africa and he is really committed to Msingi. I met a number of candidates for the role, and Ali interviewed me, really. He wanted to know, 'What is Gatsby, who is David Sainsbury, what is he really trying to do?' Through the process of introducing him to David, you could tell that Ali wouldn't do this unless he was committed, and it was a personal commitment to David. And you can't buy that – having that sense of commitment from someone like Ali to chair an organisation is priceless for us.

At the time of writing Msingi is still in the first phase of its programme, identifying those industries that have the greatest potential to become competitive and create jobs. Like Fundación Chile, the first industry Msingi has chosen to focus on is aquaculture, which meets the stringent criteria it has set: strong demand for local fish, good potential for profitability, limited obstructive vested interests and the potential for technology to improve productivity. It has set a target of over 50,000 smallholders engaged in fish farming, as well as 12,500 jobs in larger-scale aquaculture, leading to higher household incomes and increased food security. Gatsby has set Msingi up with a time horizon of twenty years. Such patience is a hallmark of Gatsby's activities, and contrasts with the sometimes over-hasty approach of wealthier donor organisations.

Msingi will help firms to develop robust systems of accountability and expertise in researching markets and writing business plans, all in the interests of drawing in new investors. It will also have the resources to make its own investments to establish early-stage industries and attract further investors to contribute. In the longer term, as well as developing the broader business environment within which its target industries operate, it will strive to increase opportunities for innovation to thrive across the region, brokering relationships between industry, academia and government and advising on investment and intellectual property.

By mitigating the very high risks that inhibit entrepreneurs from taking bold initiatives as they develop new businesses, Msingi aims to act as a nursery for innovation and growth across East Africa.

Learning the hard way: Gatsby in Mozambique

One thing Gatsby has learned is that the initial circumstances – political, social, geographical – can have a profound influence on how long it might take to effect change. Quite separately from the Gatsby Africa programme, in 2004 (when David Sainsbury was in government), Christopher Stone, as head of David Sainsbury's family investment office and working under the blind trust administered by Judith Portrait, agreed to invest in a project proposed by a new member of his staff: a potentially exciting, large-scale, agricultural development in Mozambique. The idea was to demonstrate that private investment in a developing country could both be financially worthwhile and achieve the social impact that is the aim of all Sainsbury's charitable projects.

With the apparent goodwill of the Mozambican government, and optimism about the climatic, geographical and social conditions, Aquifer, the UK-based investment company created to execute this plan, bought three small businesses that had recently been set up: a horticultural enterprise in Vanduzi growing chillies, baby corn and mangetout for European and other markets; a business developing improved strains of rice in Chokwe; and a logistics business to support the transport of goods for the food-producing concerns.

It soon became apparent that Aquifer, led by expat staff with no previous experience in the country, had seriously underestimated the challenges. Mozambique had returned to democracy only ten years before, after nearly two decades of civil war, and lagged well behind other sub-Saharan African countries, such as Kenya, in its infrastructure and skills base. The fleet of trucks ordered from Europe for the logistics business could not be serviced when they broke down. Corruption at every level was a constant drain on effectiveness. Subsistence farmers, who all their lives had supported their families from their own small plots of land, proved unwilling to become labourers in the company's fields: the very concept of working for a wage was alien to them, and only profit-busting rates of pay would persuade them it was worthwhile.

The rice and horticulture businesses went into production, eventually employing around 2,000 people, but failed to turn a profit. Stone became increasingly alarmed at the drain on funds. Soon after David Sainsbury left ministerial office in 2006, Gatsby began to take ownership of Aquifer, which became wholly owned and under Gatsby management (as a 'programme-related investment') by 2009. Despite the clear evidence that the project was not out of the woods, Sainsbury encouraged his staff to stay with it.

By 2010, Gatsby's managing director Peter Hesketh, who had taken on responsibility for the project, could point to some successes for Aquifer's wholly owned company Mozfoods SA. He had closed the logistics operation as a non-starter, but the agriculture projects seemed promising. Vanduzi enjoyed up to 33 per cent of the UK market share in its products at peak production – it remains Mozambique's largest exporter of fresh produce. Yields of rice from Chokwe were up by 300 per cent and the brand was 'flying off the shelves' in local shops. But income still fell well short of costs. Then, in January 2013, a major flood in Chokwe District destroyed the 25,000 hectares of newly restored paddy fields that were the foundation of the rice business. Gatsby contributed humanitarian aid to support the 200,000 displaced people, but, learning that such floods occurred approximately every ten years, Hesketh closed down the rice-production venture, only retaining its hard-won expertise in the development of improved seed varieties.

Today the horticulture business at Vanduzi is stable: yields have risen, the area is increasingly prosperous, the company is Mozambique's biggest taxpayer. There is little prospect that Aquifer will ever recover its investment, but it has prepared the ground for others who should not have to make the same mistakes. 'It's looking like there might be a happy ending,' says Hesketh. 'I'm confident that in the next few years other principled investors will move into Vanduzi. We have learned lessons about what not to do. But a lot of good has been achieved.'

An African future

US President Barack Obama was the most high-profile leader, inside or outside Africa, to raise the issue when in 2015 he told an audience in Kenya, his father's homeland, that they must rid their country of the 'cancer of corruption'. Gatsby had addressed this issue in its own activities from the outset. 'We worked hard to select people who were above board as trustees and chairmen of the country trusts,' says Laurence Cockcroft. In 1993, introduced by the chair of the Kenya Gatsby Trust, Joe Githongo, to the founders of the anti-corruption charity Transparency International (TI), Cockcroft became one of its co-founders and later set up chapters in the UK, Tanzania and Uganda. Under pressure from TI, in 2010 the UK passed legislation that, for the first time, outlawed bribes paid abroad.

'One of the strengths of Gatsby in the early days was that we were working under the eyeline of government,' says Cockcroft.

'The more recent projects are dependent to a greater or lesser extent on government policy.' A recent report on the political economy of four East African countries published by the Overseas Development Institute (ODI) is only the latest to spell out the way that politics and business are entwined in most of them, accusing companies of paying into party coffers in return for lenient tax regimes and lax regulation.[17] President Magufuli's 2015 election in Tanzania on an anti-corruption ticket is one demonstration of the wider population's growing impatience with this state of affairs, and of its demand for change in order to realise the region's potential.

The challenges are serious, but Gatsby's executives believe that this goal is within reach. In 2015, the Gatsby Africa programme underwent a major restructuring. Instead of providing grants to employ consultants, Gatsby Africa had gradually become a 'funder-implementer', employing its own staff on the ground. Says Highstead:

> We have moved from being a funding organisation that writes cheques, employing only one or two people, to become an organisation that is trying to think through, analyse, organise and shape programmes. We are developing relationships with governments, the private sector, and other implementing agencies. We have built up teams – we now have over 130 people on the ground, 110 of whom we have recruited locally. We've broadened our funding models to include loans and equity. And we've greatly increased our leverage – we never previously had outside funding. Now we have massive amounts of co-funding, mostly from DFID. We could not work at this scale without that leverage. Our direct level of grant capital hasn't changed massively – in dollar terms it has maybe even declined slightly – but what we do has increased.

In order to provide a distinct legal structure for the new style of operation, Gatsby Africa Ltd has been set up as a separate entity, which in 2016 acquired charitable status. It is based in London, with branches in Kenya and Tanzania, and has its own trustees and executive board. It looks to all intents and purposes like an NGO or a consultancy, but with two important differences. 'We are different because we have our own funding,' says Highstead. 'That gives us autonomy, independence and purpose. Everyone knows we are not in it for the money. It's very nice for DFID, for example, to have a trusted partner who is not incentivised to make money out of them.' DFID is only one of a number of aid agencies that now works in partnership with Gatsby.

The second difference is that Gatsby Africa Ltd's own long-term survival is not important. 'The question is, what are we trying to build and leave behind?' says Highstead. 'The purpose isn't to build an NGO, it's to build the institutional capacity so that things last.' The commitment to local ownership is reflected in projects such as KMT and Msingi. 'We have got local senior advisors, and all of the staff are local,' he says, 'but the difficulty is to find local people to lead our projects.'

The problem is that the pool of suitably trained and experienced African managers is small, and there is global competition – from business, NGOs and public institutions – for their services. And the countries have not invested sufficiently in their own people: Hatim Karimjee concedes that in his country, Tanzania, 'the education record is dreadful – we have the least educated manpower of the East African countries.' While in Kenya and Uganda the record (at least in primary and secondary education) is better, the lack of investment in relevant skills has propelled a constant brain drain from rural areas to cities, from the public sector to the private, from East Africa to South Africa, and from Africa to the USA or UK. 'For a top-tier Kenyan postgraduate engineer with ten years' experience, I would be paying 30 or 40 per cent more in Nairobi than I would in London,' says

Highstead, 'because the same pool of companies is chasing the same talent.'

By operating on timescales that are longer than the typical three-year consultancy contract, Gatsby Africa aims to train and develop people, and so build strength and sustainability in the institutions, from farmers' co-ops to government departments, that mean success or failure in each market sector.

Highstead says:

When there is the capability to manage a sector, to respond to challenges and threats, to innovate, and to build staff and skills, so that it can keep adapting and won't go off the rails in a year or two's time, that's when we step aside ... I can't point to a single industry where we've achieved that, but we are peeling back the layers of why it doesn't work ... In the end there will be twelve or thirteen industries across East Africa [where we have intervened], where we will have had two or three success stories, and probably five or six moderate successes and three or four failures. A lot of our strategy is not just about what we can implement – it's about having a portfolio that is sufficiently large to generate success stories that we can then share. We want to use those lessons to influence the way that governments work, the way that donors fund this kind of work, or the way that other implementing agencies undertake this work.

Case study: Tea in Tanzania and Rwanda

Tea is an ideal crop for Tanzania, with its acid soils, tropical climate and seasonal rainfall. Yet by the mid-2000s productivity, quality and prices were all in decline. In September 2009, Gatsby and the Wood Foundation jointly founded the $9 million Chai project. Established by Sir Ian Wood, founder of the oil and gas services company Wood Group, the Wood Foundation's aims are closely allied with those of Gatsby. Chai's initial aim is to double the amount of made tea (dried ready for packaging) and double the net income per hectare of the 30,000 smallholder farmers who grow much of the country's product.

The Chai project identified four key areas of intervention: building supportive relationships between factories and farmers, improving cultivation practices, a pricing mechanism that increased the farmer's share of the made tea price and improved regulation of the industry. Working with private sector tea factories and farmers through grants, training and improved technology, Chai addressed all these areas, while providing advice to government on price regulation. By 2015, farmers' average yields were well up, and profits per hectare had increased from $170 to over $400. With further support from DFID, Chai then set up a tea farmer service company to expand the tea sector in Tanzania, through putting new land under cultivation and reducing the risk for companies starting new operations by providing inputs to farmers on 'patient credit' (over ten years or more).

Fortified by their experience in Tanzania, Gatsby and the Wood Foundation next turned their attention to Rwanda. Rwandan tea is considered of exceptionally high quality and, along with coffee, represents the country's most significant export. Yet output is a fraction of that in the more advanced Kenyan tea sector. Moreover, the smallholders who produce more than 65 per cent of the output were receiving only 25 per cent of the cost of made tea, as opposed to the 75 per cent earned by farmers in Kenya.

In the process of recovery that followed the civil war and genocide of the mid-1990s, the Rwandan government sold off its interests in the country's thirteen tea factories to the private sector. In many cases the result was a stripping of assets and a failure to invest in improved productivity. In 2012, noting that tea prices in Rwanda were well regulated and the government

The Chai project, a partnership between Gatsby and the Wood
Foundation, aims to expand tea cultivation, increase productivity,
improve quality and boost returns to smallholders in Tanzania.

committed to good governance, Gatsby and the Wood Foundation formed
East African Tea Investments (EATI) to buy controlling interests in the last
two factories to be sold, at Mulindi and Shagasha. 'We decided to buy the
factories on behalf of the farmers,' says Highstead, 'turn them round, make
them profitable, pay ourselves back from the profits and then hand over the
ownership and the equity to the farmers.'

By 2016, both factories were making profits and the farmers were much
better off. EATI expects to be able to take its investment and leave within the
next decade. As well as the investment vehicle EATI, Gatsby and the Wood
Foundation jointly fund the Imbarutso (Catalyst) project in Rwanda, which
provides grant funding to support a variety of interventions, including the
distribution of improved plants and fertiliser, the training of farmers and
factory managers, and a transformation, using mobile phone technology,
of farmers' access to credit.

The success of both tea projects has led Unilever, the world's largest tea
producer and owner of the PG Tips and Lipton brands, to consider major
investments in both countries, building new factories and extending
the areas where tea is planted. EATI plans to work with the multinational,
ensuring the investments reach more people and pay them higher returns.

5

THE POWER OF PLANTS

A lifeline for cutting-edge science

Plants are fundamental to the well-being of us all. Photosynthesis, the process by which plants capture the sun's energy and use it to make food, is the bedrock of the global food chain. Agricultural crops are the dietary staples of all humans and domesticated animals, and plants help to maintain the delicate balance of atmospheric gases that keeps us alive and modifies the climate. Global challenges that plant science might help address include feeding an extra 2 billion people by 2050, mitigating the effects of rising carbon dioxide in the atmosphere and developing sustainable plant-based sources of energy and materials.

Yet for decades the resources devoted to research in plants have been a fraction of those lavished on understanding the biology of humans in health and disease. In the UK, only 4 per cent of UK public research funding goes to plant science.[1] Food and agriculture research no longer has a dedicated government funding source, but must fight with other priorities for funds from the Biotechnology and Biological Sciences Research Council (BBSRC).[2] Medical research, in contrast, has a dedicated research council (the MRC), plus the option of a wide variety of medical research charities – starting with the Wellcome Trust, which has overtaken the MRC in its annual expenditure. In the

USA, the National Institutes of Health spends $15 on R&D for every $1 spent by the US Department of Agriculture.[3]

'The difference in spend between medical research and plant science is huge,' says Professor Dick Flavell, former Director of the John Innes Centre in Norwich and a long-standing advisor to Gatsby. 'If you have a broader view of the role of plants in the world, this is silly. More people are kept alive by food than by medicine.' Sir David Baulcombe, Regius Professor of Botany at the University of Cambridge, wryly quotes an anonymous verse, possibly dating back to the time of Charles Darwin:

> *Botany*
> *Is monotony.*
> *The study of plants*
> *I leave to my aunts.*

Britain is highly rated internationally in plant science, coming second only to the USA in the impact of its publications. Gatsby has been critical in enabling British research institutions to retain and enhance their reputations in the field. Since 1985 it has become the second-largest funder of research on plants in the UK after the BBSRC, contributing around 20 per cent of the total and establishing two world-leading research laboratories, a training and advocacy network and a non-profit company dedicated to turning discoveries into commercially available technologies. The work has the potential to transform agricultural productivity, not only in the commercial farms of the industrialised countries but in the developing world, and to help meet the challenge of feeding the rapidly growing global population while minimising the impact of agriculture on the natural environment.

Why plants?

David Sainsbury grew up in a household where science was never mentioned, received little scientific education at Eton, and went to Cambridge to study history. In this new intellectual environment, he began to learn more about the exciting advances in genetics and neurobiology that were taking place in Cambridge at the time. Francis Crick, Sydney Brenner and others were on the point of cracking the genetic code in DNA, and physiologist Horace Barlow was just publishing his first work on how the visual system might process information. So thrilled was Sainsbury by what he found that he switched to natural sciences, following a two-year course in experimental psychology for which his lack of basic physics, chemistry and biology was not too great a handicap. (His continued engagement with the science of the brain is the subject of Chapter 8.)

One of his closest friends at Cambridge was Roger Freedman, a voluble, restlessly divergent student of natural sciences, with a tendency to all-consuming enthusiasms that he freely describes as monomania. His intellectual exuberance captivated his no less thoughtful but more reserved friend. After Cambridge, their paths diverged: Sainsbury went into the management of the family firm, Freedman to the Laboratory of Molecular Biology to do a PhD with Brenner on the genetics of microorganisms. But they always kept in touch. In the late 1970s Freedman developed a new passion, for growing and breeding pelargoniums. Trained as a geneticist, he had been fascinated to discover that you could just chop a piece off a plant, stick it in the soil, and it would grow into a new individual. His voracious curiosity drove him to learn more about the biology of plants, so in the early 1980s he went to the Plant Breeding Institute (PBI) outside Cambridge – then one of the top research institutes in the world developing new cultivars for farmers – and asked the head of molecular genetics, Dick Flavell, if he might sit in on a lecture course for master's students.

The course revealed the exciting turn that plant biology had taken: the technology that made it possible to manipulate plant genes meant that at last researchers might be able to answer hundreds of questions about how plants work. How do they grow? How do they respond to changes in their environment? How do they fight disease? The answers could potentially transform not only the basic understanding of plant biology, but also the development of new crop varieties, resistance to disease, and environmental management.

Yet fewer and fewer universities retained departments of plant science: they incorporated the subject into biology or bioscience departments, where it was always the poor relation. Bright students choosing PhD topics were much more likely to opt for the enticing world of biomedicine. The few places where British plant science was not only hanging on but leading the world were the institutes funded by what was then the Agricultural and Food Research Council (AFRC): these included the John Innes Institute (JII) in Norwich, and the PBI, where Roger Freedman experienced his epiphany. And, in the harsh economic and political conditions of the time, even here cuts were beginning to bite.

Freedman pointed out to Sainsbury the new horizons that were opening up thanks to plant molecular biology. 'I think Roger has a genius for understanding what's happening in science, and where it's going to go,' says Sainsbury. He took his old friend on as a Gatsby advisor, and in 1985 the foundation made its first grant to the John Innes Institute. For the next four years, the trustees allocated Freedman an annual budget to spend on research projects of his own choosing. Freedman soon realised that he needed some heavyweight backup, and recruited two further advisors. They were Dick Flavell, who then headed the research group at the PBI that had been the first (in 1977) to clone a plant gene, and David Ingram at the University of Cambridge, who worked on diseases of crop plants, such as mildews and blights. (Within Gatsby circles they were jointly referred to as 'Fling'.)

'We made a small number of grants to hand-picked researchers,' says Flavell. 'The only criterion was that the work was of excellent quality. We recognised that we were starting something that could have a more significant future.'

Cutting edge I: The Sainsbury Laboratory Norwich

Advised and encouraged by Roger Freedman, David Sainsbury was convinced of the need to make a long-term and focused commitment to plant science, beyond what would be possible through handing out grants to scientists at existing institutions. He began to think about funding an independent research institute, with long-term, core funding so that researchers would not be constantly scrabbling for grants. Freedman and the other advisors recommended a focus on the genetic basis of resistance to disease in crop plants such as wheat, potatoes and tomatoes.

Farmers are engaged in a constant battle with weeds, pests and diseases that currently depress the yield of crops worldwide by 30–40 per cent. Historically the best-known example is the outbreak of late potato blight in Ireland in the mid-nineteenth century. The pathogen *Phytophthora infestans* is thought to have reached Ireland from Central America only a few years before. For social and political reasons, more than a third of the Irish population depended almost wholly on potatoes for sustenance, so when the entire crop failed year after year, a million people died and the same number emigrated, a catastrophe that had a permanent impact on Irish politics and society. Today, late blight is still thought to account for $6.7 billion of lost crops annually across the world.[4] A significant proportion of the cost of contemporary commercial farming goes into pesticides that are repeatedly sprayed on crops, with detrimental consequences for the environment. Meanwhile, pathogens continue to evolve to become resistant to the pesticides.

The good news is that plants are not without their own defences: for reasons that have only recently become clear, most plants are not diseased. Like us, they have a system of immunity that gives them a variable amount of resistance to infection: over time, evolution can improve this resistance, but at the same time the pathogens will evolve to evade the plant's defences. Plants bred commercially for uniformity are potentially more vulnerable than their wild cousins.

This arms race between plant and pathogen, taking place at the level of the genes, was to be the focus of the new institute. The rationale was the conjunction of two research traditions: the decades of classical plant genetics that had demonstrated consistent variation in the susceptibility to disease of different strains, and the newer research in molecular biology that sought to explain it at the level of the DNA. 'There was a huge amount of data on resistance,' says Sainsbury, 'but no way you could do experiments until the technology of genetic manipulation came along. It was immensely interesting.'

Sainsbury believed strongly that the new institute should be a partnership with a university. He considered Cambridge University at first, but it proved to be too inflexible to accommodate the independent style of management and governance that the Gatsby advisors envisaged. After hearing a formidable research presentation from director Harold Woolhouse and his colleague Alison Smith of the JII, Sainsbury and his advisors decided to site their new institute beside it near the campus of the University of East Anglia (UEA) in Norwich. Not only was the JII a world-leading centre for research, but also Gatsby already had good relations with UEA through its support for the Sainsbury Centre for Visual Arts (see Chapter 10). In 1987, Gatsby made a grant of almost half a million pounds to UEA to recruit the first staff members and set up The Sainsbury Laboratory (TSL).

The way the laboratory has been funded from the start is highly unusual in today's scientific environment. Grants are awarded to people, not projects, with an ambition to recruit as group leaders some of the best plant molecular biologists in the world with an interest in disease mechanisms. They are able to spend their budgets as they see fit, freeing them from the relentless grind of grant applications, but their appointments are for only five years at a time. A governing council scrutinises the research programmes at twice-yearly meetings, and decides whether the five-yearly appointments should be renewed. The principle is 'fund then filter' – the opposite of the usual practice whereby research councils filter hundreds of tightly defined grant applications before deciding what to fund, or issue 'calls' for applications in predefined areas. It goes without saying that the Gatsby funding is generous (as are the salaries), and the research groups are backed up by excellent support services in bioinformatics, proteomics and plant transformation. The system of oversight ensures that no one can get too comfortable, and the sense of purpose at TSL is palpable: at the same time, there is a freedom to respond to new situations, a 'nimbleness', that the governing council sees as one of the greatest assets of the laboratory.

Nevertheless, for established scientists holding or looking for tenured appointments, taking a post at TSL could be a big risk. The founders set out to recruit four group leaders willing to take that risk: initially they were only able to find three, but thereafter the reputation of the lab has ensured high-quality successors. Another unusual principle of TSL's management is that of 'primus inter pares' – each senior group leader in turn holds the post of director for three to five years before returning full time to his or her own research. The Laboratory's first director was Mike Daniels, a senior scientist from the JII. He brought his projects on plant–pathogen interactions across to TSL, and remained at the lab until his retirement in 2002.

To begin with he and his colleagues were all housed in Portakabins, with the laboratory in a converted gardeners' tearoom. In the summer of 1989, TSL moved into its own purpose-built laboratories, which have proved their worth over more than twenty-five years' service. The following year the molecular biology research teams from the PBI moved in alongside. Two years previously the PBI's commercially successful plant-breeding activity had been sold off to Unilever by the Thatcher government – a disastrous mistake in the eyes of the plant science community, separating research from commercial application and cutting off a source of funding for innovation. The research arm of the PBI was effectively orphaned, but, says David Baulcombe, the 'vision and charisma' of Harold Woolhouse was able to put forward the JII in Norwich as a credible adoptive parent. In 1994, Dick Flavell became head of a new John Innes Centre (JIC), which incorporated JII, the 'Cambridge laboratory', as the refugees from the PBI were known, and the Nitrogen Fixation Unit, which moved from the University of Sussex in 1992. The Sainsbury Laboratory was therefore part of one of the strongest concentrations of plant science expertise in the country, if not the world.

It quickly established itself as a leader in the field, with a major discovery in its first few years. At the PBI, Baulcombe had developed an interest in plant viruses that did not sit well with the priorities of that lab, so he made a successful application to become one of the founding group leaders at TSL in 1988. 'I accepted with trepidation,' he says. 'I had a job for life at PBI. But Roger said, "If you're anxious about it, you're not the person we need."'

In the early 1990s, he was experimenting with using transgenic technology to 'immunise' plants by giving them viral genes. 'The experiments were working remarkably well,' he says. 'I was getting plants that were totally immune to the virus.' To his great surprise this immunity did not depend on any viral protein. Instead, he discovered that the viral genes were being silenced by their own messenger RNA (ribonucleic acid). Baulcombe and his colleague Andrew Hamilton subsequently discovered that this process, known as RNA interference, is at work naturally in plants, with specific small RNA molecules targeting genes to regulate their activity.[5] RNA interference has been found to operate in animals as well as plants, and is involved in cancer, heart disease and viral infections. It remains one of the hottest areas of research across the whole of biology, with potential applications in medicine both to make new discoveries and directly as therapy. Without the security of the long-term funding offered by the Sainsbury Lab, Baulcombe doubts he would have been able to pursue a result that initially he saw as 'a weird phenomenon that didn't make sense'.

In 2006, the Nobel prize for Physiology or Medicine went to American scientists Andrew Fire and Craig Mello for their discovery of the action of small RNAs in nematode worms. They had precedence in terms of publication date, but other scientists, including Baulcombe, had laid much of the groundwork and were neck and neck in making the discovery. The *Scientific American* website lists him among its 'top ten Nobel snubs'. [6] In 2007, Baulcombe moved to Cambridge University as Regius Professor of Botany. A knighthood in 2009 for his services to plant sciences is only one of the many honours he has since received.

All in the genes

Today the Sainsbury Laboratory houses seven research groups, and a total of 100 scientists and support staff. While still enjoying generous core funding from Gatsby, its researchers also regularly win competitive grants from other funding bodies such as the BBSRC and (at least, in the pre-Brexit era) the European Research Council. While it has remained a small institution, the impact of its research is out of all proportion to its size. In 2010, the *Times Higher Education* surveyed almost 9,000 institutions worldwide and placed TSL and JIC in joint first place for the most influential papers of the previous decade in plant or animal sciences.[7]

'It's hard to imagine going anywhere better,' says Jonathan Jones, who was one of the founding group leaders in 1988 and has remained ever since, serving two terms as head of the lab. Not long after he arrived, Jones hosted David Sainsbury on a visit to TSL. At the end of his presentation on the laboratory's work, Jones thanked him for his support and said, 'I hope you'll be reassured that we are not frittering away your money too recklessly.' Sainsbury turned to him with a smile and said, 'I thought that was the general idea.' Jones says he has never been so shocked. 'It's a fantastic privilege to have the flexibility to test your hunches about where the next big thing might be,' he says. 'As long as you are right some of the time, you then have the evidence you need to support grant proposals to other funding bodies.'

Jones, known to all as JJ, had studied as an undergraduate with David Ingram, and as a graduate student with Dick Flavell at the PBI. 'Gene cloning in plants took off there while I was a student,' he says. He had gone to the USA and was working for a plant biotechnology company in Berkeley, California, when he got talking to Roger Freedman at a conference. 'Roger said, "We're going to start a lab – you might be just what we are looking for",' he remembers. The five years Jones had spent in industry, working out what it took to express genes at a high level in plants with an eye to developing new varieties for the world's farmers, gave him a practical perspective beyond what he had received through his purely academic training.

Jones has focused on genes for disease resistance in plants, known for simplicity as R genes. These genes constitute the armoury of a plant's defences against the bacteria, fungi and other microorganisms that constantly besiege them. Unlike animals, plants have no circulating immune cells that can generate specific antibodies in response to infection. Instead they have an 'innate' immune system of receptors inside and outside the cell. Some offer a first line of defence against a broad variety of organisms; others are more specific, recognising the 'effectors' carried by particular pathogens. Much of the work at TSL has focused on identifying these receptors, understanding how they work, and using genetic manipulation to transfer the genes that encode them to crop plants that lack the resistance they provide.

One strategy for crop improvement is to look for R genes in

related wild species, which might stand the best chance of doing the same job in cultivated varieties. Wild members of the potato family, for example, have proved a rich source of R genes that confer resistance to late blight. In a field trial in 2012, Jones and his team demonstrated that a single gene from a South American wild potato, *Solanum venturii*, completely protected a test crop in the UK from a late blight epidemic.[8] TSL has worked with the American company Simplot to incorporate this gene into a blight-resistant GM (genetically modified) potato that has been approved for production by the US Food and Drug Administration – the first commercial use of R genes in potatoes.[9] Farmers who previously sprayed their crops with fungicide fifteen times per year will need to spray the transformed potatoes only twice or three times.

'What we've learned from the use of resistance genes is that you should not rely on one mode of action, because the bugs will invent around them pretty damn quick,' says Jones. The goal of all the researchers at TSL is to confer durable resistance through the strategy of 'stacking' three or more different R genes in transformed varieties. Jones and his colleagues have developed technology that allows them to recognise and clone new R genes from wild relatives much more quickly than before: in 2016 they published the discovery of several new genes that protect against late blight in another potato relative, *Solanum americanum*.[10] Jones heads a five-year project with multiple funders, including the same industrial partner, to develop a new potato that will contain not only three genes conferring resistance to blight, but others that protect against nematode worms, reduce bruising (so avoiding waste) and alter the levels of reducing sugars to avoid the formation of toxic acrylamide at high temperatures. The new potato will therefore have benefits not only for farmers, but also for retailers and consumers.

It is a source of frustration to Jones and his colleagues that political opposition to GM crops in Europe makes it unlikely that this potato, even if field trials are successful, will be adopted there in the near future. 'The irony is that UK charitable and taxpayers' money has gone into producing something that's going to make life easier for American potato farmers,' he says. 'Because of the neurosis in the UK and Europe about GM crops, that's a lot further off here.'

Jones's work is complemented by that of senior group leader Cyril Zipfel, who took on the rotating headship of the Laboratory in 2014. Zipfel has been instrumental in demonstrating the importance of the other branch of innate immunity in plants, which enables them to recognise the arrival of a broad range of pathogens, particularly bacteria. The grandson and nephew of forest engineers in his native Alsace, Zipfel switched from forestry to the more exciting field of molecular biology as a student. Fortuitously, he arrived at Basel to do a PhD at the Friedrich Miescher Institute soon after colleagues there had discovered the first example of a 'pathogen-associated molecular pattern' (PAMP), the protein flagellin, which is common to bacteria and recognised by receptors on the surfaces of plant cells. Working with the weed *Arabidopsis thaliana*, a member of the cabbage family widely used in plant molecular biology for its compact genome, fast generation time and ease of cultivation, he soon afterwards helped to discover a second PAMP called EF-Tu (elongation factor Tu), and to identify its receptor, EFR.

'Most geneticists thought this form of immunity was less important,' says Zipfel. 'Now it's in all the textbooks.' A chance encounter with Jonathan Jones at a conference led to an invitation to work with him as a post-doctoral fellow from 2005. Only two years later he was promoted to group leader. The early promotion was an example of the 'nimbleness' made possible by TSL's funding and governance.

'I had been offered, and accepted, a group leader position at the JIC,' says Zipfel. 'Within two weeks TSL had made a counter-offer, which I accepted. I can't think of anywhere else that would be able to do that.' By 2010, Zipfel and his colleagues had successfully transferred the gene for EFR into tomatoes and potatoes.[11] After going through the stringent regulatory process, they conducted the first field trials in 2015 and the results were striking: photographs show a row of blackened, dead and dying infected tomato plants facing a row of green and vigorous specimens protected with the transferred gene. The early success of the approach encouraged TSL to set up another research group working on pattern recognition receptors, led by Zipfel's former colleague from Basel, Silke Robatzek, who joined the lab in 2009.

As well as working on immune responses in plants, TSL scientists study the pathogens that provoke them, and this is the province of senior group leader Sophien Kamoun. Originally from Tunisia, he was working in the USA – as a tenured full professor at Ohio State University – when he chose to move to TSL on a five-year contract in 2007. He has never regretted it. 'We are trying to understand how pathogens trick plants into letting them infect them,' he says. 'We now know so much more about how the molecules from each side interact.' Complementing the work of other colleagues at TSL, he focuses on the organism that causes potato blight, *Phytophthora infestans*, and in 2009, with colleagues at the Broad Institute at Massachusetts Institute of Technology (MIT), succeeded in sequencing its genome. The sequence opened up the opportunity to find out much more about how the pathogen had such devastatingly destructive effects. 'The secret of its success is that it is very adaptable,' he says. While most parasites and pathogens tend to evolve reduced genomes, the *Phytophthora infestans* genome has just gone on getting bigger.

Kamoun has discovered that this is because it is bloated with long, repetitive non-coding sequences – what are sometimes misleadingly called 'junk DNA'. In these regions genes are scarce, but Kamoun discovered that they had something in common: they were largely the virulence genes that encode the effector molecules the plant immune system has to battle. These genes, unlike essential 'housekeeping' genes that change little from one species to another, have evolved very rapidly, specifically infecting particular species of wild potato. Kamoun coined the phrase 'two-speed genome' to describe this phenomenon. 'Just by sequencing the genome, we discovered this important concept,' he says. Others have since discovered two-speed genomes in wholly unrelated species.

Kamoun and his colleagues are exploring a variety of reasons why keeping its virulence genes in these gene-sparse regions makes the pathogen more effective – and more difficult for plant pathologists to combat. This is where TSL really benefits from the investment it has put into developing new research technologies. The latest is gene editing: instead of inserting genes from other strains or species of plant, it is now possible to make precisely targeted changes to the DNA of the host plant that are indistinguishable from natural mutations, using technologies such as CRISPR/Cas. 'This has huge potential to reduce the time it takes to develop new varieties,' says Kamoun. The regulatory bodies in Europe have yet to catch up with this new development. In the USA, new varieties that have been created with gene editing cause little concern to regulators, because the product is essentially indistinguishable from conventionally bred varieties. In Europe, it is the process that is regulated, not the product, and for the time being gene editing is still classed as genetic manipulation. In 2014, Kamoun and other plant scientists took the initiative in briefing journalists about these new developments and their implications for crop improvement at the Science Media Centre in London, garnering favourable reports in several newspapers.[12] TSL's successful editing of a tomato plant was chosen as one of four 'good things that happened in 2016' by the BBC World Service's *The Inquiry* programme.[13]

Meanwhile the formidable array of technical expertise built up at TSL makes it the first port of call globally for tackling emergent infections. In February 2016, Bangladesh experienced Asia's first outbreak of wheat blast, a fungal disease that infects up to 3 million hectares of wheat fields in Brazil and neighbouring countries. In affected parts of Bangladesh, it caused losses of up to 90 per cent in yield, and fields had to be burned to try to contain the outbreak. When his Bangladeshi colleagues appealed to him, Kamoun stopped what he was doing and within six weeks had identified the pathogen as the same one that was devastating South America. Rather than sitting on the data until it could be published, he then set up a website, Open Wheat Blast, and posted it online. Open Wheat Blast is based on TSL's earlier success with Open Ash Dieback, a collaborative website set up in response to the first emergence of the disease in the UK in 2012 (see Case study, page 134). The site is encouraging researchers all over the world to collaborate by sharing data and bringing their expertise to bear on analysing it, with a view to containing the outbreak before it spreads further in Asia. Without the flexibility to use his research funds as he saw fit, he would not have been able to do this – yet another example of TSL nimbleness.

'As an institute, we aim to establish durable resistance to disease in agricultural crops,' says Zipfel. 'That's a quantitative statement, not a qualitative one: in the end, the pathogen will always win. But we aim to make it more difficult.'

From lab to field: the Two Blades Foundation

While David Sainsbury has always championed the importance of basic research in advancing technology, his goal is its ultimate application in improving human welfare. And he recognises the perils of the so-called 'valley of death' – the vulnerable period when discoveries made by publicly funded scientists in research institutions have to make their way in the world before they become a convincing product likely to attract commercial investors. Via his private investment vehicles, he has funded venture capital initiatives to tackle this gap, with any dividends going to charitable causes. Through these vehicles, Roger Freedman was given a free hand to spend part of this money on projects designed to improve crops.

In 1983, the government had set up a company, Agricultural Genetics Company Limited, with several commercial partners, which was given the exclusive rights to develop all discoveries in government-funded institutes – including JIC and the PBI. As Dick Flavell wrote in 1989, most research scientists and commercial companies found this highly unsatisfactory and complained that it acted as a brake on developments in the UK while plant biotechnology in the USA and elsewhere was rushing ahead.[14]

David Sainsbury was only one of many who raised this restrictive policy with the agriculture ministry, and by 1994 Agricultural Genetics' exclusive rights had been relaxed. Gatsby and JIC jointly took the opportunity to set up a new company, JIC Innovations, to develop and market discoveries at JIC and the Sainsbury Lab on a 'mutual voluntary' (that is, non-exclusive) basis. The company later changed its name to Plant Biosciences Ltd (PBL) and now provides services to research organisations all over the country, funded through its licensing agreements and a number of government grants. It has a policy of providing licensing free or at low cost where there are humanitarian considerations, and shares its income with inventors and their institutions.

Freedman was initially a non-executive board member of Plant Biosciences and had been instrumental in setting it up. However, he was concerned that for the kind of research TSL was doing, working to achieve durable disease resistance in plants, the PBL model was inadequate: it could not support the high-throughput screening, field trials and other processes needed to get through the 'valley of death'. Meanwhile David Sainsbury had become Minister for Science and Innovation in 1998, and was enduring many hostile press attacks because of his known support for plant biotechnology (see Chapter 7). Freedman had an idea about how to move forward, but could not consult Sainsbury, as both his private and Gatsby funds were 'blinded' for the duration of his ministerial appointment.

Resigning from his seat on the board of PBL, Freedman decided to use funds from David Sainsbury's private investment company to develop a new initiative in the USA, where he already had many contacts, GM technology was widely accepted and David Sainsbury largely unknown. The result was the Two Blades Foundation (2Blades), a not-for-profit charitable company with a single mission: to develop durable disease resistance for major pathogens of major crops. A tiny organisation based in Evanston, Illinois, its role is to support near-market research, apply for patents on behalf of inventors, and license successful technologies to major companies. All its income is either ploughed back into the company or spent on developing technologies; in this way, commercial investment can be used to develop varieties that will ultimately benefit developing countries. Freedman recruited Diana Horvath, then science director of venture capital fund Agricultural Technology Partners, initially as chief operating officer and now president and de facto CEO of 2Blades.

'We do much more than technology transfer,' says Freedman. 'We identify needs and technical possibilities, and we identify people and stratagems, and we put the whole package together, and project manage it until we get to something that is ready to go into a company.' Right at the start Freedman made a very astute purchase, acquiring the rights to a gene-editing technology called TALEN (transcription activator-like effector nuclease) that had been developed by Jens Boch and his colleagues at Martin-Luther University in Halle, Germany. The technology is a Swiss Army knife of a tool, with applications across the whole of bioscience. 2Blades has gained a multimillion-dollar income from selling non-exclusive sub-licences to other companies, as well as giving a nice return to the inventors.

Since David Sainsbury came out of government, the foundation has received core funding from Gatsby and, with further income from licences and grants, 2Blades is a significant supporter of near-market research. It now funds a research group at TSL, led by Dutch scientist Peter van Esse, explicitly to bring discoveries in the lab to the point where they are ready to attract a commercial partner. An early project to engineer resistance to bacterial spot in tomatoes using Bs2, a gene from red peppers discovered by TSL advisor Brian Staskawicz at the University of Berkeley in California, has gone through six years of field trials in Florida and been found to double yields. Now efforts are under way to combine it with the EFR gene discovered by Cyril Zipfel to protect tomatoes against bacterial wilt as well.

Most significantly, 2Blades has negotiated a partnership with Dupont Pioneer that has successfully developed a variety of soybean that is resistant to Asian soybean rust, a disease that currently costs Brazilian farmers $1.7 billion per year in fungicide, using a gene from the wild legume pigeon pea.[15] Field trials have been undertaken in the USA; van Esse estimates that with not just one but a 'stack' of resistance genes, and once all the regulatory hurdles have been negotiated, a resistant variety should be commercially available to Brazilian farmers within a decade.

In 2015, a $2.3 million grant from the Gordon and Betty Moore Foundation to 2Blades established a collaboration between four international plant science centres of excellence, including TSL, to collect information on genetic diversity in plant disease resistance genes, using the rapid sequencing technology developed by Jonathan Jones's group at TSL. All the information will be placed in a publicly available database, ensuring that both academic and commercial plant scientists will have the opportunity to develop further products.

'2Blades has taken the basic knowledge of disease resistance and turned it into methodologies that enable you to produce products,' says Sainsbury. 'One of the few things I am certain about in life is that in fifty years people will look back and say one of the great agricultural revolutions in the history of mankind took place at the beginning of the twenty-first century. Because the ability to genetically alter plants enables one to transform productivity in agriculture.'

Cutting edge II: The Sainsbury Laboratory Cambridge

When David Sainsbury emerged from his eight-year stint as science minister in the Blair government in 2006, he was quick to catch up with what was happening in the Gatsby projects. TSL was going from strength to strength. But there were other areas of research that were ripe for investment. 'Roger had seen that there was a possibility to study how plants grow and develop,' says Sainsbury. 'Microscopy, genetics and computer modelling were all coming together to address questions that were relevant to plant productivity and response to environmental stresses such as climate change.'

'In David's absence, it had been difficult for the trustees to decide on a major new initiative,' says Freedman, 'so to try to move things along I organised a two-day closed meeting in 2004, bringing together leading scientists in the field but designed as an instructional opportunity for the trustees.' Invited to that meeting was Elliot Meyerowitz, George W. Beadle Professor of Biology at the California Institute of Technology (Caltech) and one of the world's leading plant developmental biologists. He was enthusiastic about the idea, provisionally floated at the meeting, of a lab dedicated to the subject.

Gatsby took the decision to go ahead at the end of 2006. 'I was now licensed to work towards the establishment of a new laboratory,' says Freedman. 'I had become convinced that the particular approach that Elliot was developing was the right way to go. Elliot wasn't ready to commit to leaving Caltech to lead a new lab, but he generously agreed to help bring the new lab into existence – we assembled an advisory board which he chaired.' Meyerowitz says:

> There are two big frontiers. One is understanding the funda-
> mental developmental mechanisms that control how the one-
> dimensional instructions from a DNA molecule are read out
> into a three-dimensional, dynamic set of cells that make up
> a plant's organisation. Then there are environmental factors,
> such as temperature, water and light, as well as the presence
> of other organisms, that alter development. Unlike animals,
> which have a fixed body plan, plants are very plastic in the
> way they develop.

Meyerowitz's approach to dealing with all this complexity is to complement experimental research with computer modelling. 'You have to be careful in making models that accurately represent the variables in your experiment,' he says. 'So if you change the experiment, you have a prediction about what the result will be.'

Freedman organised a series of small meetings, inviting both younger and more experienced plant developmental biologists and computational scientists from around the world to present their work. Ottoline Leyser, then Professor of Plant Sciences at the University of York, was one of those invited. As a graduate student she had helped to pioneer the use of *Arabidopsis* as a model organism to study the genetics of development, and when the AFRC started a UK *Arabidopsis* initiative it funded her to train as a post-doc in the USA before she set up her own plant molecular biology lab at York. 'Roger's meetings became semi-notorious in the community because nobody could figure out whether they were recruitment events or just scoping events,' she says. 'Initially I wasn't thinking about it as anything other than a very good thing for UK plant science.'

The idea was to site the lab on the footprint of some old

buildings on the northern edge of the University of Cambridge's Botanic Gardens, and to make it an independent institute affiliated to the University. Through negotiation with Freedman and the Gatsby director Peter Hesketh, Cambridge had become more amenable to the Gatsby model of governance: Gatsby also provided generous funding to the Cambridge Department of Plant Sciences to enable David Baulcombe to set up his lab when he moved there as Regius Professor in 2007. Freedman eventually persuaded Meyerowitz to take a two-year sabbatical from Caltech and move to the UK as inaugural director. He also invited Ottoline Leyser, who was considering a job offer from overseas, to bid for extra support from Gatsby for her lab in York, and then persuaded her to apply to join the new lab as associate director and Meyerowitz's de facto successor.

Initially both Freedman and Sainsbury planned to commission a functional building to accommodate the new institute. 'I said "Science changes",' says Freedman. 'You shouldn't put a lot of effort into building something wonderful, because you're going to knock it down in twenty years.' This fitted well with the views of Cambridge University's building services department, who wanted to work with an architect that had built a lab before and that they already knew. But at this point Sainsbury's wife Susie intervened: 'I said, "But you've been given one of the most beautiful sites in the country – why can't you have a beautiful building?"'

Sainsbury's previous experience of working with Foster + Partners on his parents' great legacy, the Sainsbury Centre for Visual Arts (SCVA; see Chapter 10), had given him an understanding of the potential complexity of major building projects. Susie Sainsbury was vice-chair of the governors of the Royal Shakespeare Company (RSC), and was heading the transformation programme that would see its theatre rebuilt (also covered in Chapter 10). The last thing she thought was needed, as her husband's first major building on a hugely sensitive site, was

125

what she called 'a red-brick box'. She suggested the names of leading firms of architects she thought could reliably deliver a beautiful building. Meanwhile, Freedman went off to visit other labs around the world and ask them what was right and what was wrong about the buildings in which they worked. 'You need to hang around and talk to the graduate students,' he says. 'The principles that came out of that are maximum natural light, adaptability and the promotion of conviviality and interaction.'

The choice of architect eventually fell on Stanton Williams, a partnership established in 1985 by Alan Stanton and Paul Williams, with a track record of distinguished buildings and a willingness to explore the needs of the scientists as they developed their design. Presented with options from the absolutely basic to state of the art, David Sainsbury agreed to an enhanced budget from Gatsby of £82 million. He appointed Stuart Johnson, who had come in as project manager during a major refurbishment of the SCVA, to help keep the whole thing on track.

To work with Stanton Williams, Freedman brought in Robert McGhee, who had worked for the Howard Hughes Medical Institute in the USA on their Janelia Research Campus in Ashburn, Virginia, as advisor, together with Alan Cavill, who had previously been the lab manager at the Sainsbury Laboratory in Norwich.

The Sainsbury Laboratory Cambridge University (SLCU) is a defining statement of David Sainsbury's commitment to plant sciences. Stanton Williams Architects created a stunning two-storey building that integrates seamlessly with its natural surroundings. The interior is as carefully thought through as the exterior: it provides abundant natural light and numerous opportunities for interaction between the scientists, to encourage discussion and collaboration. 'And a view out into the garden,' says Meyerowitz, 'so that nobody can take their minds off the central issue, which is how plants are growing.' Accompanied by the Duke of Edinburgh, who was also the Chancellor of

Laboratories at the Sainsbury Laboratory Cambridge University
(SLCU) conduct research into plant growth and development,
with multiple research groups sharing space and facilities.

Cambridge University, Her Majesty the Queen opened the laboratory on 27 April 2011. (David Sainsbury would be nominated to succeed Prince Philip as Chancellor a month later, and was elected in October 2011.) The building went on to win the Royal Institute of British Architects premier prize, the Stirling Prize, in 2012.

As planned, Meyerowitz returned to Caltech after two years, and Leyser took over: much of her job in the early years was to complete the task of filling the place with top-class scientists. By 2016, the laboratory had reached its capacity of twelve research groups, with leaders recruited from all over the world. They include physicists and mathematicians who develop models of plant growth that can then be tested both theoretically and practically. As well as the computing network and plant growth rooms, the lab has state-of-the-art microscopy facilities that enable the scientists to watch live cells developing in real time and track the movements of key molecules. Crucially, the lab has a team of support staff that keep all this equipment running. Says Leyser:

> The reason development emerged as best focus for the lab is that there is this extraordinary range of tools available. Genomics, amazing live imaging, atomic force microscopes – we can probe changes in the cell walls that are enormously important for plant growth. And then there has been enough foundation work over the years to identify the core signalling pathways involved in many of the events in plant development to allow the development of predictive dynamical models. The lab has been founded at exactly the time when there is this ongoing transition from collecting up of the parts to figuring out how they actually work to deliver an organism. Just now is really the first time when it's been possible to put together these pieces.

Integrating theory and practice is at the core of how the lab works. It is also founded on principles of collaboration that affect even where people sit. 'We have an open-plan lab system where groups are randomly interspersed,' says Leyser. 'There's no zoning per group. We have maximum group sizes: nobody's group is allowed to be more than twelve people, and that has driven very good collaborations. There's a whole range of things we've done to create an environment where people are excited about their science and what they can discover, rather than feeling deeply anxious all the time about delivering. It's actually very exciting! And it would have been totally impossible without Gatsby funding.'

Just as had happened in Norwich, the long-term funding has helped groups to take a gamble on unproven research. 'We wanted people to be limited by nothing but their imagination,' says Meyerowitz. 'The Gatsby fellowships give group leaders enough money to keep going even when grant funding isn't coming in. You know that if you try something risky, you can keep trying – you are not going to be shut down in a year and your post-docs and students are not going to pay the price.'

His own work is a case in point. Though based in California, Meyerowitz still retains a research group at SLCU, working in collaboration with SLCU computational biologist Henrik Jönsson. They are interested in what goes on at the tip of a growing shoot, where the hormone auxin prompts undifferentiated stem cells to develop into flowers or leaves. Much of the recent focus has been on the plant cell wall, which gives the plant its structural rigidity. Plant biomass is mostly made up of cell walls, yet for a long time they were neglected as a topic of research. The research at SLCU in recent years has shown that the cell wall is an active participant in development.[16]

'The entire pattern of what cells are doing has to do with what is happening in the cell wall,' says Meyerowitz. 'No one had looked at this in this way before. It took us about five years – I don't think we could have got there without the long-term vision of Gatsby. We would have lost our grant, if we'd ever been able to get a grant in the first place.'

Leyser's group focuses on shoot branching, the process by which buds adjacent to leaves on the main stem grow into new shoots, and how it is tuned by changes in the environment. 'The same genotype can result in a single, unbranched shoot or a spectacularly ramified bush,' she says. 'This developmental plasticity has numerous applications in agriculture. There is no doubt that changes in shoot-system architecture have been fundamental to the domestication of crop species. Understanding how that works in an era of low-input agriculture is an important goal.' Working with the model plant *Arabidopsis*, Leyser and her colleagues have unravelled the complex communication systems within the main stem that mediate competition between the leading shoot and side shoots, and among the side shoots themselves, for access to auxin transport paths down to the root. 'We've discovered that this downward stem auxin transport system has what is effectively both a fast lane and a slow lane,' says Leyser. 'This is important for regulating the export of auxin from the side shoots.'[17]

Over and above the specifics of her own and her colleagues' research, Leyser has a strong commitment to raising the profile of plant sciences in the world at large. 'Plant sciences is moving up the agenda largely because of food security – people have finally noticed that it's an important thing for humankind,' she says. 'For a long time that wasn't the case. Now we are looking at both environmental and agricultural crises that are dependent on understanding plants to mitigate them.' The lab has an active public engagement programme, as well as a series of seminars and workshops to share the latest information within and beyond Cambridge.

'This building is a marker that plant sciences is worthy of this level of investment,' says Leyser, who was made a Dame Commander of the Order of the British Empire in the 2016 New Year's Honours list. 'If someone invests in you to the extent that David Sainsbury has invested in us, the responsibility to do something significant with that money is extraordinary. I don't feel I need to do anything to raise the level of ambition of my colleagues.'

Plants from cradle to grave

Funding top-class researchers was worth doing only if there was a pool of bright young scientists waiting to be recruited into their teams, but in the 1980s plant science was not a popular option for PhD students, and there were many attractive opportunities in biomedicine. The Gatsby plant science advisors recommended that the trustees fund a small number of graduate student-ships for plant science projects. 'I devised a system involving virtually zero administration [for Gatsby],' says David Ingram. 'We would choose eight supervisors and ask each of them to select a student to be interviewed by us: we then selected four to receive an enhanced stipend. It was very unusual for students to be interviewed competitively in that way.' The number of supervisors or 'Gatsby mentors' has increased over the years, but the studentships remain highly competitive.

Each year Gatsby holds a networking event for students and alumni of the scheme, together with their mentors. After nearly thirty years, this 'Gatsby plant sciences network' has turned into a powerful advocacy group for plant science, as well as a tool for professional collaboration. It has enabled Gatsby to adopt a 'cradle to grave' approach in their funding of plant science education and training.

'For the public to be better informed about plant science,' says Ingram, 'school was the right place to start.' But for many teachers, presenting biology in relation to the human body seemed more likely to keep students engaged, while plants were indelibly associated with the outmoded 'nature study' of their own schooldays. Ingram wanted to find a way of supporting science teachers to use plants in the classroom. Paul Williams in Madison, Wisconsin, had set up a successful programme of school practical projects using 'fast plants': a variety of brassica that would grow from seed to mature plant in just a few weeks under fluorescent lights. In 1989, Gatsby funded Richard Price, a former science teacher then working for the Cambridge Local Examinations Syndicate, to visit Williams to learn more about his programme.

'I came back and reported to Gatsby that I thought it would be possible to set up a similar programme for schools in the UK,' says Price. The result was Science and Plants for Schools (SAPS), established with its own board of trustees initially chaired by David Ingram. Price oversaw the production of 'fast plant' kits for schools, offered grants to schools to buy the kits and lighting, and through in-service training sessions recruited a gradually widening network of teachers who were not only enthusiastic about using the kits in their lessons, but came up with ideas to extend the programme. Beginning with 200 schools, the scheme quickly expanded, and Price became its director. When in 1999 the Wellcome Trust commissioned a survey asking teachers to rate fifteen organisations (including themselves) who were working to support biology teaching, SAPS came top. Meanwhile David Ingram, who had been appointed Director of the Royal Botanic Gardens in Edinburgh, oversaw the development of a SAPS programme in Scotland, geared to the different qualifications taught in Scottish schools. One of the first projects of the SAPS Scotland team was to devise a low-cost kit to introduce plant DNA technology into the classroom.

Headed from 2009 until 2016 by Ginny Page, who previously worked on the education team at the Royal Society, SAPS continues to offer free resources including videos, lesson plans and practical notes, grants to develop new practicals, and an associates' scheme for teachers and technicians in secondary schools with opportunities for continuing professional development.[18] The number of associates – teachers and technicians – rose from 2,000 to 5,000 between 2009 and 2016. One associate who has contributed to the SAPS package of resources is Richard Spencer, head of science at Middlesbrough College on Teesside, who was shortlisted in 2015 for the £1 million Global Teacher Prize. Spencer taught a whole A level Biology syllabus centred around the mint plant. 'He challenged himself to find as many links as possible,' says Page. 'He had all his students looking after mint plants that they grew from cuttings, and enabled them to engage better with some difficult scientific concepts. That's what you'd love every teacher to be able to do.'

As part of the wider Gatsby science education programme (see Chapter 6), Page continued to engage in policy work in an effort to raise the profile of plant science in GCSE (General Certificate of Secondary Education) and A level curricula. For example, the practical that is now in many science specifications is one developed by SAPS that involves algal balls, photosynthesising algae encapsulated in alginate gel, so that students can explore processes that are notoriously difficult to demonstrate. 'We took that very successful practical and said to the awarding bodies, "Look what can be done in biology lessons, we know teachers and students enjoy it – and plants are fundamental to an understanding of the natural world",' says Page. She observes that SAPS is remarkable for the length of time it has been generously funded by Gatsby. 'We are able to produce high-quality resources,' she says. 'It's always been important for us that plant science does not look in any way like a Cinderella subject.'

Two further programmes bridge the gap between SAPS and the graduate studentships. In 2005, Celia Knight, a Gatsby mentor at the University of Leeds, applied for a grant to run a week-long summer school for eighty undergraduates at the end of their first year, to be recruited through the Gatsby plant science network. It proved such a success that it has continued ever since, and is now part of the Gatsby Plant Science Education Programme at the University of Cambridge. An evaluation after five years found that students on the summer school were more than twice as likely to do a final-year project in plant science as their peers who did not attend, and more than three times as likely to do a plant science PhD.

In addition, Gatsby's network of mentors invites second-year undergraduates to apply for grants to carry out a summer project in a research laboratory. Like applicants for PhD studentships, the students are interviewed, and the advisors award about seven studentships per year. Many go on to graduate study in plant sciences.

Case study: Open Ash Dieback

In 2012, Anne Edwards, a scientist at the John Innes Centre (JIC) at the University of East Anglia (UEA), noticed while walking in the ancient Ashwellthorpe wood nearby that the ash trees were diseased. With colleagues, she showed that the pathogen was *Hymenoscyphus fraxineus* (previously *Chalara fraxinea*), or ash dieback, a fungal disease that had been spreading through Europe since the early 1990s. The discovery made national news, as the UK feared losing its entire population of ash trees, some hundreds of years old – a repeat of the epidemic of Dutch elm disease that destroyed nearly all mature English elms between 1970 and 1990.

It was fortuitous that being exposed to winds from Europe, it was Norfolk that first encountered ash dieback in the wild – on the doorstep of the UK's largest concentration of plant pathologists. Researchers from three Norwich research institutes, including The Sainsbury Laboratory (TSL), immediately formed an open consortium, pooling their existing funds to start sequencing both ash trees and fungi. They were quickly joined by researchers in Denmark and Norway, who had identified trees that could survive infection, and at the Universities of York and Exeter. The group, dubbed Nornex, soon won £2.4 million funding from the Biotechnology and Biosciences Research Council (BBSRC) and other agencies to take forward its project.

The task of setting up Open Ash Dieback, the crowdsourcing hub that would host Nornex's data, fell to Dan MacLean, head of bioinformatics at TSL. 'It's frustrating when science isn't quick enough to respond in emergencies,' he says. 'Open Ash Dieback is a different way of doing science. The fact that it stayed open encouraged foreign partners to become involved. For example, Erik Kjær in Copenhagen did not have the funds to generate sequence data, but he had been working on ash dieback for years and he shared his tree samples.' Very soon, the group had enough information to enable it to predict, on the basis of their genetic sequences, which trees would be able to tolerate the fungus. 'In Oxfordshire and Devon, 90 per cent of trees turned out to be tolerant,' says MacLean, 'but the ancient woodland in Norfolk has trees that are more like those in Poland and Denmark, where many trees have died. All this has happened in two years – computational management and open access has massively sped up what we were able to do.'[19]

Fraxinus, an online game that allowed volunteers to match
genetic sequences in the fight against ash dieback.

MacLean went on to develop a 'citizen science' initiative that allowed
Facebook users to help spot genetic variants in the fungus by playing an
online game. Fraxinus, launched in August 2013, invited players to match
sequences taken from different specimens against a reference sequence,
winning points for accuracy. 'People can do this better than machines,' says
MacLean, explaining that, while genomics projects make use of automated
alignment, after a certain point it is too expensive and time-consuming
to pursue further. With thousands of willing volunteers, it is possible to
discover more variants at the level of single 'letters' in the genome – variants
that might be significant in predicting resistance in plants or virulence in
pathogens. Players also proved to be much better than machines at aligning
larger mismatches known as 'indels' – insertions and deletions of multiple
letters. The game ran for just under a year: in that time 25,000 players helped
to provide 74,356 answers to 10,000 puzzles, providing the scientists with
7,000 improved variant sequences. MacLean also collected useful information about the behaviour of the players: it turned out that most visited the
site only briefly, while 50 per cent of the work was done by just 49 people.[20]

The outlook for ash trees in Britain is still uncertain, but thanks to Open Ash Dieback the guardians of our woodland are much better equipped to mount surveillance over existing trees, ban the importation of infected saplings and select resistant strains for future planting.

··

6

SKILLS FOR THE
TWENTY-FIRST CENTURY

Scientific and technical education

In 1986, the historian Correlli Barnett published *The Audit of War*, a scathing account of British government policy in the postwar years.[1] A particular target of his ire was technical education. David Sainsbury read his book, and it struck a powerful chord. In his early days in the personnel department at Sainsbury's he had witnessed the failure of one national system of technical and vocational training after another. 'Every ten years we wake up to the fact that we do not have good technical education,' he says.

> Some person is asked to write a report. The report is in three parts: the first says we have a terrible problem, the second says we must have some organisational change, and the third says we must try harder. And we have a new organisation, and it doesn't make a difference, and we wait for the next change. And no one ever sits down and says, 'What do we need, what has worked previously, what works elsewhere?'

Since the mid-1980s Gatsby has been developing initiatives that seek to address the issue. For the first twenty-five years or so the foundation gave grants to education authorities, university departments, professional bodies and other charities 'to support an improvement in educational opportunity in the UK for a workforce that can better apply technology for wealth creation by incubating innovative programmes that promote excellence in teaching and learning'.

The education programme at Gatsby has evolved over the years, with projects in science, technology and engineering aimed at every level from preschool children to university researchers, at a cost of some £200 million. It has scored some notable successes. A scheme to train graduates without physics degrees to teach physics, now adopted nationally, boosted the number of physics teachers by 30 per cent. Innovative teaching resources brought cutting-edge materials and techniques into science and DT (design and technology) lessons in every secondary school in the country. A distance learning scheme in further maths reversed the decline in sixth forms offering the subject at A level and trebled the number of candidates. A national STEM (Science, Technology, Engineering and Mathematics) network, together with a National STEM Centre (now STEM Learning Ltd), supported science teachers with training and resources for practical work. The Sainsbury Management Fellows Scheme gives business training and mentoring opportunities to graduate engineers, many of whom have gone on to become business leaders.

A recent OECD report placed the UK twentieth in a world ranking of the science and maths achievement of 15-year-olds. The top five places were all taken by East Asian countries, led by Singapore; in Europe, the Netherlands, Switzerland, Poland, Estonia and Finland all made the top twelve. The OECD argues that improving the skills of school leavers is a powerful driver of economic growth. Yet the problem of a shortage of suitably trained young people to meet the needs of science-, engineering- and technology-based industry is still far from solved.

Since 2010, Gatsby's educational work has sharpened its focus, describing its mission as 'Strengthening science and engineering skills in the UK by developing and enabling innovative programmes and informing national policy'. It has advocated reforms to apprenticeships and technical education in colleges; promoted professional registration for technicians and a greater recognition of the importance of technician roles; and championed a coherent approach to STEM education and better careers advice and guidance.

The Engineering Education Continuum/BEST

In 1977, Sir Monty Finniston, the Glaswegian metallurgist who had just stepped down as Chairman of British Steel, chaired a departmental inquiry into the training and role of engineers in industry. He found that what he called the 'engineering dimension' was neglected in most British manufacturing firms, relative to what he found in other countries. Engineers were the exception rather than the rule on boards, and there was no attempt to plan for future innovation.[2]

The trouble started at the grass roots. Basic science at school neglected applied and practical activities, while university-level engineering degrees were too narrowly focused on technical subjects and did not prepare students for the business environment. None of this was a surprise: the absence of scientists and engineers from positions of leadership and influence had been a source of concern to many since the nineteenth century. But the newly installed Conservative minister at the Department of Trade and Industry (DTI), Keith Joseph, did not act on most of Finniston's recommendations.

Technical education first appeared as an area of Gatsby's interest in the mid-1980s, though it had been a concern of David Sainsbury's for longer. There was no immediately obvious way to address the question, so Hugh de Quetteville went looking for an advisor. Roger Baker was a Professor of Engineering who had worked at Cambridge University, Imperial College London and later at Cranfield Institute of Technology. He had successfully applied for funding from one of the Sainsbury family trusts to develop ways of enabling engineers with disabilities to make use of computers in their work, and one day de Quetteville came to visit. By the end of their conversation de Quetteville was sufficiently impressed to invite Baker to become Gatsby's advisor on technical education projects. A few years later Baker joined SFCT as Assistant Director.

Baker thought that part of the problem was that able school students had too little knowledge of industry, so that even those with a technical bent were unlikely to choose an engineering degree. He proposed what came to be called the Engineering Education Scheme (EES). 'I lived in St Albans,' says Baker, 'so I suggested they pilot the scheme with Hertfordshire County Council. The idea was to get local industries to suggest projects, which teams of students would carry out.' Selected sixth-form students spent up to a hundred extracurricular hours on these projects, supervised by an engineer, as well as undergoing week-long placements in the partner company. At the end of the year they presented their projects before an invited audience. By the end of 1989, 1,168 pupils had taken part and twenty-five local education authorities had asked Hertfordshire to help them set up similar schemes in their own areas.

In 1990, the Fellowship of Engineering (since 1992 the Royal Academy of Engineering) took over the management of the EES from Hertfordshire. In the same year Gatsby put up the funds to extend the project into an 'Engineering Education Continuum', embracing the EES, a university scheme, and an MBA programme for graduate engineers, the Sainsbury Management Fellowship scheme (see next section). The avowedly elitist object was 'to place some of the most able students from our schools in positions of leadership in engineering industry, and to enhance their education and training in order to equip them for such positions'. Other initiatives included the Year in Industry, industrial placements for school leavers who would later take up degree courses in engineering, and Sainsbury scholarships for selected undergraduate engineers.

In 2001, the Royal Academy of Engineering (RAEng) renamed the Continuum as BEST (Better Engineering, Science, Technology) and reaffirmed its aim to 'recruit, train and retain the brightest and most motivated young people into and within the engineering profession to fulfil the needs of the economy and society'. Despite its original aim to withdraw after five years, after more than a decade Gatsby was putting between £1 million and £1.5 million per year into BEST. From 2004, Gatsby and the RAEng agreed a tapering away of Gatsby funding as the Academy built up funding from other sources – the total Gatsby had invested with the Academy since 1989 amounted to £19 million.

In 2008, one of Gatsby's key advisors on technology transfer, Professor of Engineering Neil Alford of Imperial College London, became co-chairman of BEST. 'By that time, they were reaching a huge number of students, and had got a number of industries involved,' he says. 'It was quite clear that what Gatsby had wanted to happen had taken place. It ended up as a success story, though it took a long time to get off the ground.' Today the key elements of the programme are still offered by the Engineering Development Trust, a not-for-profit agency set up by the RAEng for this purpose, and funded from a variety of industrial and charitable sources.[3]

Sainsbury Management Fellows

In 1986, having consulted some young engineers through what is now the RAEng, David Sainsbury decided to give very bright engineers with experience in industry the opportunity to go to business school. 'You need more people running companies who really understand the technology,' he says. 'If you don't, you're not really running them from an entrepreneurial viewpoint.' He himself had taken an MBA at Columbia University a few years after leaving Cambridge. 'We thought they should go abroad,' he says, 'because that widens their horizons.'

Gatsby funded twenty Sainsbury Management Fellows (SMFs) in each of the first two years, most of whom went to INSEAD in Paris. Since then the Fellowship has grown by about ten new fellows per year, reaching 330 in 2016. Leading business schools in the USA and UK are now accredited to the programme, as well as those in continental Europe. The statistics on the performance of SMFs are impressive. Over 153 have founded or co-founded businesses with a total value of over £4.6 billion, and created over 18,000 jobs. Over 275 start-ups are still in business. More than 40 per cent of SMFs currently hold executive board roles.

They are an extremely diverse community. Tom Delay is founding Chief Executive of the Carbon Trust, making the business case for investment in sustainability. Imoni Akpofure is a Senior Associate at Kina Advisory and one of four Senior Advisors to the Africa50 infrastructure fund, set up by the African Development Bank to support large-scale national and regional infrastructure projects in Africa. Mark Johnson is leader of marine innovation at Raymarine, a world leader in high-performance marine electronics, which bought his company and continues to produce his award-winning designs.

When the number of SMFs reached 60 – by this time they had set up their own society – they hired Cathy Breeze to act as a central point of contact and catalyst for networking. 'I make contact when they are about to go to business school and invite them to a welcome dinner with all the existing SMFs,' she says. 'I will be communicating with them while they are at school, and if they wish, I'll match them up with an SMF mentor.'

The SMFs are not an exclusive club, however. 'If any engineer gets in touch with me, or is at school and thinking of becoming an engineer, or acquiring business skills, I will find them a mentor,' says Breeze. 'The door is always open to anyone who is, or is interested in becoming, an engineer.' SMFs work with young engineers: they help with the RAEng's Engineering Leadership Awards and Executive Engineers programmes, and participate in the selection of future SMFs. Recently they have begun a publicity drive to improve the image of engineering, publishing an annual Hard Hat Index to persuade editors and advertisers not to represent engineers as though they were all construction workers.

Since 2010, the SMFs have been seeking to establish an independent future for the Fellowship. The society was incorporated as a company limited by guarantee in 2011, and registered as a charity the following year – its twenty-fifth anniversary – under the name Engineers in Business Fellowship. Seeking to inculcate a 'culture of giving' among its own members, it launched a fundraising campaign in 2014 to build up an endowment. Within two years the campaign had raised almost £2 million of the £10 million target – David Sainsbury is matching donations pound for pound during the first five years of the campaign.

Support for the curriculum

The late 1980s were a time of great change in English education. A new examination for all students at age 16, the GCSE (General Certificate in Secondary Education) replaced O levels, which had catered only for the top 30 per cent of the ability range, and CSEs (Certificate in Secondary Education), which were taken by the next 50 per cent. The new science and technology GCSEs aimed to include content more relevant to the students by demonstrating its application in a variety of social and industrial contexts.

At the same time the Education Act of 1988, introduced by Conservative education minister Kenneth Baker, for the first time prescribed what was taught in all schools in England, Wales and Northern Ireland. The National Curriculum specified a number of subjects that students were 'entitled' by law to be offered at different points during their school career. It also provided for national testing at the ages of 7, 11, 14 and 16, so that schools could be ranked in league tables on their students' performance at each stage. For the first time, science was made compulsory for all students up to the age of 16, along with English and mathematics, and design and technology also became statutory, although students were later able to drop it after the age of 14.

At this time most primary teachers did not have science qualifications and many lacked confidence in teaching science, while the extra demand for teaching the sciences and design and technology in secondary schools also had huge implications for classroom resources and teacher training. Gatsby was one of a number of bodies that developed schemes to support them. It remains a relatively crowded field, with the Nuffield Foundation, the Wellcome Trust, the Salter's Company, the Smallpeice Trust, the Association for Science Education, the Design and Technology Association (DATA) and professional bodies in engineering, science and technology all active to some degree.

Science and Technology in Society

As early as 1984, the Association for Science Education (ASE) decided to support teachers as the new curriculum came into effect by producing a series of topic-based units, initially for the 14–16 age group and later for younger students. They seconded John Holman, head of science at Watford Grammar School for Boys, to direct the project, which they called SATIS (Science and Technology in Society), and began to look for funders. Starting in 1985, Gatsby made an increasingly generous succession of grants to ASE that helped to ensure the success of the SATIS project.

Sir John Holman, knighted in 2010 for his services to education, has been a leading advisor to Gatsby and other bodies ever since. 'SATIS turned out to be very successful,' he says; 'very widely used in the UK and also overseas. We would take a topic that was already in the syllabus, find some interesting application and write about that.' There were eventually ten books, all linked to some topic in the GCSE science curriculum: examples of unit topics included noise, physics and cooking, and air pollution. The first set, for 14- to 16-year-old students, were distributed to every school in the country, and were so popular that they were twice updated, most recently in 2008–10. Among the later topics were making things waterproof, designing a bicycle, and sport and fitness.

The Technology Enhancement Programme
While the National Curriculum's assertion that all children should be offered lessons in science and technology could be seen as positive, there was widespread concern among engineers about the content of the design and technology (D&T) curriculum. 'People tried to shoehorn into one curriculum metalwork, woodwork, needlework and cookery, all lumped together,' says Holman. 'D&T became very loose and lost a lot of rigour.' A number of organisations, including the ASE and DATA, approached Gatsby about projects to support the new curriculum. Impressed by the work Holman had done with SATIS, the Gatsby trustees asked him to coordinate these different approaches into a new Technology Enhancement Programme (TEP), producing textbooks and classroom resources to help teachers of Design and Technology develop skills and activities that would inspire their charges to consider careers as engineers or technicians.

At this stage Gatsby itself still had no staff of its own: both de Quetteville and Roger Baker, together with one or two further officers, worked across all the Sainsbury trusts, and there was no capacity within the organisation to run such a scheme. Looking for a partner to host and manage TEP, they chose the Engineering Council, the body that sets and maintains standards in the British engineering industry. Gatsby asked John Williams, head of the Engineering Council's general education programmes, to take charge. 'I found some really good people', he says, 'who had been technology advisors in local authorities and had experience of going into schools. But I needed to find someone who could write.'

Eventually he found the ideal person: John Cave, Professor of Education at Middlesex University. 'We had just finished a major government contract to devise SATs [standardised assessment tasks] for the National Curriculum,' says Cave. 'That alerted John [Williams] to the fact that we were a live force.' However, Cave's engagement meant that TEP became much more than a textbook publisher. In 1986, he had started a small, not-for-profit spin-out company called Teaching Resources, which created and distributed basic scientific and technical equipment for schools. Cave suggested that as well as textbooks TEP would fund work into the development of similar materials. 'John developed a huge range of unique, cutting-edge physical resources for TEP,' says Williams. 'TEP was able to give schools access to modern technology at ultra-low cost.'

By the end of 1995, 1,000 schools and further education colleges had joined the programme as associates, and almost 4,000 had bought products or services. Cave remained with TEP for almost twenty years. 'Everything we did was premised on the restoration of significant technical content in the provision that schools were offering,' he says. 'And we succeeded in many ways. Since we were heading towards a multimillion-pound turnover by 2005, we must have been doing something right.'

Cave's company, Teaching Resources, won a Queen's Anniversary Award in 1998 for 'combining enterprise and entrepreneurial activity with an education agenda'. 'David hosted a lunch at the House of Lords to celebrate,' says Cave. 'I suspect the award would not have happened without TEP. That gave us both the investment we needed and the incentive to develop new products.' One of the most successful products was called the 'bit-by-bit controller'. Schools in the 1990s had only limited access to computers, too few to allow small groups of students to experiment with control systems. 'Industry ran on controllers

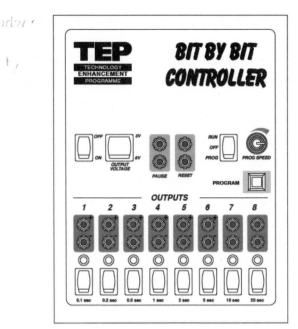

Teacher's manual for the bit-by-bit controller
developed for schools by John Cave as part of Gatsby's
Technology Enhancement Programme.

called PLCs [programmable logic controllers],' says Cave. 'They
were sub-computer-level systems, and we replicated that.'

One of TEP's aims was to help teachers to refresh the curriculum by introducing new technologies and new materials to
demonstrate the principles and processes their students had
to understand. Discovered in 1996 and patented by the British
company Peratech, one such new material was called quantum
tunnelling composite, or QTC. It had the property that it changed
from an insulator to a conductor when it was compressed,
making it a natural touch or pressure sensor. 'We approached
the company, and applied for a specific grant from Gatsby to
secure the first large-scale supply,' says Cave. With an additional small contribution from the Department for Education

and Skills (DfES), Gatsby bought 100 pill-sized pieces of QTC for every secondary school in the country and donated them as a 'science gift'. 'For the first time ever, schools were on the cusp of an invention that was just emerging from the laboratory,' says Cave. 'It was a great incentive for teachers and students to take an interest in new materials.'

Meanwhile Baker had asked Williams to 'think big' and to come up with a development plan for TEP. He proposed, in addition to developing classroom materials and trialling them in schools, to develop courses for initial teacher training and continuing professional development, and to monitor and evaluate the work in schools so that Gatsby could influence the content of the curriculum and examination syllabuses. Williams says:

> I costed it, and could not get it below £4.3 million. And this was in 1993. I took the proposal to David Sainsbury and the trustees at a meeting at the Sainsbury's head office. He had read the document, and was wonderfully enthusiastic. And a lot of that did happen – we had a serious impact on examination syllabuses, beyond anything that I expected.

An evaluation of TEP by the National Foundation for Educational Research in 1999 estimated that 90 per cent of the schools in the UK had benefited from its work.

In the long term, however, the philosophy behind TEP could not compete with the agenda that came in with the appointment of Michael Gove as Education Secretary in 2010, focusing heavily on academic subjects. While in principle schools could continue to teach a wide range of subjects for GCSE, their performance would be assessed largely on those included in the 'English Baccalaureate' – English, maths, science, history or geography and a modern language. 'A lot of the momentum has gone out of the technology curriculum because of that,' says Williams. 'It's a great pity. It was a practical subject that gave young people all sorts of skills.'

There are, nevertheless, surviving legacies of TEP. The classroom materials have been digitised and archived at the National STEM Learning Centre in York (see page 158), and the teachers' subject association DATA, which received Gatsby funding, continues to support the subject in schools.[4] After John Cave's retirement, the University of Middlesex relaunched his not-for-profit company Teaching Resources independently as Mindsets, which continues to supply equipment for science and technology teaching to schools.[5] 'Its main purpose is still to provide a modernising influence in curriculum matters,' says Cave. 'One legacy of Gatsby's interest in this area is the company and its mission and philosophy.'

Gatsby Technical Education Projects: a separate charity

In 1994, the Engineering Council underwent a restructuring. Its board no longer consisted of a selection of the 'great and good', empowered to make decisions, but instead each of its many member institutions sent a representative. Decision-making suffered, and Williams felt strongly that the education programmes were no longer a priority for the Engineering Council. He expected that Gatsby would cancel TEP, but Baker and the Gatsby trustees thought laterally. 'They came up with the idea of taking it back in house,' he says. 'They asked me to come with it and bring the whole team.' Following the example of the country trusts in Africa, Gatsby established a separate charity to handle its education projects, with its own trustees and its own staff working alongside the SFCT staff. Williams continues:

> We used to manage and run some programmes from Gatsby Technical Education Projects [GTEP], but wherever possible we found external programmes and we oversaw those. The trustees became really tough. On their behalf, we demanded milestones, targets, and outcomes from grant beneficiaries every three months. By the early 2000s, the number of

programmes had risen to around sixty. Some were small, some several million pounds. And we put in place evaluation programmes: at one point there were about thirty research programmes going on at the same time.

The Science Enhancement Programme

In 1998, GTEP launched the Science Enhancement Programme (SEP), initially to address the decline in students opting for physics at A level. Entries were falling steadily from 55,000 in 1983, eventually to reach a low of 27,368 in 2006. Following the model of TEP, SEP's aim was 'to find ways of making experimental work more interesting, up-to-date and high quality'. Gradually the scheme expanded to include other subjects, with John Cave and his team at Teaching Resources supporting SEP as well as TEP. 'We designed a low-cost centrifuge in partnership with Reading University,' he says, 'which had a transformative effect on the way DNA could be looked at in schools.'

By 2005, however, the Gatsby trustees felt that SEP had become somewhat diffuse, with lots of good, but unconnected, projects being pursued at the expense of a clear strategy. On the retirement of SEP's director, John Williams encouraged Nigel Thomas, then the Royal Society's head of science communication and education, to apply for the post. Thomas joined the team in June 2005 and undertook a strategic review of SEP. He proposed refocusing the programme around a single aim: to stimulate innovative practical and experimental work in school science lessons.

'My idea was to focus SEP really tightly', says Thomas, 'and deliver it through two clear strands of activity: production of curriculum-related material which brought cutting-edge technologies into the classroom, and a programme of professional development for teachers to enable them to use our materials to full effect.' The trustees were supportive of Thomas's approach and, between 2005 and 2010, agreed £6 million of funding for SEP. By the end of the five-year period, over 10,000 secondary science teachers – around a third of the entire workforce and representing 93 per cent of all secondary schools – were regularly engaging with SEP materials. Over 200,000 hard copies of curriculum resources had been requested and sent to schools, with many more being downloaded from the web.

SEP's professional development training in practical work delivered over 600 courses to more than 6,000 teachers in the same period. At the same time, SEP partnered with the Weizmann Institute based in Tel Aviv, Israel, and later also the Nuffield Foundation, to develop a complementary professional development programme: Learning Skills for Science (LSS). This supported science teachers to develop higher-order research and problem-solving skills in pupils and proved extremely popular. Originally designed for 14- to 16-year-old students, LSS was later extended to cover both the 11–14 and 16–18 phases.

The success of SEP, and TEP before it, in driving immediate changes in classroom practice was identified again and again by independent evaluators. But by 2009, trustees and senior staff had decided that Gatsby's focus should move away from this type of open-ended programme. 'David has ambitions around long-term, systemic change,' says Thomas 'and you can't really achieve that with projects like SEP and TEP. You need to persuade governments to implement on a national scale what you have demonstrated works in smaller, well-evidenced pilot projects.'

A pipeline for physics teachers

One reason for the decline in the uptake of physics was the desperate shortage of qualified physics teachers. While he was still at the Engineering Council in the late 1980s, John Williams had been frustrated that the Department for Education (DfE) could not supply information on the qualifications of science and technology teachers. So he had commissioned his own research from Alan Smithers, then Professor of Education at the University of Manchester. 'I said, "I don't want [academic] papers, I want it in the press",' says Williams. 'It was absolutely shocking – there were schools without any properly qualified teachers in maths and physics. It really hit the headlines.' By 2005, things were no better: many of those who did have physics backgrounds were close to retirement, and head teachers were having to replace them with non-specialists or general science teachers.[6]

GTEP had already begun projects in initial teacher training, focusing on recruiting and supporting specialist teachers. In 2003, working with the Training and Development Agency and the Institute of Physics, it had funded a pilot programme to recruit graduates from different subject backgrounds and give them bursaries to attend an intensive six-month course in physics before they began their teacher training the following autumn. The new recruits would also benefit from specialist mentoring throughout their training and into the classroom. In the face of scepticism from all sides, the Physics Enhancement Programme (PEP) proved immensely successful: at its peak, it was responsible for around a quarter of all new physics teacher trainees, and independent evaluations found no difference in subject knowledge between the PEP teachers and teachers with physics degrees.

'Our work has allowed graduates in oceanography, ceramics, engineering – a very broad range of technical backgrounds – to become specialist teachers,' says Nigel Thomas. The model, now called Subject Knowledge Enhancement (SKE), has been embraced by the DfE and extended to other subjects in which there is a shortage of teachers.[7] Working in partnership with others, Gatsby developed a larger programme of work to recruit and retain physics teachers and saw the number of trainee teachers increased from fewer than 300 in 2005 to a peak of 900 in 2012. The work, though, has not been without threat. In 2011, Secretary of State Michael Gove introduced major changes to the teacher training system, moving from university-led to school-based training and consequently reducing the SKE provision. 'Numbers haemorrhaged,' according to Thomas, and the scheme was soon reinstated. 'It shows what a fragile ecosystem Gatsby is working in.'

Mostly maths

The performance of British school students in mathematics relative to those in many other countries has long been a cause for concern. The economist Sigbert Prais, who conducted a number of comparative studies of business growth in Britain and continental Europe for the National Institute of Economic and Social Research (NIESR), concluded that British industry suffered from poor education and training in technical subjects relative to successful countries such as Germany and Switzerland. Gatsby had supported his work in this area since 1990. In 1994, he undertook a comparative study of mathematics teaching in primary schools. John Williams says:

> On the continent they start at a later age, and the class moves at the speed of the slowest pupils. They get a really thorough groundwork and catch up compared to English schools. In England, kids worked through their books in isolation: in Switzerland, they sat in a horseshoe around the teacher, and the teaching was interactive – the pupils came up and did examples on the board.

On the strength of Prais's findings, GTEP funded NIESR to run a pilot project teaching numeracy using Swiss whole-class methods in six schools in Barking and Dagenham.[8] The project aroused great interest, with visits from the Chief Inspector of Schools, Chris Woodhead; the Secretary of State for Education, Gillian Shepherd; and the Labour spokesman on Education, David Blunkett. GTEP then set up a five-year, £2 million study of the methods in Newport (Gwent), Stockton-on-Tees, York and

Gloucestershire as the Mathematics Enhancement Programme Primary (MEPP). 'We wanted quantitative proof that the method worked,' says Williams. From the start MEPP included control schools, which received extra training but continued to use previous methods, so that there was a basis for comparison.[9] 'We paid more for the evaluation than we had spent on the programme itself,' says Williams. 'It was a good, interesting experiment.'

In parallel the government had launched its own National Numeracy Project, and the two initiatives shared their findings. 'The Gatsby approach is to develop a model, preferably hand in hand with government from the start, and then present the model with evidence that it has worked,' says Williams. In 1999, after the change of government, the Department for Education introduced the National Numeracy Strategy, requiring primary teachers to use whole-class methods as piloted by MEPP. The strategy was in place until 2011, when all the government-funded National Strategies in education were discontinued. During that time, the performance of students in English primary schools improved to become among the top four in Europe, and the gap between children from deprived and less deprived backgrounds closed.[10] By 2015, England's 9- and 10-year-olds had slipped to fifth place, excluding the five East Asian countries that consistently hold the top spots.[11]

Another programme focused on the maths skills of students as they entered university, enabling them to study further mathematics at A level through distance learning (see Case study, page 170).

The Teacher Effectiveness Enhancement Programme
From the evaluation of the MEPP project, and other academic research, emerged the idea that there were general principles of effective teaching that could not only be identified but also be taught and implemented in the classroom. In 2002, Gatsby launched an ambitious programme of continuing professional

development for teachers called the Teacher Effectiveness Enhancement Programme (TEEP).

The programme developed an approach to planning lessons that had five key strands: assessment for learning, thinking skills, accelerated learning strategies, collaborative problem solving and effective use of IT. It also introduced the concept of the 'learning cycle' that progresses from lesson preparation, through ensuring that students understand what the lesson is for, presenting new information and ensuring it is understood and can be applied, and finally reviewing what has been learned. It is a 'learning-centred' approach that encourages teachers to tailor their lessons to the particular strengths and requirements of their students. It is also highly collaborative, giving students and teachers a common language that they can use to discuss their learning, encouraging students to work together and teachers to share their practice with one another.

Between 2002 and 2010, more than 4,000 teachers took the five-day Level 1 TEEP course, and more than 500 Level 2, which trains subject leaders to embed the TEEP approach in their schools. While the programme initially focused on science and mathematics, the framework turned out to be equally applicable to all other subjects. The demand became so great that in 2010 Gatsby passed the management and development of TEEP to the Specialist Schools and Academies Trust (SSAT, now the Schools, Students and Teachers Network).[12]

While some teachers were sceptical at first, the longer TEEP has been implemented in their schools, the more enthusiastic they have become. A typical comment was, 'It changed our whole ethos and it made us fall in love with teaching again.'[13] Another said, 'I used to teach: now I think what I do is help students to learn. The focus has shifted completely from what I was doing, to what the students are doing.' TEEP training starts from the premise that 'the students are the crew and not the passengers'.

Numerous evaluations have shown the programme to be

hugely effective. As well as increasing staff morale and confidence, schools using TEEP have both increased their percentage of GCSE grades A*–C relative to the national average, and closed the gap in A*–C grades between children on free school meals and the rest. Where TEEP has been adopted as part of a school improvement programme, schools have moved from being in special measures to being judged 'Outstanding' by the school inspection agency, Ofsted. The project continues to flourish as TEEP-trained teachers become 'ambassadors' for the approach among their colleagues.

A single voice for maths

As well as working directly with schools and teachers, Gatsby helped the mathematical community to speak more coherently to government through establishing and funding the Advisory Council on Mathematics Education (ACME), based at the Royal Society. 'ACME is a good example of how Gatsby trustees are willing to take risks when there is the potential for significant benefit,' says Thomas. In 2001, working at the Royal Society, he had been approached by a group who wanted to establish such a body, giving a single voice to educational and professional organisations in the field of mathematics. 'We approached the Department for Education and Employment but they wouldn't fund it,' he says. 'Everyone back then felt ACME's chances of success were really slim – the maths community was hugely diverse, with several factions arguing over just about everything, so the idea of a "single voice" was pretty revolutionary.'

He talked to John Williams at Gatsby, who agreed that ACME's only chance of success was to obtain significant funding and status from day one. 'John persuaded the Gatsby trustees to take what, back then, was a real punt on ACME and offer a grant of £247,000 over three years', says Thomas. 'This in turn allowed me to convince the Royal Society Council to establish ACME under its aegis.' ACME succeeded beyond all expectations.

Gatsby funded it for twelve years and, since 2005, the DfE has contributed to ACME's core costs. It continues to be hugely influential with government. 'There's no doubt ACME would not have become what it did without Gatsby,' says Thomas, 'and I can't think of any other organisation that would have taken a chance on it back then, or indeed on a similar, unproven proposition today.'

Building lives in the city

With less long-term success, Gatsby also took a chance on an organisation called Women's Education in Building (WEB). Its trustees and advisors were well aware that opportunities to acquire technical skills were limited for people without much of an education. When in 1993 Allison Ogden-Newton approached Gatsby for support with her project to train disadvantaged women in construction skills, it ticked both the foundation's technical training and social renewal boxes.

Ogden-Newton had started WEB in a couple of arches under the Westway flyover in Ladbroke Grove, London. She knew that there were employment opportunities in construction, yet only 1 per cent of those in skilled trades were women. So she offered practical training in carpentry, joinery, plumbing and electrics to women with no educational qualifications who were desperate for work. Gatsby helped to bring the training workshop up to the standard needed for NVQ (National Vocational Qualifications) courses, and then supported Ogden-Newton to start a second workshop in southeast London. By the early 2000s, the programme was producing 300 trained craftswomen per year (90 per cent of whom went straight into jobs) and turning over £3 million. The hope was that the government would step in and absorb it into the further education sector. But the DfES baulked at the high unit costs needed to maintain flexible provision and support for child care, ignoring the great social value. In 2004, WEB got into cash-flow difficulties and went into liquidation.

'We lost some money but we learned a lot,' says Victoria Hornby, a Gatsby officer who worked on social enterprise projects. 'It was very typical of a Gatsby grant – there was always a willingness to look at interesting things and back something that looked promising.'

National STEM Centre and STEMNET

From the early 1990s Gatsby funded the Engineering Council to set up a network of regional technology centres and industry clubs to support science and technology teaching. Soon afterwards the Secretary of State at the DTI, Michael Heseltine, launched a series of initiatives under the heading Action for Engineering. One of these was SETNET, a regional network of SETPOINTS to act as 'one-stop shops' providing local information to schools and industry on link schemes and funding opportunities. Later SETNET also coordinated the Science and Engineering Ambassadors programme (now STEM Ambassadors), bringing thousands of volunteers from science and industry into schools to help with lessons and talk about careers. Gatsby co-funded SETNET for its first six years, jointly with the DTI and the DfE. As ever, its aim was to arrive at a coherent, nationally coordinated programme that would eventually be able to stand on its own feet or gain government support.

SETNET survived from one year to the next, often kept in doubt about future government support, until the energetic and persuasive physicist Gareth Roberts, founding president of the Science Council, produced his report for the DTI *SET for Success* in 2002. The resulting ten-year investment strategy (devised by David Sainsbury as science minister) included both new government funds for SETNET (which became STEMNET in 2008), and a network of nine regional Science Learning Centres (SLCs) that would offer continuing professional development for teachers.

Gatsby advisor John Holman, who had been appointed to the Chair in Science Education at the University of York, led a bid that won the £25 million contract to build the National Science Learning Centre (NSLC), the hub for the SLC network, and funded by the Wellcome Trust. Holman was appointed national STEM director following a joint report of the DTI and the DfES setting out a programme of action towards greater rationalisation of STEM enhancement and continuing professional development for teachers.[14]

'When David came out of government in 2006, he became very proactive,' says Holman. 'He is a man for whom my admiration is almost boundless. One of the things he wanted to do was support the National Science Learning Centre. I proposed to extend its remit to STEM – science, technology, engineering and mathematics.' In 2008 Gatsby provided a grant of over £4.5 million to set up the National STEM Centre at the NSLC, and to run it for six years: the grant has since been renewed. The National STEM Centre was a national resource for teachers of science, technology and mathematics and included a library of books, worksheets, lesson plans and practical kits that teachers could borrow or download. These materials included those developed through Gatsby's TEP and SEP programmes. It also acted as a coordinating hub for science enhancement activities offered through other bodies, including STEMNET and professional bodies such as the Royal Society of Chemistry and the RAEng.

The founding director of the National STEM Centre was Jenifer Burden, who is now an executive on the education team at Gatsby.

The big idea was to digitise and catalogue educational resources, all of which would be free to use. Digitisation was new – it was a great time to be working with bodies such as the Institute of Physics, who were hugely supportive of our making their resources available. And as funding for a lot of projects started to dry up, the Centre was a place to capture materials that would otherwise disappear. We also supported teachers to make sense of the resources – for example, we had 'top 20' lists of resources linked to curriculum objectives.

In August 2016, there was a further rationalisation, with the merger of the National STEM Centre, NSLC and STEMNET as a single company, STEM Learning Ltd.[15]

Interactive science centres

The effervescent psychologist Richard Gregory, who had taught David Sainsbury when he was a student at Cambridge University, was one of the British pioneers of centres where young people could engage with science and technology through 'hands on' activities. Taking his inspiration from Frank Oppenheimer's Exploratorium, which opened in San Francisco in 1969, he founded the Bristol-based Exploratory in 1983. Gatsby provided some of the start-up funding he needed to build exhibits and launch a series of exhibitions trialling the 'plores', or hands-on science exhibits. The Exploratory operated in dedicated premises at Bristol Temple Meads station from 1989 to 1999. Gregory's inspiration was taken up by At-Bristol, the Millennium project that opened in 2000 as part of the regeneration of Bristol's floating harbour, and Gatsby helped to fund projects that eased the sometimes difficult transition from the Exploratory to At-Bristol.

Gatsby then engaged a consultant, Steve Pizzey, to manage a fund for the development of further science centres and promote the concept nationally. Centres that received Gatsby support included Techniquest in Cardiff, Technology Testbed at the Merseyside Museum, Jodrell Bank's visitor centre and INTECH (now Winchester Science Centre and Planetarium). For the most part these ventures have been successful, attracting large numbers of visitors; however, they have had to be inventive in their funding models, adding a mix of diversified activities (such as the car park at At-Bristol) and local authority or local business support to their income from ticket sales.

Training technicians

Since the review of Gatsby's education policy that took place when David Sainsbury came out of government, Gatsby has returned to the central issue that launched its education programmes: the training, qualifications and status of technicians in science and engineering. These are skilled, usually non-graduate, employees who are essential in a variety of research, manufacturing and operational areas.

David Sainsbury has spent more time than most studying this problem. 'You can't just copy the German system,' he says.

> It depends on the fact that they have very good trade unions and trade associations that help to run the technical education system. And we have rather poor trade unions and trade associations. First, you have to have a national system of qualifications that everyone understands and that works in the marketplace. If the employer doesn't recognise your qualification, then word very quickly gets about that it's not worth doing.

He believes that the advent of NVQs was a backward step, because, unlike previous vocational qualifications such as City & Guilds and BTEC, they are not recognised by many employers. While City & Guilds and BTEC are still available, they are now delivered commercially by competing agencies, which threatens standards. 'The idea that you have competing bodies is truly ridiculous,' says Sainsbury. 'You lower the standards so more people can pass, so more people take your course. But word gets round that the qualification is meaningless, and so it doesn't help employers to select able recruits.'

The two other essentials for technical training, he believes, are a system that funds people while they get qualifications, and properly equipped places where they can receive training. 'The reason we don't have a good technical education', he concludes drily, 'is that we don't have any of those three things.'

And the need is urgent. 'If the UK is to maintain its competitiveness,' says Nigel Thomas, 'it has to develop its intermediate-level skills. We need 700,000 more STEM technicians in the next ten years. Meanwhile there are 400,000 16- to 24-year-olds who are unemployed. We can't assert that none of those could make the transition to rewarding, exciting jobs as technicians if they were only given the opportunity.'

Apprenticeships

Apprenticeship is a system of vocational training dating back to the Middle Ages. Originally it involved a five- to nine-year contract signed by the parents of a young teenager with a craft master, who would train the boy in return for his labour. For centuries, it was illegal to practise certain trades unless the tradesman had followed an apprenticeship, and standards were maintained by the craft guilds. For much of the twentieth century apprenticeship remained a recognised way of obtaining a rigorous and respected training in manufacturing. However, with the decline of manufacturing industry on the one hand, and increased emphasis on academic qualifications on the other, by the mid-1990s the opportunities for apprenticeship were in severe decline.

Since the 1990s there has been a series of efforts to reform the apprenticeship system, offering incentives to companies and public sector bodies to train apprentices. One problem, however, has been that the tiered system of NVQs that was supposed to certify their competence was not aligned to the standards for registration demanded by professional bodies, leading to the charge that they were 'not worth the paper they were written on'. Gatsby has worked energetically to change this. In 2013, with support from Gatsby, the government introduced the 'Trailblazers' scheme, by which groups of employers in different sectors developed standards for specific categories of employment. By July 2015, 140 Trailblazer groups were well on the way to delivering over 350 apprenticeship standards, with a requirement that these focus on occupational competence and be aligned with the relevant standards for professional registration.

Technician registration

Within the engineering profession alone, there are thirty-five professional institutions licensed by the Engineering Council, each with its own system of standards and scheme of professional registration that it applies as a means of self-regulation. However, registration has not been the norm for technicians. Without registration, and with the confusion that has bedevilled vocational qualifications, it has been harder for them to progress in their careers.

'Status is about competency,' says Thomas. 'You don't just pass an exam – you have to practise and demonstrate competence in the workplace. Then you submit an application to a professional body, and sign up to their code of ethics.' Working with the Engineering Council and a number of engineering professional bodies, Gatsby has helped to promote the professional registration for engineering technicians (EngTech). It has also worked with the Science Council to introduce two new levels of registration below Chartered Scientist (CSci): Registered Scientist (RSci) and Registered Science Technician (RSciTech). The Chartered Institute for IT is also being supported by Gatsby to develop Registered IT Technician (RITTech). 'Registration is "owned" by the professional bodies,' says Thomas. 'But you can make it work only if employers value it. The idea is that registration helps to guarantee the quality of apprentice training, and that it gives the technician transferability in the labour market.'

Technicians will be able to qualify for registration through a variety of routes, including learning on the job. 'Up till now there has been an alphabetti spaghetti of qualifications,' he says. 'Employers can't keep up. And for some qualifications on offer, students would have earned more if they hadn't done the course.' Coupled with the government commitment to significant changes to formal technical education qualifications that followed a review led by David Sainsbury in 2015/16 (see below), a system of registration creates a clear vocational pathway to the professions, which have previously been difficult to access without a degree.

And furthermore

Traditionally apprentices and students following vocational paths would study at further education colleges, either full-time or on day or block release. Yet in December 2015 the government's own Public Accounts Committee warned that the FE sector faced 'financial meltdown', with seventy colleges at risk of closure.[16] Those that remain have cut back on expensive courses in workshop-based disciplines in favour of popular but cheaper options such as hairdressing or business studies.

Following a government decision to devolve investment in skills to Local Enterprise Partnerships (LEPs) from a central Skills Funding Agency, Gatsby supported a pilot project across Greater Manchester to map technical training provision in relation to local needs. The project brought together FE colleges, employers and local agencies, recommending greater partnership and coordination between all players in order to provide training facilities equipped to a suitably high standard.[17] At the time of writing, plans are being drawn up to extend this work in Greater Manchester and also to explore similar work in the Sheffield City Region.

Gatsby has also contributed to the core costs of the Baker Dearing Educational Trust as it develops University Technology Colleges (UTCs). This innovative model of secondary school for

14- to 19-year-olds is linked to neighbouring universities and local employers and has a focus on technical and vocational skills.[18] The first opened in 2010, and over fifty will be running across the country by 2017 (though a small number have closed).

Advocacy and policy

While Gatsby's programmes have touched the lives of millions of individual children and young people, they have had to face the same obstacle as all other education initiatives in the UK: the vulnerability of education policy to the whims of successive political leaders, who seem intent on valuing what they can measure rather than measuring what they value.

For example, Gatsby's school science and technology initiatives have tried to make the subjects more stimulating and challenging by raising the quality of practical work in the classroom. Much of its work in technology became necessary after the introduction of the National Curriculum in 1989 radically reduced the opportunities for students to practise the practical skills that industry was crying out for. More recently the 'English Baccalaureate' acts as a disincentive to schools to put effort into subjects such as Design and Technology that are seen as 'less academic'. As recently as 2015, Gatsby was joining other science bodies in a salvage operation to ensure that at least some practical work would be assessed in GCSE and A level science, after education officials proposed dropping practical examinations because, they said, it was too difficult to achieve consistency in marking.[19]

The extent to which education is a political football is perhaps illustrated by the five changes of name and responsibilities that the relevant government department has undergone since Gatsby started work in education: Department of Education and Science, 1964–92; Department for Education, 1992–5; Department for Education and Employment, 1995–2001; Department for Education and Skills, 2001–07; Department for Children, Schools and Families, 2007–10; and back to DfE (since 2010). Any attempt to effect long-term change must build up an evidence base strong enough to withstand the ever-blowing winds of change.

Gatsby's work on apprenticeships and technician registration epitomises its current focus on research, dissemination and persuasion rather than directly managed projects. However, attempting to gain the ear of ministers and their advisors is by no means a new activity for the education programme. John Williams took an early opportunity to brief Labour Minister of Education David Blunkett on GTEP's activities in 1997, and after an encouraging meeting with schools minister Stephen Twigg in 2004, GTEP got together with the Nuffield and Sutton Trusts to try to develop a mechanism whereby successful charity-funded pilot studies might be taken over and rolled out by the DfES.

The initiative foundered on the indifference of the then Department's civil servants. As Williams noted in his annual report, 'One of the lessons that took us a long time to learn was that the only sure way to get government to take on programmes that we were piloting or supporting was to get them involved as a committed partner right from the word go, rather than to bring them in late in the day.'

More recently, Gatsby has had greater success in convincing government of the wisdom of its vision, with David Sainsbury and Nigel Thomas having had regular dialogue with successive ministers and civil servants since 2007. The Trailblazer apprenticeships currently being rolled out by the government are required to link to professional registration only because Gatsby's arguments for this were considered sufficiently persuasive. Equally, the government's intention to invest in the creation of a number of prestigious 'Institutes of Technology', which will focus on developing the all-important technician-level STEM skills, is in response to a Gatsby proposal submitted in early 2015 to the then skills minister, Nick Boles.

Boles was sufficiently impressed by a number of proposals

Gatsby had put forward that, in August 2015, he asked Nigel Thomas to be seconded to his office as senior policy advisor. In November that year, Boles convened an independent expert panel to review England's national system of technical education, and asked David Sainsbury to chair it. Thomas led the supporting secretariat of officials from the DfE, the Department for Business, Innovation and Skills (BIS) and Gatsby. The report of the Sainsbury Review was published in April 2016, and recommended a move to a coherent, well-funded system replacing thousands of courses from competing providers with just fifteen high-quality routes to a technical qualification.[20] These would be available both to apprentices and college-based students. The government published its formal response in July 2016 as the *Post-16 Skills Plan*.[21] 'We are determined to make technical education an option that leads to long-term success,' wrote Boles in his foreword, 'and to see through the continued delivery of lasting change in the skills system, which is why I am so delighted with the recommendations by Lord Sainsbury's independent panel.'

A week later Boles, who had supported the Remain campaign to stay in the European Union, followed the example of Prime Minister David Cameron and resigned from his post. With the installation of Theresa May as prime minister, there was a reorganisation of departments, removing all responsibility for careers, further education and training from BIS, which became the Department for Business, Energy and Industrial Strategy (BEIS), and transferring it to the DfE. Despite these changes, there were strong indications that the skills reform agenda established under Boles would continue to be implemented: the newly appointed Secretary of State for Education, Justine Greening, was unequivocally positive about her intention to implement the Sainsbury Review recommendations.

The other key area in which Gatsby thinking has shaped the national agenda is career guidance for young people. Most young people have only a hazy idea of the job prospects that are available if they have good qualifications in science and maths. They are confused by the options available post-16, and intimidated by the financial burden they will face if they embark on a university degree. 'Good career guidance has never been more important,' says Thomas, 'yet career guidance in English schools is often inadequate and patchy.'

When John Holman retired from directing the NSLC in 2010, he began to work on a number of research projects for Gatsby. 'We became very interested in careers education,' he says. 'If young people don't understand the range of careers that involve scientific and technical qualifications, they're less likely to take them.' 'John and I were in agreement', adds David Sainsbury, 'that, rather than add to the pile of reports criticising the current system, what was needed was work which would identify good practice in career guidance – both here and abroad – and then point the way to embedding such practice in all of our schools.'

Gatsby commissioned Holman to undertake a major comparative review. With experts from the University of Derby, he visited the Netherlands, Germany, Finland, Hong Kong, Canada and the Republic of Ireland, and compared what they found with what was typical practice in English schools. His report sets out a framework of eight benchmarks for assessing the quality of careers advice, and includes an assessment of the cost of implementing his recommendations across the school system.[22] 'It's been very influential,' says Holman. 'The government has picked it up and used it for career guidance policy.' In 2016, in partnership with the Careers & Enterprise Company, Gatsby launched a free online tool for teachers to enable them to monitor and evaluate their careers teaching against the eight 'Gatsby benchmarks'.[23] At the time of writing the signs are good that Gatsby's work in this area will be a cornerstone of the government's strategy.

'In all our advocacy and policy work, ' says Thomas, 'we

genuinely try to offer pragmatic and workable solutions – to work with what is changeable. I think that's what sets us apart.'

On 24 November 2016, David Sainsbury received the Lord Dearing Lifetime Achievement Award at the Times Higher Education Awards, in a glitzy ceremony held at the Grosvenor House Hotel. He declared himself pleased 'that the work I have done in the field of education has been recognised, as I thought it had gone largely unnoticed'. Announcing the award, the Vice-Chancellor of the University of Exeter, Sir Steve Smith, made it clear that people had certainly noticed his contribution to higher education while in office (see Chapter 7). 'Lord Sainsbury was without doubt the most effective and supportive science minister for a generation,' he said. 'Our research base has never had a better friend, and colleagues in all subjects from anthropology to zoology owe him their thanks.' There was not a word about the Gatsby Foundation's record in education, which had indeed gone mostly under the public's radar. But, asked in an interview for the *Times Higher Education* what he would do if he were the higher education minister today, Sainsbury replied, 'I would try to bring back polytechnics. We need to strengthen our system of technical education, not create more universities.'

Case study: The Further Mathematics Support Programme

Between 1980 and 2000, the number of students taking A level further mathematics (essential for mathematics courses at some universities, and highly desirable for physics and engineering students) fell dramatically. 'At one stage there were 15,000 students taking further maths,' says John Williams. 'That dwindled to 5,000.' Schools were unwilling to offer such a minority-interest subject, and many teachers did not have the confidence to teach it.

The idea of using modern information technology, such as CDs, to help A level students access further mathematics had arisen in a discussion on 'virtual education' hosted by Gatsby in the 1990s, but had gone no further. The chief executive of Mathematics in Education and Industry (MEI), Roger Porkess, then came to Gatsby with a much more developed proposal. 'He came up with the idea that he would develop a structure for the subject,' says Williams. 'MEI would set up lead centres around the country, and provide distant support for students.' The DfES had refused even to co-fund a pilot, but Williams was impressed with previous work MEI had undertaken and the trustees agreed to put up the full £360,000 for three years. The GTEP board recognised that the model 'could be followed or adapted to other specialised subjects where the subject expertise was spread thinly across the country'.

For the pilot of MEI's Further Mathematics Support Programme, project coordinator Charlie Stripp (who succeeded Roger Porkess as CEO of MEI in 2010) set up lead centres in Warwickshire and in Tyne and Wear, launched a website and produced topic modules. The lead centres were immediately inundated with requests for support: they worked with schools in the Midlands and the north to trial the materials, before offering the course to students in those areas who would sit their A levels in 2002. The first evaluation found that the students received grades at least as good as those they received for subjects they had studied conventionally within their schools.

The pilot project was so successful that the DfES, despite having declined to fund the pilot, took it over and rolled it out nationally under MEI's direction.[24] 'Charles Clarke [the Secretary of State for Education and Skills] became really interested,' says Williams. 'He recognised that the decline in

170

further maths was a serious problem.' Clarke decided to fund a network of lead centres throughout the country, with an injection of £1.5 million into the forty-seven regional Learning and Skills Councils. Since 2005 the number of students taking further maths has trebled, and the number of schools teaching it has risen from fewer than 40 per cent to over 66 per cent. As expected, the model proved attractive for other groups of users. With further Gatsby support, Stripp went on to develop distance learning packages for students of single maths at A level, gifted and talented students, and even first-year undergraduates who needed extra help with their maths.

'Double maths is really important for students who are going to go on to study maths at university, as well as for computation and engineering, and we were losing that in the UK,' says Williams. 'Gatsby helped to save the subject.'

7

A NEW AGENDA

Programmes for change

Members of the Sainsbury family have often taken an active interest in politics and public life. In his youth, Alan Sainsbury, David's uncle, stood unsuccessfully as a Liberal candidate, before switching to the Labour Party in 1945. The first in the family to be ennobled, he entered the House of Lords as Lord Sainsbury of Drury Lane in 1962, sitting on the Labour benches, though he later joined the centrist Social Democratic Party (SDP). He did not pass on his political affiliation to his sons: the youngest, Timothy, was Conservative MP for Hove from 1973 until 1997, holding several junior ministerial posts; and the eldest, John, also a Conservative supporter, was made a life peer in 1989 as Lord Sainsbury of Preston Candover.

David Sainsbury never aimed for a political career in the conventional sense. However, he grew up in a socially progressive household and has been politically engaged ever since his days as an undergraduate at Cambridge, joining the Labour Party when he came to work in London in 1963. Over time, however, his perspective on how government operates has matured. 'I used to have the idea that people in politics took a long-term view – that the state was not subject to short-term concerns, and that politicians took an enlightened view of public interest,' he says. 'In contrast, I thought business was totally profit-oriented and short-term in its outlook.' Years of experience working for Sainsbury's taught him that the truth was quite the reverse. A family business such as theirs owed much of its success to taking a long-term view, while government policy initiatives could be limited by the lifetime of a ministerial appointment, often as little as two or three years, thwarting any prospect of consistent, progressive change.

The interaction between the state and the economy – how governments can create an environment in which business thrives, while ensuring that the benefits are equitably shared – became an abiding interest for Sainsbury, expressed publicly for the first time in a pamphlet he wrote for the Fabian Society in 1981.[1] The ideas are more fully developed in his recent book *Progressive Capitalism*.[2] The conviction that business had an essential role to play in a progressive society put him at odds with the increasingly left-wing leadership of the Labour Party in the early 1980s, and he threw his personal financial support behind the break-away SDP. However, as Labour moved towards the centre ground under the leadership of Tony Blair, his allegiance to the party revived.

When Labour came to power in 1997, after eighteen years in opposition, Sainsbury became the third chairman of Sainsbury's to be given a peerage and entered the House of Lords as Lord Sainsbury of Turville. He felt that his years of experience as a businessman, and as a long-term supporter, through Gatsby, of science, innovation and economic growth, gave him something to offer, and he accepted the post of Minister of Science and Innovation in the Department of Trade and Industry (DTI) the following year. His appointment came suddenly, and there was no time for lengthy discussions with Judith Portrait and Christopher Stone about the management of Gatsby while he was in government. At the time, he did not see this as a problem, as he thought he would probably stay for only two or three years at most. In the event he stayed for eight, and is eternally grateful for the thoughtful and careful way they ran Gatsby while he held his ministerial post.

His longevity was a plus for his relationship with the British science and industry community, who could see that for him the junior post was no stepping stone to higher office. But for the team left running the multimillion-pound operation that the Gatsby Charitable Trust had become, it had major implications. Even though its activities were charitable, under parliamentary rules Sainsbury could no longer participate in Gatsby's management. The Trust, for as long as he held office, would be 'blind' – the trustees would have to manage the affairs of the charity entirely without his intervention. When Sainsbury eventually left his ministerial post in 2006, having long since given up any responsibility for the management of J Sainsbury plc, Gatsby became the central focus of his working life. His experience in running Gatsby had certainly influenced the work he did as a minister: his time in government would subsequently have a lasting impact on the way he ran Gatsby.

Yes, minister

Taking office in the new Labour government brought David Sainsbury into the glare of public view to a degree he had never previously experienced, even as chairman of Sainsbury's. There were rumblings in the press about the fact that he was unelected, a member of the House of Lords and a known Labour donor, and more concerted protests from the Green lobby about his supposed commercial interests in plant biotechnology. However, as time went on it became so evident that he stood to gain nothing personally from the post that the furore died down. 'I think I was asked to be minister of science because the prime minister wanted to have someone in the job, and in the DTI, who had both an interest in science and experience in industry,' Sainsbury told the journal *Nature*. 'The more interesting question from my point of view is whether the scientific community and high-tech industry think he made a good choice.'[3]

They did. Under the previous Conservative administration, the British scientific community had felt itself to be under siege, with real-terms cuts to the science budget. Sainsbury was determined to put science and innovation squarely on the political agenda, not just in their own right, but as activities that were economically important. On his arrival, he discovered that the government chief scientific advisor, Sir Robert May, had already collected quantitative data on the productivity of the science base that would make it possible to monitor the UK's performance relative to other countries. They demonstrated that, despite its funding difficulties, UK science was already outranking larger advanced nations in scientific productivity. 'We were able to say that the UK had 1 per cent of the world's population, 5 per cent of the world's scientists, 9 per cent of published papers and 12 per cent of citations,' says Sainsbury. 'I was extremely lucky that in Bob May and his successor Sir David King, I had two outstanding scientific advisors.'

Finding that in the early 2000s spending on R&D as a percentage of GDP was lower in the UK than in comparable countries, Sainsbury lobbied hard for an increase, putting together a credible case for the importance of research to economic prosperity. By the time he left office in 2006 the science budget had doubled, and was ring-fenced to protect it from later cuts. This was part of a ten-year science and innovation investment framework, launched by Sainsbury to aid in strategic planning. The framework was designed to support the components of what he called a 'system of innovation', underpinned by strategic government spending on key elements of infrastructure. 'It is … necessary for the Government to provide the significant range of public goods for a knowledge-driven economy to create competitive advantage,' he wrote, 'such as a strong science and technology base, incentives for knowledge transfer and business

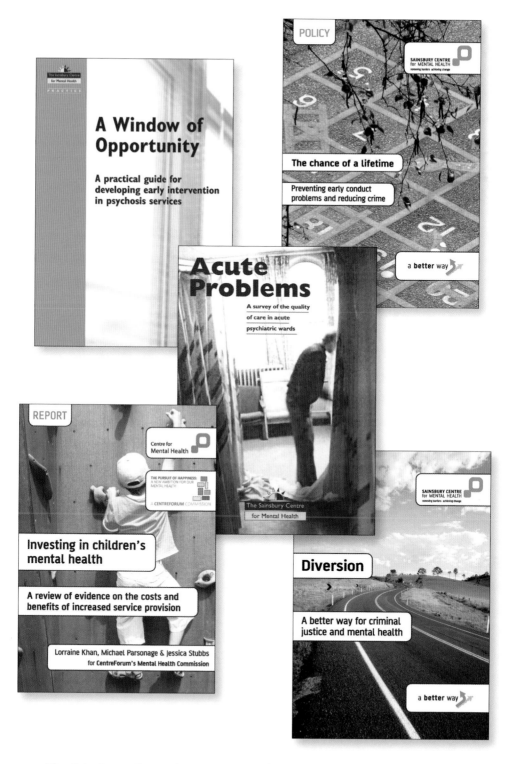

The Sainsbury Centre for Mental Health and its successor, the Centre for Mental Health, published a series of hard-hitting reports on aspects of mental health care.

Cecilia Ogony (above, at right) is one of the farmer teachers trained by the International Centre for Insect Physiology and Ecology in Kenya to demonstrate the 'push-pull' approach to pest management as part of its Gatsby-funded maize stem borer project.

Trees are raised from cuttings at the Tree Biotechnology Project in Kenya.

Gatsby's partnership with the Wood Foundation is supporting tea growers in Tanzania and Rwanda through giving them a stake in the processing and marketing of their crops.

Gatsby's Tanzania cotton programme works with cotton processors, known as ginners, and farmers to raise their productivity and improve the quality of the cotton.

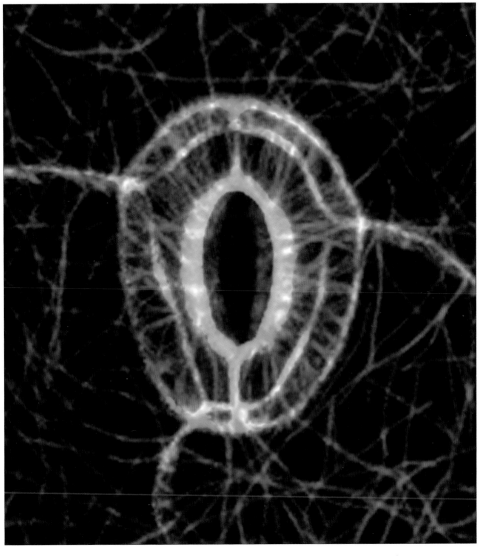

Research at The Sainsbury Laboratory, Norwich, explores how
stomata – pores in the plant surface – close in response to pathogen attack.

The non-profit Two Blades Foundation, which has a lab within
The Sainsbury Laboratory in Norwich, is developing a variety of tomato
protected against bacterial spot with a gene from peppers.
The photographs show untransformed (at top) and transformed
varieties exposed to the same infection.

The Sainsbury Laboratory Cambridge University (SLCU), designed by
Stanton Williams Architects, pursues research into plant development.

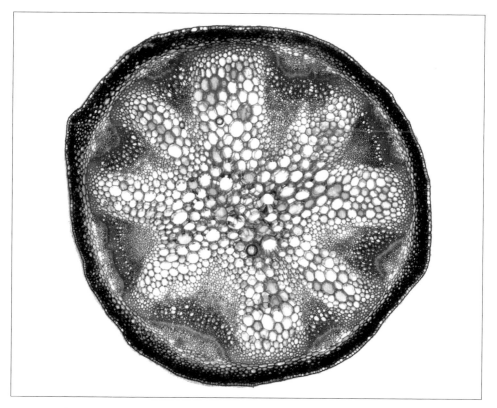

High performance microscopy reveals detailed plant anatomy at SLCU.

Training technicians is central to Gatsby's work in education.

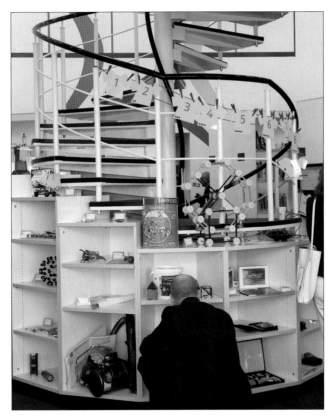

The National STEM Centre at the University of York opened in 2010.
Part of the National STEM Learning Centre since 2016, it holds a
wide range of resources for teachers.

The National Science Learning Centre (subsequently renamed the
National STEM Learning Centre) at the University of York coordinates
a network of science learning centres in the UK.

The Sainsbury Wellcome Centre for Neural Circuits and Behaviour (SWC), designed by Ian Ritchie Architects Ltd, opened in 2016 for research into the brain's connectivity.

The SWC is designed with double-height labs to increase the sense of connection between researchers on different floors.

Researchers at the SWC combine biochemistry
and microscopy to image connections in the brain.

Eyewire, an online game developed by Sebastian Seung at Princeton
University with Gatsby support, recruits citizen scientists to help refine the
mapping of brain circuits.

Tristram Hunt MP delivers a lecture on 'The urban century' at the People's History Museum in Manchester in 2016, at an event hosted jointly by the Centre for Cities and the *Manchester Evening News*.

The Institute for Government moved into its own building in Carlton Gardens in 2009.

The Sainsbury Centre for Visual Arts (SCVA), designed by Norman Foster.

The Living Room at the SCVA displays items from the
Robert and Lisa Sainsbury collection.

Curtain call following Rupert Goold's production of *Romeo and Juliet*, one of the first to be staged in the remodelled Royal Shakespeare Theatre in Stratford-upon-Avon in 2011.

The Chamber Orchestra of Europe performed at the Korani Culture Hall in Kofu as part of a ten-concert tour of Japan in November 2016.

The *Weeping Window* from the installation 'Blood Swept Lands and Seas of Red' on tour at Caernarfon Castle, supported by Backstage Trust as part of the 14–18 NOW arts project. Poppies and original concept by artist Paul Cummins. Installation designed by Tom Piper. By Paul Cummins Ceramics Ltd in conjunction with Historical Royal Palaces, originally at HM Tower of London 2014.

Research and Development (R&D), and high standards of education at all levels.'[4]

For example, he introduced incentives for universities to engage in knowledge transfer, first through competitive applications to the University Challenge Fund, and later on a continuous basis through the Higher Education Innovation Fund (HEIF). These had an almost immediate impact. Patents awarded to universities more than doubled between 2000 and 2006, licensing agreements almost quadrupled, and income from licences more than trebled.[5] Unlike most of his predecessors, Sainsbury appreciated the importance to industry of shared standards, and reinvigorated the highly respected National Physical Laboratory by encouraging it to develop standards in emerging areas of manufacturing such as nanoscience.

For innovations within industry he set up the Technology Strategy Board in 2004, initially within the DTI. The board's members are drawn mainly from industry, and its role is to coordinate activities to promote business innovation, through such means as collaborative R&D and knowledge transfer networks. In 2007, it was given executive responsibilities as a non-departmental public body, now called Innovate UK.

While Sainsbury modestly claims that 'because science was not politically a big issue, I was allowed a lot of freedom to get on and do what I wanted,' he had some battles to fight. There was a proposal to establish a European Research Council (ERC), which would hold funds collected from member states and distributed as research grants to excellent scientists, with an initial budget of over €1 billion per year. The Treasury was opposed to Britain's participation, but believing that the strength of British science would ensure that the UK would do very well out of it Sainsbury gave his approval. The UK has since secured between 20 and 25 per cent of ERC grants, for which scientists from thirty-two countries compete. It is hard to disentangle how much of the UK's overall contribution to the EU has gone to the ERC, but

As science minister, David Sainsbury (at centre)
visits satellite manufacturer EADS-Astrium.

it is generally agreed that the balance has been very much in Britain's favour.[6]

Another battle whose outcome has had long-term consequences concerned the animal rights campaign that threatened the survival of the drugs-testing company Huntingdon Life Sciences (HLS). By 2006, a small number of members of animal rights groups had successfully intimidated the staff of a large number of HLS's suppliers, including their bank, Royal Bank of Scotland, which had severed their contacts with the company. HLS's share price had plunged, the company was in danger of going under, and other pharmaceutical companies based in the UK were talking about taking their businesses overseas. At around the same time, a new biomedical research lab at Oxford University was the target of similar tactics, with builders working on the project requiring police protection.

With the prime minister's support, Sainsbury launched a

broadly-based campaign to save HLS, with initiatives ranging from guaranteeing its financial security to stepping up the police campaign to arrest and charge those guilty of violence, harassment, intimidation and blackmail, and a doubling of the penalties for harassing suppliers. In 2009, seven of the key figures were given sentences of up to ten years in jail for offences such as conspiracy to commit blackmail and arson. Since then, although the campaigns against animal research continue, the use of harassment, intimidation and violence has been dramatically reduced. 'If we had not done that work,' says Sainsbury, 'we would have lost most of our pharmaceutical and biotechnology industry.'

A battle he was not able to fight, though he was probably uniquely qualified to do so, was over the regulation of trials of genetically modified (GM) crops and the countering of misleading communications from the anti-GM lobby. John Ashworth, Gatsby's senior advisor for many years, had by this time become Director of the London School of Economics. In that capacity, he had helped to set up social research projects on public perceptions of plant biotechnology before the Labour government came into office. 'David was one of the few properly prepared science ministers,' he says, 'partly because of his experience of those earlier discussions about GM crops and public risk.' However, because of widespread media claims that he stood to gain personally from any initiative that promoted the plant biotechnology industry, Sainsbury was advised to avoid political fallout simply by stepping out of any discussion concerning the topic. While members of his team within the DTI worked on the issue, decision-making rested with a different minister.

He remained wholly convinced that the only way to tackle public perceptions of risk more broadly was through greater openness and dialogue between the scientific community, the media and the public. This was the conclusion that had been reached by the House of Lords Select Committee on Science and

Technology in its 2000 report on science and society, chaired by Lord Jenkin.[7] The hard-hitting report had argued that 'public understanding of science' and 'outreach' activities by universities were not enough: they must proactively engage in dialogue, and not expect any special treatment from the press.

The problem with implementing this requirement was that journalists often work to a time horizon of less than twenty-four hours, while scientists are more used to horizons of weeks, months or years. The result was that reporting of topics such as cloning or food scares was often ill-informed. Sainsbury convened a meeting to discuss the issue, attended among others by Susan Greenfield, who had been director of the Royal Institution (RI) since 1998. The outcome of the meeting was the establishment of the Science Media Centre in 2002, funded by a variety of government, charitable and industry partners (including Gatsby, see page 226), and hosted by the RI. An independent charity since 2011 and now hosted by the Wellcome Trust, the Science Media Centre acts as a press office for science, maintaining a database of authoritative contacts on key topics and proactively engaging the media with informed briefings before potentially contentious topics come into the public eye.[8]

The depth of Sainsbury's understanding of the issues that came across his desk as science minister grew directly out of the interests he had been able to pursue through Gatsby initiatives, and the network of 'hugely valuable' contacts he had developed. He was personally acquainted with forward-thinking vice-chancellors, such as Gareth Roberts at Sheffield and Howard Newby at Southampton, both of whom had participated in a technology transfer fact-finding mission to the USA that Gatsby had organised (see Chapter 9). Both universities had gone on to become highly successful centres of knowledge exchange, and their experience fed into the DTI's innovation strategy. With decades of experience exploring new models of science and technology education, Sainsbury deterred over-enthusiastic officials from launching new initiatives into an already crowded market, but set about supporting, streamlining and rationalising existing provision.

Sainsbury was protected from many of the slings and arrows of a political career by the fact that he self-evidently had no interest in further political advancement, or in any prestige that a title might bring: the relatively junior post of science minister was all he wanted. The fact that he stayed as long as he did enabled him to keep plugging away at policy initiatives until they gained traction within Whitehall and Westminster, and could be implemented. He had not originally envisaged staying so long, and wished to return to his charitable activities full-time. However, he had undertaken to see the Company Law Reform Bill – the longest bill in parliamentary history – through the House of Lords, and it finally reached its enactment as the Companies Act in 2006.

On his departure, the British political and scientific community lined up to commend his achievements: after the prime minister and the chancellor, he had been the longest-serving minister in the Labour administration. Tony Blair called him a 'huge asset to this country', President of the Royal Society Lord Rees said he was 'a fine ambassador for science around the world', and the Society elected him to an honorary fellowship. Colin Blakemore, then head of the Medical Research Council (MRC), commended his courage in engaging publicly with opponents of animal experiments, and pursuing the prosecution of animal rights extremists.[9] Mark Walport, chief executive of the Wellcome Trust, said he had been 'an outstanding science minister and shown extraordinary passion and commitment to his portfolio'.[10] Denis Noble, founder of Save British Science, says that Sainsbury 'did much to repair the damage of the 1980s. Over the period of his office, the science budget roughly doubled: almost exactly the target that the campaign had proposed to Blair before the 1997 election.'[11]

His vision for the future of British science and innovation came together in his report *The Race to the Top*, produced at Gordon

Brown's request as preparation for the 2007 spending review.[12] The report, written after his resignation but with the support of a crack team of Treasury officials, developed the ideas contained in the series of White Papers he had written for the DTI during his time in office,[13] with some additions. 'Realistically you can only implement two or three big initiatives,' he says, 'but you have to have 25 in a white paper, most of which are not significant. I wrote a whole series of documents that gradually took the central ideas forwards.'

The Race to the Top argued that Britain's economic prosperity depended not on driving down wages and taxes to compete with emerging economies, but on investing in the infrastructure that would support business innovation. It pointed out that in recent years the contribution to value added in the UK economy from high-value manufacturing, such as aerospace, pharmaceuticals and computer manufacturing, and from knowledge-intensive services, had outstripped growth in low-technology sectors at a faster rate than in other European economies such as France and Germany. To support this growth, it recommended coherent approaches to technology strategy, knowledge transfer, venture capital funding, the training of young scientists and engineers, and international collaboration.

As prime minister, Brown accepted its recommendations in full. Provisions such as a new executive role for the Technology Strategy Board (now Innovate UK) have remained in place since the election of a coalition government between the Conservatives and Liberal Democrats in 2010, and of a majority Conservative government in 2015. Recommendations on support for science in schools led to the network of Science Learning Centres, and the National Science Learning Centre led by Sainsbury's long-standing advisor at Gatsby, John Holman, both still in place in 2016.

With a vastly increased understanding of how the machinery of government works (slowly, inefficiently and unaccountably),

David Sainsbury returned to Gatsby determined to continue his mission through tightly focused spending on selected projects, and informed advocacy.

Back at the ranch

In 2003, in a rare moment of public recognition, David Sainsbury took a brief break from government to accept the Carnegie Medal of Philanthropy on behalf of the Sainsbury family, among whose foundations Gatsby was cited as the 'flagship of the fleet'.[14] The medal had been inaugurated in 2001 and given to a handful of exclusively American donors: it has since been given in alternate years, and the Sainsburys were among the first non-Americans to receive it. In his speech, Sainsbury reiterated his commitment to focused, proactive, adventurous and long-term philanthropy.

For the trustees and staff who had been left to manage the shop while he held ministerial office, it was a difficult ambition to live up to. 'We had to guess what David would want, and try and deliver that,' says Andrew Cahn, a senior civil servant who joined the trustee board in 1996. 'The real difficulty was that David would want Gatsby to develop and do unusual and unexpected things. And yet that completely contradicted the idea that we were there to keep things going, and not to take decisions he might be unhappy with. I certainly felt that was a real tension at that time.'

Judith Portrait, Gatsby's longest-serving trustee and legal advisor, and trustee of the 'blind' Trust, found herself with the heavy responsibility of ensuring that the separation between Sainsbury's government office and his personal and charitable financial activities was legally watertight, and of allaying any concerns of the permanent secretaries in the DTI about possible conflicts of interest. The intense scrutiny from the media, much of it hingeing on Sainsbury's support for plant molecular biology, was particularly unwelcome.

With very little fanfare and no public outcry the Sainsbury's supermarket chain, under David Sainsbury's chairmanship, had successfully introduced tomato paste made from genetically modified (GM) tomatoes in 1996. But, soon after Labour's election victory, the media of all political persuasions mounted campaigns against the importation into Europe of the agrochemical multinational Monsanto's genetically modified soybeans – and by implication, all GM crops. The tomato paste was withdrawn. As well as supporting basic plant science research through Gatsby, Sainsbury had previously made some private investments in commercial plant biotechnology projects. As science minister, he was committed to supporting the UK biotechnology industry, though he was deeply frustrated by Monsanto's arrogant disregard for public opinion. The press, particularly right-wing papers that objected to his political affiliation, tried to create the impression that in his roles as both minister and charitable funder of plant science, he was seeking to force GM tomato paste on an unwilling public for the sake of his own company's profits.

For an intensely private man, whose interest in economic growth has never been about personal gain, the vitriolic nature of the attacks was an unpleasant shock. Nor were his closest associates spared. Portrait remembers being doorstepped by members of the press: 'It was a miserable eighteen months,' she says. To remain transparently impartial as a minister whose area of responsibility – at least on paper – included plant biotechnology, Sainsbury had to limit his contact with Gatsby to one meeting with the trustees per year to receive the annual report.

The fact that the office continued to run as effectively as it did during Sainsbury's absence owes everything to the strong team that had been built up. In 1985, Christopher Stone, a former fund manager who since 1983 had been managing David Sainsbury's private financial affairs, had joined Portrait on Gatsby's board of trustees. Andrew Cahn joined the board in 1996, when David Sainsbury felt that it needed another voice. Susie Sainsbury also attended meetings, as did the Gatsby senior advisor John Ashworth. From 2000, Stone was listed as chair of the trustee board in annual reports; until he went into government, Sainsbury had chaired the meetings himself. One innovation that the trustees introduced around this time was an informative, illustrated introduction to accompany the accounts in the annual report: previously these documents had been terse to the point of baldness, containing the very minimum required by the reporting regulations. For the first time, outsiders could see the breadth and depth of Gatsby's activities.

Meanwhile the staff of the SFCT office had steadily grown: by the time of his retirement in 1995, de Quetteville was leading a team of around fifteen people. In 1989, he had taken on Paul Spokes as director of finance: previously all the accountancy had been undertaken by an outside firm, Crowe Clark Whitehill. It wasn't just that the accountancy work had become so demanding that an in-house appointment was justified. Spokes was also charged with updating the creaky systems, wholly inadequate to support grants now running at several million pounds a year. 'The grants system was so slow that it needed to run overnight to update,' he says. He bought in a new IT network and created a grants administration system called Poseidon that is still the basis of SFCT's operations. 'If you go into a grant, it has all the supporting documents linked to it,' says Spokes. 'There are several million documents in the system, and it's continually under development.'

As the staff grew, Spokes took on the responsibility for finding appropriate office accommodation. In 1990, they left the cramped offices that a dozen staff had occupied in New Row, next to a pub in London's theatre district, and moved into their own, fully refurbished and air-conditioned building on five floors in Red Lion Court, Holborn. 'The family always worked on the basis that the trusts would be run to the standard of J Sainsbury plc,' says Spokes. 'Everything was to be done well, but not extravagantly.' The new office was quickly outgrown. Spokes supervised another move, to a commercial office block in Victoria Street called Allington House, in 2002. Finally, with massive development of the area in prospect and their building under threat of demolition, in 2012 SFCT became the first tenants of The Peak, a brand-new office building opposite Victoria Station, where they occupy the entire third floor.

In 1995, de Quetteville retired after twenty years as the founding director of the SFCT offices. Michael Pattison, a former civil servant who had moved on to be chief executive of the Royal Institution of Chartered Surveyors, stepped into his capacious shoes. Pattison says:

> There was a small but excellent team when I arrived. Three of the four senior family members were all still involved in the [Sainsbury's] business. It took me a year or so to realise that the set-up was unique: three generations of family charitable interests being run through a single office, which provided great economies of scale. The younger generation were being encouraged to start their own trusts, and given a break by the others on the admin costs. The family decided that each member should do his or her own thing, and Judith Portrait was trustee and legal advisor to most of them.

He was required 'to give bright staff their heads, to know what was going on in each of the trusts, and where necessary keep the peace between them,' says Pattison. 'I went in thinking I had a broad knowledge of what goes on in the world. Within six weeks I realised how much I *didn't* know. There were corners of British life where people were falling out of society. I learned a lot in a fascinating and impressive few months. A lot of the skill was in finding the right people to engage with.'

Pattison began to introduce additional expertise to the small team running Gatsby. He recruited Matt Williams to look after health and social care programmes across the office; Victoria Hornby came in also to work across several trusts, including assisting Laurence Cockcroft with the Gatsby Africa programme and development projects in the other trusts; Yvonne Pinto came to work with GTEP, though she later moved to the Africa programme; Elaine Ponte took on children's projects; and finally Peter Hesketh joined as deputy director for Gatsby. (Hesketh had previously worked in the aerospace industry, a background that raised eyebrows in some quarters: Pattison remembers an old Oxfam hand in Cameroon observing, perhaps not entirely in jest, that Gatsby had 'brought in an arms dealer' to head its programmes.)

Pattison had a clear understanding with the trustees that Gatsby must be prepared to take risks, and that this approach would lead to failures even if they produced lessons of value. The trick was to judge what proportion of failures would be acceptable, but until 1998 the degree of David Sainsbury's enthusiasm for a project had been a significant factor in determining how long to keep going. Targets and key performance indicators were not part of the culture; trust and close communication with beneficiaries were.

By 1998, the areas that Gatsby was funding were mental health (through the SCMH, which had its own board), and projects for disadvantaged children (Chapter 3); developing countries (the African country trusts and transfer of agricultural technology; see Chapter 4); plant sciences (chiefly the Norwich laboratory, SAPS and the Gatsby studentships; see Chapter 5); science and technology education (through GTEP, also with its own board; see Chapter 6); neuroscience (the Gatsby Computational Neuroscience Unit; see Chapter 8); an assortment of social and economic projects such as the British Social Attitudes survey and the Institute for Manufacturing (see Chapter 9); and the arts (mainly the Sainsbury Centre for Visual Arts and the Royal Shakespeare Theatre; see Chapter 10).

From 1998 to 2006, the proportions allocated to different areas stayed broadly the same: science and engineering education received 26 per cent of the total, social and economic R&D just 6 per cent, and the others somewhere in between. The amount available to spend continued to grow, however, so that project areas that might, if subjected to greater scrutiny, have been scaled back or terminated, continued to be generously funded, and few new initiatives were undertaken. The decade to 2007 saw Gatsby spend £300 million, three times as much as it had given in grants in its first three decades. Staff and trustees were aware that some of this spending was less effective than it might be, but felt they lacked the authority to change direction.

Andrew Cahn says:

> David had to be hands off, and was hands off. The trustees had a very large burden, and I certainly felt that. Truly to do what David wanted we should have continued to be quite experimental, but it was a risky thing to do. We did not manage to do much, and were right not to go very far. When you start something at Gatsby you are not starting a two- or three-year commitment – you are starting a 20-year commitment.

Michael Pattison felt the same: '[David's] disconnect from the Foundation had to be carefully policed – we were allowed to have dinner with him every two years or so,' he says. 'Which was a pity, because it meant the intellectual drive and connection was broken.'

Defining priorities

Towards the end of his time in office, David Sainsbury made two significant and not unrelated public announcements. One was that he intended to give away at least £1 billion; the other was that he would not endow his foundation to keep going indefinitely, like a Carnegie or Rockefeller, but instead Gatsby would 'spend out' its endowment during the remainder of his life.[15] Both decisions implied a reassessment of all the programmes, and a new agenda for the remainder of the life of the foundation. 'David's experience in government helped him greatly with being a better settlor,' says Cahn. 'He came out with much clearer intentions.' On his return to Gatsby, Sainsbury was 66 years old: there was a sense that the time he had left to achieve his ambitious objectives was limited. 'I realised that you could end up doing lots of small things that didn't add up to very much,' says Sainsbury. 'I decided to focus on a few big projects that had an impact.'

For a year or two after his return in September 2006, there was a general changing of the guard. Christopher Stone retired from the trustee board in 2008, to be replaced successively by Bernard Willis, and then Joe Burns in 2014 – both, as Stone had been, were members of staff in Sainsbury's private office. Judith Portrait and Andrew Cahn, meanwhile, have retained their distinctive roles. The board has always been very small, very closely connected to Sainsbury and with most trustees of very long standing. They repay Sainsbury's trust with loyalty to him and his vision, and the governance of the charity has been exemplary. 'It can only work with a settlor as engaged, as intelligent and as strong-minded as David,' says Cahn, who has been a trustee for more than twenty years, 'but then it is a very good system.'

Michael Pattison had also reached retirement age: during his eleven years as director of SFCT, Gatsby's annual grants had risen from £17 million to £49 million. Pattison was succeeded by Alan Bookbinder, a former BBC TV producer who had most recently been the Corporation's head of religion and ethics.

In practice, SFCT deputy director Peter Hesketh was already taking the lion's share of responsibility for Gatsby: Sainsbury had been very impressed with his performance, and in 2009 formally appointed him to work exclusively on the foundation's projects as its director. Immensely effective and energetic, Hesketh made certain that all Gatsby projects over a wide-ranging portfolio, including the building of two enormously complex laboratories, were delivered on time and on budget. He also provided leadership to the highly creative and thoughtful team of Gatsby executives, who were given greater authority and scope than they had had previously. Bookbinder continued to look after the Sainsbury Centre for Visual Arts and other arts institutes in Norwich.

The changes were not just in personnel. On his return, Sainsbury asked the trustees to review all Gatsby's activities and to move forward with fewer, but more ambitious, projects. There were to be major increases in spending on plant science, neuroscience and public policy; a shift from small-scale businesses to sector development in Africa; a tighter focus on technical training in education; and a gradual withdrawal from the areas of mental health and disadvantaged children. There were to be two brand-new public policy-focused institutes, the Centre for Cities and the Institute for Government (Chapter 9). All this was unsettling for those staff and beneficiaries that saw their projects wound down, but it also injected a stimulating sense of urgency. As Nigel Thomas, recruited in 2008 to head the education team, puts it, 'We know that Gatsby's not always going to be around. All the impact we will ever achieve has already happened, or is in train, or we must do it. That's exciting and very empowering.'

One of the things that had changed in the eight years Sainsbury was in government was the coming of age of the fifth generation of Sainsburys, both as individuals and as philanthropists: of the seventeen family trusts currently active, ten were founded by the children of John, Timothy and David Sainsbury.[16] Between them they fund a wide range of causes, including the arts, the environment, third world development and the welfare of children. For Victoria Hornby, who worked across all the family trusts, that provided an important context for the change of gear. She says:

A lot of the growth in the organisation [SFCT] was about that next generation. I remember that at the same time as David was shedding some things, others were growing, so it felt OK. In the areas where he retained interest there was no drop-off in activity; it just became much more focused. His ambitions were very well articulated about what he wanted to achieve, which was a great example to others.

8

BETWEEN BRAIN AND MIND

Computation, circuits and cognition

Neuroscience – the study of the brain – is one of the most competitive fields in bioscience; the questions it raises are uniquely challenging, and the answers ever more urgent as ageing societies face the consequences of dementia and neurological conditions such as stroke. The brain is very complicated, and very hard to mend when it goes wrong. The two things are related: most brain cells do not regenerate if they are damaged, and most of the signals that guide the immensely intricate wiring in the developing brain are no longer available once it is complete. The brain also holds the key to some of humanity's most fundamental questions: What makes us who we are? How do we think, learn, remember, feel, love, fear, touch, hurt, move, dream?

Neuroscience is not by any means a Cinderella discipline. All the major biomedical research funding institutions have programmes in neuroscience: the National Institutes of Health in the USA and the MRC in the UK; charitable organisations such as the Howard Hughes Medical Institute (HHMI) and the Wellcome Trust; and disease-specific charities such as Alzheimer's Research UK. More recently 'new philanthropists' such as Microsoft co-founder Paul Allen, mathematician and hedge fund manager Jim Simons, and entrepreneurial engineer Fred Kavli have made multimillion-dollar investments in cracking the brain's secrets. New institutes with an interest in the brain have been founded in Seattle (the Allen Institute for Brain Science), near Washington, DC (the HHMI's Janelia Research Campus), at Columbia University (the Zuckerman Institute) and in Lisbon (the Centre for the Unknown, funded by the Champalimaud Foundation), while the Simons Foundation has launched an international Collaboration on the Global Brain. But understanding the brain is a very big challenge; bigger by far than that faced by physicists in their hunt for the Higgs boson, which by one estimate cost $13.25 billion.[1] There is plenty still to do.

Gatsby has made a long-term, focused commitment to understanding how the activity of billions of neurons underpins our behaviour, from the simplest reflex to our thoughts about the future. New institutes, the Gatsby Computational Neuroscience Unit and the Sainsbury Wellcome Centre for Neural Circuits and Behaviour, opened in London in 1998 and 2016 respectively, while strategic grant funding to organisations around the world has helped to forge international collaborations and push forward new technologies. The emphasis is on basic research, but the findings will ultimately underpin new approaches to disease: a new partnership with the Royal College of Psychiatrists is ensuring that those training for a career in psychiatry are up to speed with the latest on the science of the brain (see Case study, page 219).

The 'hard problem'
As a history student at Cambridge, David Sainsbury found himself required to write an essay on 'Consciousness' for his college, King's. His research turned up a little book published a decade before: *The Physical Basis of Mind*, edited by the Cambridge historian and BBC radio producer Peter Laslett. The book contained transcripts of a series of talks broadcast on the BBC Third Programme during 1949. The speakers included

the Nobel prize-winning physiologist Sir Charles Sherrington, then in his nineties, and his fellow Nobelist Edgar Adrian, as well as philosophers Freddie Ayer and Gilbert Ryle. 'It didn't say anything about consciousness,' says Sainsbury, 'but it introduced me to the whole idea of neurophysiology, and I was rather intrigued by that.' Thinking about the problem for the first time, he immediately accepted the idea that mind and brain could not be separated, and decided it would be fun to switch from history to psychology so that he could study it further. 'To King's' great credit, they said, "You'll get a worse degree, but if that's your journey, go for it,"' he says. 'Maybe they thought that it didn't matter, as I was likely to go into the family firm; but I like to think of it as an extremely enlightened educational decision. It certainly changed the course of my life.'

As mentioned previously, Sainsbury's closest friend at Cambridge, Roger Freedman, was studying natural sciences, including physiology. He says,

> That course covered all of physiology, for medical students. I had the incredibly good fortune to be supervised by Horace Barlow, one of the great minds of neuroscience, for my first two years. I remember reading Horace's celebrated paper on the visual system of the frog. It was a mindblower for me, about the reduction of redundancy in sensory coding: one of those things that changes the way you see the world.

One of Sainsbury's own lecturers in psychology was the visionary and irrepressible Richard Gregory. 'He gave me a totally different view of what a scientist was,' says Sainsbury. 'He had this wonderful laugh, and was full of ideas about all kinds of things.' Gregory would later both help to set up the UK's first department for the study of artificial intelligence (AI) in Edinburgh, and jump-start the movement for interactive science centres in the UK (see page 160). Working with visual illusions, he developed the idea that visual perceptions are hypotheses constructed by the brain on the basis of evidence and experience, rather than photographic records of the physical world.

At the same time, Cambridge was experiencing the ripples of excitement coming from the latest discoveries in North America. Working at McGill University in Montreal, Canada, Donald Hebb had published his classic text *Organisation of Behaviour* (1949), proposing that learning depended on the strengthening and weakening of connections in networks of neurons. A decade later David Hubel and Torsten Wiesel at Harvard University recorded the activity of single cells and discovered how the mammalian visual cortex is organised into discrete layers and columns that respond to different features of the visual environment – work that later won them a Nobel prize. 'I think I had understood that the interesting question was "How do neural circuits process information in order to produce behaviour?"' says Sainsbury, 'though I'm not sure I would have expressed it like that at the time.' On graduating, Sainsbury considered pursuing research in neuroscience, but regretfully decided he did not have a strong enough scientific background and went into the family business as expected. Years later Gatsby gave him the opportunity to renew his interest in the study of the brain. The science had moved on, driven by technologies that enable scientists to explore the living brain in unprecedented detail.

We already know a great deal. We know that different regions of the brain control different functions: vision, hearing, movement and so on. We know how signals pass between the 90 billion neurons (nerve cells) in the brain. We know what happens when brain cells are damaged or diseased. But we are still barely beginning to understand how this lump of tissue weighing less than 1.5 kg learns, remembers and thinks. Far less do we understand how the combined activity of all those neurons gives us the experience of being conscious selves.

Cognition and computation

In the late 1990s, encouraged by the success of the Sainsbury Laboratory in Norwich with basic plant science, David Sainsbury began to think about funding research into how the brain works. Once again, Roger Freedman was closely involved in helping him decide how Gatsby might best support neuroscience. At the time advances in technologies for investigating the brain directly had slowed: it did not look like a 'breakthrough' moment. Instead of an experimental laboratory, Freedman suggested a unit that would explore the potential of networks of brain cells through computer simulation.

His researches had led him to exciting work at Oxford University in the area of 'neuromorphic engineering' – a term coined by the Caltech engineer Carver Mead to describe a new way of designing computer chips with analogue circuitry so that they worked more like networks of neurons.[2] The research of Rodney Douglas, Kevan Martin and Misha Mahowald in Oxford's MRC Anatomical Neuropharmacology Unit was underfunded, and Gatsby made them a grant at a critical juncture. But, in 1996, Douglas and Martin took the opportunity to leave Oxford to establish the renowned Institute for Neuroinformatics in Zurich.

Meanwhile, wanting to know more, Freedman signed up for the three-week workshop in neuromorphic engineering held each year at Telluride in Colorado. There he met one of the chief architects of neural network theory, Geoffrey Hinton, an Englishman working at the University of Toronto. Hinton is celebrated as a co-author of a 1986 paper demonstrating how an algorithm known as back propagation could enable artificial neural networks to learn from their mistakes by modifying the strengths of the connections between layers of neurons.[3] 'I was always interested in artificial neural networks, things that were only loosely related to the brain,' he says, 'and at that time they had fallen into disrepute. The idea [of back propagation] was seventeen years old and hadn't worked in a practical sense. It hadn't worked because computers were too slow, but there was no way anyone would have funded a grant for it.'

Freedman invited him to come to London and head a new unit in London that combined machine intelligence with theoretical neuroscience, all funded by Gatsby. The Gatsby Computational Neuroscience Unit (GCNU) opened at University College London (UCL) in 1998, with the aim of 'building neurobiologically realistic and computationally sound models of the way the brain computes'. Tim Shallice, a former colleague of Hinton's and director of UCL's multidisciplinary Institute for Cognitive Neuroscience (ICN), was instrumental in bringing the unit to UCL. The Gatsby grant enabled UCL Provost Derek Roberts to rent a former office building in Queen Square: the GCNU took the top two floors, while the ICN, previously a 'virtual' institute, moved in downstairs. The strength of neuroscience research across UCL's departments provided an ideal environment for GCNU's theoreticians to interact with people working on real brains.

Once the unit was established, Hinton took advantage of the unrestricted research funding that came with the job, and returned to his work on neural networks. 'I went back to an old idea [restricted Boltzmann machines] that had never worked properly and made it work nicely,' he says. 'It was a way to initialise neural networks so that back propagation would work very well.'[4] Hinton continued this line of research after he returned to Toronto in 2002, and almost a decade later so-called 'deep learning' in many-layered artificial neural networks finally took off. Deep learning algorithms are now taking over areas of AI such as image recognition, natural language processing and machine translation. 'The seeds of the resurgence in neural networks and deep learning came from the work I did while I was working at the GCNU,' says Hinton. 'It was thanks to the Unit encouraging pure basic research. If I had stayed in Canada there's no way I could have written a grant proposal to do that.'

When Hinton moved to London he brought with him another Englishman, Peter Dayan. 'I had been a post-doc of Geoff's,' says Dayan, 'and was then an assistant professor at MIT. He asked me if I was interested in coming back to Britain to help found this unit.' When Hinton went back to Canada, Dayan succeeded him as director of the GCNU. 'Neuroscience doesn't have a very mature relationship between theory and experiment in the way that physics does, where the distinction has been well understood and celebrated for a long time,' says Dayan. The role of the unit is to provide the theoretical underpinning that will help experimental neuroscientists make sense of the data they collect, and generate predictions about how real brains might work.

'These very complicated systems are solving very complicated computations,' says Dayan. 'What theoretical neuroscience does is deliver three sorts of analyses. Mathematical analysis offers theories that provide a bridge between different levels of explanation: between the level of the cell and the level of the circuit, for example.' It is also a fruitful way of trying to keep pace with the highly dynamic operation of neural circuits, from the millisecond trace of activity in a single neuron, to the seconds that we can hold items in short-term memory, to the long-term memories we keep for a lifetime.

The second important role for the theorists is to analyse the increasingly unmanageable torrent of data collected by experimental scientists. 'You could record from 1,000 neurons: you might be interested in how closely correlated different neurons were,' says Dayan. 'That's a statistical question. How long do I have to record in order to know what those correlations are like?' Other areas where computer analysis is invaluable are in capturing the information in still or video images. The 'connectome' is the total set of connections within the brain, and several research groups around the world are intent on mapping it completely. This will involve imaging a large number of 40-nanometre slices (2,000 times thinner than a human hair), and then analysing the images to find out where all the synapses are.

The third type of analysis is explicitly computational. 'The brain solves computational problems,' says Dayan. 'Computational analysis investigates which and how.' This area of work is the key link to building machines that can learn. He says:

> The brain is solving a lot of problems that we would like computers to be able to solve, such as vision, and so we need to have a way of understanding this. What's great about biology is that there's a reason why things are the way they are. That should provide us with a lot more clues about how things work. Animals do sensible things, they learn in sensible ways, they respond to uncertainty in the world appropriately, they absorb information correctly – they learn. So we need ways of characterising that.

Keeping machine learning and theoretical neuroscience people together in the same, close-knit environment has proved its worth. 'Artificial neural networks have led to a huge wave of successes in artificial intelligence that are being used everywhere,' says Hinton, who now works part-time for Google, 'and that's leading neuroscientists to consider whether the algorithms that work really well in practice might be implementable in the brain. For many years, neuroscientists were utterly confident that nothing like back propagation was going on in the brain. And they are suddenly beginning to get interested in it, because it works so well.'

Dayan's own research focuses on modelling the way that the expectation of rewards and punishments – positive and negative reinforcement, in the jargon of behaviour theory – affect how animals make decisions in their daily pursuit of survival. He is also interested in the 'unsupervised learning' – without rewards and punishments in any conventional sense – through which they form a representation of the environment in which they live. His four fellow group leaders, Peter Latham, Arthur Gretton, Aapo Hyvarinen and Maneesh Sahani, work across the range of theoretical neuroscience, data analysis and machine learning, asking questions about the probabilistic nature of perception and the encoding and decoding of sensory representations.[5] Dayan's wife, Zhaoping Li, who helped to found the Unit, is now funded by Gatsby to work on machine vision in UCL's Department of Computer Science.

The unit has stayed small, with about two dozen post-docs and graduate students, but holds an influential place in international computational neuroscience through a variety of formal and informal collaborations. The most significant of these is the 'Tri-Centre' collaboration with the Center for Theoretical Neuroscience at Columbia University and the Interdisciplinary Center for Neural Computation at the Hebrew University in Jerusalem (see page 207). Teaching is also an important part of the Unit's role, through its bespoke four-year PhD programme in Computational Neuroscience and Machine Learning. Former faculty, post-docs and students have gone on to leading positions elsewhere, while often retaining connections as adjunct faculty. Zoubin Ghahramani, who came from Toronto with Hinton, left in 2005 for the University of Cambridge, where he now leads a thirty-strong machine learning group as Professor of Information Engineering. In December 2016, the AI start-up he founded, Geometric Intelligence, was bought by the transport network company Uber to form the basis of its new artificial intelligence laboratory.

In 2010, two researchers, Demis Hassabis and Shane Legg, left the GCNU to found the AI start-up DeepMind, together with entrepreneur Mustafa Suleyman. Google bought the company in 2014 for a reported £400 million.[6] Hassabis had been using AI to underpin the development of computer games since he graduated in computing science from Cambridge. 'I decided to study neuroscience to see how AI works,' he says, and he signed up for a PhD at UCL working on the hippocampus with Eleanor Maguire. His doctoral work generated a number of papers on topics such as imagination and memory, and he won a Wellcome Trust postdoctoral fellowship that brought him to the GCNU. 'My work at Gatsby was an extension of my PhD work, on how the hippocampus works, memory and imagination, not on machine learning algorithms,' he says. 'But I wanted to use neuroscience to inspire new directions for AI. I was studying aspects of the brain that we didn't know how to do well in machine learning.

'The GCNU is unique in combining machine learning and AI with neuroscience,' he goes on. 'It's one of the only places in the world that does that. That combination is embodied in Peter Dayan – he's a world expert on both sides, and there are other world-class people.' When he met Shane Legg he realised that they were both on 'a lifelong journey to general purpose AI', and that the time was ripe to found DeepMind. The company's most high-profile achievement has been to develop an algorithm that can beat a human master at the oriental board game go, which it achieved in March 2016. Unlike many chess algorithms, it was not pre-programmed. Says Hassabis,

> The algorithm learned by playing 30 million games against itself. It took a few months. We only build systems that learn how to master tasks directly from raw data or experience. We used a variation of the same algorithm recently to control the cooling in Google's data centres: it saved 15 per cent of the power, and 40 per cent of the cooling, which could save tens of millions of dollars and is good for the environment.

DeepMind is now talking to organisations from the National Health Service to CERN (European Organisation for Nuclear Research) about how AI based on deep learning might help them to cope with the massive amounts of data they generate.

Hassabis acknowledges that he and his colleagues at DeepMind owe a debt to the work on deep learning that Geoff Hinton carried out at the GCNU in the late 1990s. 'Everybody uses deep learning, which is what he invented,' he says. 'The year he spent when he started GCNU was very creative for him. The GCNU is very important – that's where I met Shane, and we hire a lot of people from the unit. It's a great thing that Lord Sainsbury has done there.'

A strategy for neuroscience

Delighted as he was by the success of the GCNU, Sainsbury still wanted to support research in experimental neuroscience – studies of real brains and real neurons. By the mid-2000s new tools were becoming available that meant the question of how the brain generates behaviour, from recognising odours to solving mazes, might just be tractable. David Sainsbury was in post as Minister for Science and Innovation and was not allowed to have anything to do with his foundation, but he still kept an eye on what was happening in the field. In 2003, at one of many dinners to mark the fiftieth anniversary of the discovery of the DNA double helix, he found himself sitting next to Roger Freedman's former PhD supervisor, the molecular biologist Sydney Brenner. From the 1960s, Brenner had led a pioneering study of the nematode worm, *Caenorhabditis elegans*, aiming to understand this tiny creature – less than 1 millimetre long – completely, from genes to behaviour. The previous year he had shared the Nobel prize in Physiology or Medicine for this work.

'I said, "I think neuroscience is becoming very interesting, who can tell me more about what's going on?"' says Sainsbury. Brenner told him he should go and talk to Thomas Jessell, a British neuroscientist who was a professor at Columbia University in New York. Sainsbury had done his MBA at Columbia and knew it well. 'So the next time I was there I went and saw him, and he introduced me to Richard Axel and Eric Kandel.'

The two Columbia neuroscientists, both Nobel prize winners for their work on neural systems, confirmed his view that the field was immensely exciting. 'Richard Axel showed me this extraordinary experiment in which you could take a fly's head, engineer the cells to fluoresce when they were active, pass the smell of a melon over and see which cells responded,' he says. After a few more conversations, he became convinced that the right way forward was to fund a new institute for experimental neuroscience.

For a long time, physiologists interested in brain activity focused on the individual neuron. By placing a fine-tipped electrode alongside, it is possible to listen into a cell's electrical activity and relate it to behaviour or sensation. But it has long been understood that cells are connected into overlapping circuits, and that these circuits underpin our interactions with our perceptual, social and biological world. In the twenty-first century, a burst of innovation is delivering technologies that at last make it possible to explore these circuits. Contemporary neuroscience integrates the power of modern computing, the latest 'wet lab' techniques in biochemistry, genetics, microscopy and imaging, and behavioural experiments on humans and laboratory animals. This is exactly the moment that a foundation such as Gatsby can most usefully intervene, supporting scientists as they open up new areas of research.

'Where you have this breakthrough technology, there is merit in having scientists from different disciplines working together in a new institute,' says Sainsbury. 'Enabling them to exchange technologies and interact with one another is the way to do it.' By this time, Roger Freedman had his hands full with the new Sainsbury Laboratory for plant science in Cambridge. So, on leaving government in 2006, Sainsbury went back to Columbia and recruited Sarah Caddick, a British neuroscientist who was heading the development of a new brain research centre there, as his neuroscience advisor. 'During 2005–2006 he would spend time with us at Columbia,' says Caddick. 'That's when plans for the institute began to emerge.'

While the Gatsby name was well known in the world of theoretical neuroscience, it had very little visibility among experimental scientists. Caddick advised Sainsbury to begin by developing a strategy and supporting a portfolio of projects around the world – the 'splashing around in the shallows' phase that had worked so well in other areas of Gatsby funding. 'I spent the first two years working out what that portfolio should look like,' she says, 'and building up awareness and credibility in the neuroscience community.' She undertook to find out what the state of play in neuroscience in the UK was, and plan a portfolio that would support a new institute. 'The thinking was that we should be finding allies, funding good science – and doing it in a way that reflects the Gatsby philosophy, which is "Do your homework, see where there are interesting things to fund",' she says. 'And we had a very specific time frame.'

Sainsbury gave Caddick his complete backing. While he expected assurances that the work Gatsby funded was of good quality, he was happy to dispense with the usual bureaucratic apparatus of hundred-page grant applications and academic review boards. Instead he was eager to see the work for himself. 'One of my strongest memories of building up that portfolio was how much time David spent going on trips around the world to visit the scientists,' says Caddick. 'To him this was never just grants.'

To establish its presence in the field, Gatsby began to contribute support for international conferences in this area. 'In the early days, we funded lots of meetings', says Caddick, 'to get a sense of what was happening and who was coming through the field.' Once she had identified researchers whose work met the strategic aims of the Gatsby portfolio, Caddick approached them and asked them to develop a short proposal. This came as a great surprise to those on the receiving end. 'Normally a foundation puts out a call for applications,' says Massimo Scanziani, now at the University of California at San Francisco. 'But here was an agent – a scout if you like – very well briefed in neuroscience, going to meetings and finding opportunities for her foundation.' In each case, generous four-year, no-strings grants have enabled the research groups to undertake risky, cutting-edge projects that would not have been possible otherwise.

One of the first major projects in the portfolio was the Connectomics Consortium, a partnership between Jeff Lichtman, Josh Sanes and Xiaowei Zhuang at Harvard, Stephen Smith at Stanford and Sebastian Seung at MIT. Taking forward previous work on the 'connectome' – the complete set of connections in the brain – in 2008 Gatsby funded this group to develop high-resolution light and electron microscopy, high-throughput imaging techniques and computational analysis to construct three-dimensional wiring diagrams of small regions of the brain.[7] Seung, who has now moved to Princeton, has gone on to develop the computer vision part of the programme into an online game, Eyewire,[8] that recruits citizen scientists to help refine the mapping of brain circuits. More recently he has expanded the project into a multi-game platform, WiredDifferently,[9] which Gatsby continues to support.

The California Circuits Consortium was another early portfolio member, bringing together Anirvan Ghosh and Massimo Scanziani at the University of California at San Diego, Karl Deisseroth at Stanford University and Ed Callaway and John Reynolds at the Salk Institute, to explore the action of inhibitory circuits in the visual system. 'We had proposed it with a small document of a few pages,' says Scanziani. 'It was a vision rather than a real proposal.' The collaboration proved abundantly fruitful, generating more than fifty papers over the lifetime of the grant, and establishing how different classes of inhibitory interneuron regulate and shape visual experience.[10]

Scanziani has no doubt that the Gatsby approach – long-term

grants to individuals with no strings attached and no expectation of a 'translational' outcome – was critical to that success. 'It is very important in the current atmosphere to have funding sources that support very basic science,' he says. He also credits Sarah Caddick with seeing the benefit of working as a consortium. 'She forced us to interact with other people and learn from them,' he says. 'This has allowed us to make extraordinary progress in understanding visual processing in the brain.'

Collaboration is a key feature of the strategy Caddick has developed for Gatsby. To complement the work of the GCNU, since 2006 Gatsby has supported work in theoretical neuroscience at Columbia University led by Larry Abbott, co-author with Peter Dayan of the field-defining textbook on the subject.[11] 'It was a dream to emulate that Gatsby unit,' says Abbott, and the first grant from Gatsby enabled him to enlarge his group. The funding also covered an annual joint meeting with GCNU.

In 2010, Gatsby gave another five-year grant to a third theoretical neuroscience centre, the Interdisciplinary Center for Neural Computation at the Hebrew University in Jerusalem, to form what they call the Tri-Centre theoretical consortium. 'We are inundated with requests for other theory groups to join the Tri-Centre group,' says Caddick. 'That reflects that when you get on with what you want to do, and do it well, people will gravitate towards you.' The annual Tri-Centre meetings are only the most visible part of the collaboration. 'We have a student here who is going to work in London,' says Abbott. 'She will get a PhD from Columbia. It's a fantastic opportunity to move around. We are all interested in the same things, but we approach the subject in different ways. Moving between the centres helps students decide which way matches that student's intellect.'

After the new portfolio had been in place for three or four years, with some of the grants drawing to an end, Caddick considered bringing all the participants together for a meeting in London. 'We had built up a portfolio based on very smart individuals,' she says. 'I chatted to David, and said it might be interesting to see if they come up with things they might want to do together. He said, "Yes, absolutely. Try to get as many as we can."' She got every single one to come, and they met in 2011 at the Academy of Medical Sciences in London. 'At that point, David had gone to meet with almost every one of them in their home location,' says Caddick. 'They were willing to move their various commitments around because they'd all met him and liked him.'

Scanziani has vivid memories of the occasion. 'We were all very nervous,' he says. 'It was our chance to show off and see what we were doing relative to the other groups. It ended up being very exciting – Lord Sainsbury was there listening to all the papers, and was very accessible. And there were people from theatre and the arts – I remember it as a very multicultural event.'

Circuits and behaviour

While the portfolio of activities was important and influential, its purpose was always to prepare the ground for the flagship project, which was the institute. Discerning a complementary interest within the Wellcome Trust, the powerful London-based medical research charity, Caddick approached Richard Morris, the Edinburgh University neuroscientist then seconded as Wellcome's neuroscience advisor. The Wellcome and Gatsby trustees agreed to fund the institute jointly – to the tune of £150 million including running costs and research costs for the first five years. The result is the Sainsbury Wellcome Centre for Neural Circuits and Behaviour (SWC), built, after stiff competition from Oxford and Cambridge, on the campus of UCL. As runner-up, Oxford University won a £10 million grant co-funded by Gatsby and Wellcome to develop its own Centre for Neural Circuits and Behaviour: it is led by Gero Miesenböck, a pioneer of the technique of optogenetics, which allows experimenters to switch genetically transformed brain cells on or off with light.

Creating the SWC was a high-risk operation. UCL is second only to Harvard in the strength of its neuroscience community, but the idea was not to cherry-pick from its existing labs. Instead, Gatsby appointed John O'Keefe, one of the architects of UCL's pitch to host the SWC, as interim director. O'Keefe pioneered the study of the circuits that enable animals to orient themselves in space, discovering specialised neurons that fire in response to location. The understanding was that he would help to recruit a permanent director and team leaders from around the world. The GCNU, meanwhile, would remain a separate entity, but would be housed in the new institute alongside twelve teams of experimental researchers.

Combining theory and experiment was central to the way David Sainsbury envisaged the SWC working. 'Up to the level of the cortex you can see what is happening,' he says, 'and then it just explodes. We have no idea what the code is or how it works. It's going to require both the experimentalists and the computational people to solve that problem, which may turn out to be immensely complicated.'

'We developed quite a high-level, philosophical approach to the question of what the Centre would do,' says O'Keefe. 'We said we wanted to investigate how activity in neural circuits represents ideas, thoughts, and actions. We did not specify what part of the brain we were going to look at, who was going to be involved, or who would lead it. The idea that you would be able to record from large numbers of cells in freely moving animals, that you now had ways of controlling cells – none of that was doable when we made the bid, but we could see that in a short time new techniques would let us do those sorts of things.'

In the event, after several possible candidates were interviewed, O'Keefe was confirmed as founding director. But the lists of requirements the other candidates had come up with proved highly useful. 'The main thing was more money,' says O'Keefe. It became clear that the funding on the table, generous as it was, would not be enough to recruit some of the best young scientists in the world in the face of competition from other centres. 'The world has changed markedly over the past ten years,' says O'Keefe. 'People now command resources that were unimaginable ten or fifteen years ago. Even young people are identified as superstars and they know they're superstars.' David Sainsbury approves the strategy of pursuing early-career scientists rather than established leaders in the field. 'I like that, because it means that you are adding to the area,' he says. 'It's more fun and more valuable to pick the bright, upcoming people – they're the ones that will do the breakthrough research. But you've got to find them and persuade them to move.'

The funders saw the point, and increased the money that was available for recruitment. O'Keefe says,

> The nice thing about the SWC is that it's a well-found institution. One of the reasons I was happy to take the job was that I don't need to go out and raise funds. Almost anyone else who runs an institute this size has to spend time doing that. It's a very nice position to be in. We can also go out and get Wellcome Trust or MRC fellowships, but we can use the core funds for doing science and not salaries.

The other big risk Gatsby took was to embark on a major architectural project in central London. Strongly influenced by David Sainsbury's wife Susie, the Gatsby and Wellcome project leaders did not play it safe. In the autumn of 2009, they awarded the design contract to Ian Ritchie Architects Ltd, who had never previously designed a lab, and who produced no drawings as part of the competition: instead, as requested in the brief, Ritchie described how he would visit labs and consult neuroscientists in order to design the building 'from the inside out'. Ritchie was charged with creating a building that was 'creative, useful, adaptable and wonderful', in Caddick's words. 'David said, "This needs to be about science and function, and not a big iconic building",' she remembers. 'We wanted an architect who would agree to spend the first couple of years working with the scientists on the design. And the whole project team had to be committed to the same approach.'

Ritchie and his colleagues spent several months visiting neuroscientists around the world to find out how they worked. Once they embarked on the design, they held a regular programme of workshops that brought together the design and client teams, including the structural and services engineers, with a group of scientific advisors. Every aspect of the design was interrogated by this group before it was incorporated into the final planning application, approved in July 2011.

Ritchie achieved the aim of making the spaces feel interconnected by creating four two-storey laboratories within the seven-storey building, each built around a glass-walled mini-atrium with a staircase. Working with the engineers, he provided each laboratory with a 'satellite' holding area for laboratory animals (mostly mice) that met the strict environmental controls required by the Home Office. This avoids stressing the animals by transporting them up and down from the main biological services unit in the basement. He placed the GCNU over three floors in the centre of the building, so that the theoreticians were in easy contact with the experimentalists.[12]

These innovative features have delighted the scientists who have moved in. As well as being practical, the building is also beautiful, with a cool blue and white colour scheme inside, and a unique façade of white, undulating, opaque cast glass. The façade both references the electrical waves that carry information in the nervous system and acknowledges the vertical rhythms of the Georgian buildings in nearby Fitzroy Square. On 23 May 2016, the SWC was formally opened by Nobel prize winner Eric Kandel, from Columbia University. The following October it was named Major Building Project of the Year at the British Construction

Nobel prizewinning neuroscientist Eric Kandel from Columbia
University opened the Sainsbury Wellcome Centre in May 2016.

Industry Awards, and Overall Winner (and Best Façade Design)
at the 2016 Leading European Architects Forum (LEAF) Awards.

At the time of writing, one senior group leader (Troy Margrie
from the National Institute of Medical Research at Mill Hill,
London) and four junior group leaders (Adam Kampff from the
Champalimaud Centre for the Unknown in Lisbon, Andy Murray
from Columbia University, Yoh Isogai from Harvard University
and Tiago Branco from the Laboratory of Molecular Biology in
Cambridge) have moved in and are setting up their labs. Each
is using combinations of the latest techniques of imaging, multi-
electrode recording, genetics, biochemistry and axon tracing to
analyse the circuits involved in behaviours including naviga-
tion, social interaction, balance and vision, while also thinking
more broadly about how the cortex functions as a whole.

John O'Keefe had himself crowned the excitement around
the new Centre by sharing the 2014 Nobel prize in Medicine or

Physiology with two former colleagues, May-Britt Moser and Edvard Moser of the Norwegian University of Science and Technology, for their discoveries of place-finding cells in the brain. He stepped down as director of the SWC in September 2016, but remains very much engaged as a senior group leader. His successor, Thomas Mrsic-Flogel from the Biozentrum in Basel, Switzerland, was announced the following month and formally took up the post during 2017. Mrsic-Flogel's wife Sonja Hofer, another group leader in neuroscience at the Biozentrum, also moved her research group to the SWC.

Mrsic-Flogel has pioneered a combination of methods to relate the fine-scale organisation of the brain's circuits to their function, focusing on the part of the neocortex that processes visual information. As mentioned above, Hubel and Wiesel established the principle that the anatomical organisation of the visual cortex is related to specific features of the visual environment – cells in specific columns of cortical tissue respond to edges at specific orientations, for example. However, the technique they used – recording from single cells – could not reveal how those cells were interconnected. 'Neighbouring cells can have overlapping trees of dendrites and axons, but that doesn't mean they're connected,' says Mrsic-Flogel. 'Connectivity is determined by function: cells that frequently fire together are more likely to connect to each other strongly, just like friends on Facebook.'

His strategy now is to try to establish principles of connectivity that can transcend different brain areas. 'The more interesting question is the principle of long-range connectivity,' he says. 'Of the many inputs a cell receives, some come from nearby cells, but many from distal parts of the brain. The challenge ahead is to understand the logic of that connectivity. Do cells that fire together wire together in distributed networks?' Such long-range associated networks could be the basis of memory – for example, hearing your grandmother's voice might elicit a memory of her face, even though speech and vision are processed in different brain areas, because the cells have learned to fire in synchrony.

The SWC will seek to develop coherent theories that can link the growing body of data from experimental observations into a whole. Mrsic-Flogel says:

> We need an intuitive, easy to understand theory of what the neocortex, or other parts of the brain, have evolved to do. It is a machine that makes associations, to enable us to make predictions about what will happen if we do something or experience something. My view is that we need to spend time thinking about how to interpret our data in a framework of a bigger theory that transcends multiple scales, from behaviour to circuits to diverse neuronal cell types. And that's one reason why exceptionally talented scientists should be in the same building. Ultimately you want experimentalists who think about theory, and theorists who think about how computations are implemented in circuits, so theorists and experimentalists speak the same language.

One way to achieve this will be the two coordinated PhD programmes that are run jointly by Adam Kampff from SWC and Maneesh Sahani from the GCNU. During the first year of the four-year programme, students from the GCNU and the SWC study a common course of experimental, theoretical and systems neuroscience before specialising in either theory or lab work from the second year onwards. 'It was a very clever idea to set it up that way,' says Mrsic-Flogel. 'Students will be speaking the same language from day one.'

The building has been designed to encourage collaboration between individuals and groups, and Mrsic-Flogel passionately believes in developing a new model of working to capitalise on the opportunity. 'Ultimately the goal is not to advance one's career, which is the current model, but to understand how the brain works,' he says. He cites the 'more selfless' approach adopted at 'big physics' laboratories such as CERN, where scientists work in teams to develop massive instruments such as the Large Hadron Collider to solve problems that cannot be tackled any other way. 'Neuroscience has failed to do that,' he says. 'There's a vicious circle in which scientists have to become increasingly self-serving to get their next three-year grant. To do that they have to get the next paper in *Nature* or *Cell*. Their motivation changes from wanting to discover something about how the brain works to wanting to publish the next paper and so get the next grant.'

The way the SWC is funded, with core costs and salaries funded for five years at a time, provides an opportunity to break this model. 'The SWC should act as a beacon for how to approach science in a different way,' says Mrsic-Flogel. To meet this aim, and prepare for the quinquennial reviews they will face with Gatsby and Wellcome in 2021, the centre is developing review criteria that take into account progress and future work rather than published papers. 'I would say that if we collectively can generate a couple of plausible theories about how parts of the brain work by 2021, that will be a success,' he says.

Research at the SWC could potentially answer many questions about how the healthy brain perceives and learns. What many find hard to grasp, says Caddick, is that David Sainsbury's funding initiatives are not primarily about trying to 'fix things'. Instead he is in for the long haul – the SWC has a fifty-year projected lifetime – during which research might begin to make a difference to our understanding. 'David is an example of how to trust your own instincts', says Caddick, 'and engage the right people to help you think through what's possible.'

A technological advance

Many of those who have joined the SWC have skills in developing technology as well as doing science, and the building includes a fully equipped and staffed fabrication workshop where their designs can be prototyped. 'There are questions where we know that we'd like to find an answer and we just can't do it with the technology we have,' says O'Keefe. 'We're always looking for new ways to answer the questions that we have.'

Gatsby has history in this area. Another portfolio project, launched in September 2013, is developing new electrical recording neuroprobes that will greatly increase the amount of data that can be gathered in experiments. Using silicon wafer technology, they make it possible to record from hundreds or thousands of cells at the same time. 'There are hundreds of little contacts, and you can do a lot of the processing right on the probe,' says O'Keefe, who contributed to its design and testing. Gatsby and Wellcome have funded UCL's work on the project as part of a larger initiative led by HHMI at the Janelia Institute and also including the Allen Institute for Brain Science. The chips themselves are made by a big silicon wafer manufacturer, Imec in Louvain, Belgium, and are due to be launched during 2017.

'It's another example of working with partners, trying to do something for the field,' says Caddick. 'David is very pleased with the progress, it's exactly what he wants to see happen.'

A wider influence

In all Gatsby's areas of interest, it aims to influence policy makers, the media and the general public in support of its goals. The biggest organisation in the world representing the interests of people working on the brain is the Society for Neuroscience (SfN), based in Washington, DC but international in its 40,000 membership. Its annual conference, attended by 30,000 participants, always brings the latest neuroscience discoveries into the public eye.

Since 1993, SfN has published successive editions of a book entitled *Brain Facts*, widely used in classrooms as well as by journalists and policymakers as a reliable source of background for stories about the brain. After Marty Saggese became executive director of the society in 2002, the incoming president of the society, Huda Akil from the University of Michigan, and many other current and past leaders of the Society, encouraged him to make it a priority to take *Brain Facts* online. There was an urgent need for a source of reliable information to counter the 'neuro-myths' at large on the internet. 'It was clear that it would take a significant amount of money to get this started, do it right and sustain it,' says Saggese.

It was something he had talked to Sarah Caddick about before she joined Gatsby and, as she developed Gatsby's neuroscience portfolio, she returned to the idea. She did not think Gatsby could meet the full cost, however, and encouraged Saggese to find another partner. In the event Gatsby and the Kavli Foundation put in equal contributions, and the site, BrainFacts.org, was launched in 2012. By early 2016 it had passed 10 million page views and, although the site's visitors include many school students, its audiences are by no means all in education. Saggese says:

> Congressional staff are accessing the site as issues such as mental health come into focus. Policymakers, including those in the White House Office of Science and Technology, tell us they look at BrainFacts. A *Washington Post* reporter told us, 'When I write about the brain I always go to BrainFacts before I start work.' We're seen as a trusted and valuable source of information by the media and by politicians. And we get traffic from specific groups among the general public, such as seniors who want to know more about dementia.

David Sainsbury himself understands very well that, depending on their complexity, major advances in understanding the functions of the brain could take decades. He says:

A fairly good starting place is what Sydney Brenner called the 'itch to scratch' issue. I have an itch here and while I'm talking to you I scratch it. How does that happen? To lots of people that might seem a dull subject. To a scientist, it's seen as immensely complicated. The message has to go from here to your brain, it sends a message to the arm which seamlessly, without consciousness, goes to the right place to scratch it. An intermediate goal is to understand the visual or auditory systems, or coordinated walking, all of which are intriguing. In the long term the prize is 'How do we manipulate ideas?' But in my lifetime I doubt if we will get further than the 'itch to scratch'.

Case study: Neuroscience training for psychiatrists

When David Sainsbury first became interested in neuroscience, one of his long-term aims was to improve the understanding and treatment of mental and neurological disorders. However, it was immediately apparent that there was still a long way to go to achieve a basic understanding of the brain before it could be applied in the clinic. Instead, for twenty-five years Gatsby invested in research into the care and management of people with mental illness.

By 2015, the picture was beginning to change. New techniques such as magnetic resonance imaging (MRI), and new discoveries in genetics, brain development and neuropharmacology, were beginning to suggest how some forms of mental illness might one day be associated with brain abnormalities or altered biomarkers, and how this new understanding might lead to new therapeutic strategies. Yet the training of psychiatrists, charged with the care of patients whose conditions ranged from mild anxiety or autism to full-blown psychotic episodes, had not changed in decades. They might learn about psychodynamic theory, psychopharmacology and psychotherapy, but very little about how behaviour integrates with brain function. Diagnosis remains largely based on behavioural symptoms, and treatment on physical or talking therapies that alleviate those symptoms.

Neuroscientists working in the area of brain disorders had become increasingly concerned about this state of affairs. In 2009, the Cambridge neuroscientist Ed Bullmore wrote an article for the *British Journal of Psychiatry* calling for a change in the way psychiatrists are trained, to include more contemporary neuroscience. 'We do not need to know the anatomy of the cranial nerves,' he wrote; 'we should know more about cognitive testing, neurobiological sequelae of early-life social deprivation and psychopharmacology.'[13] Gatsby proposed to the Royal College of Psychiatrists (RCPsych), which specifies the curriculum for postgraduate trainee psychiatrists, that it might help to fund such a revision.

The RCPsych's President, Simon Wessely, of the Institute of Psychiatry, King's College London, accepted that it was time to address the issue of neuroscience in the curriculum. 'We feel that we are lagging behind', he wrote in a letter to the membership, 'in equipping the next generation with some of the new developments that have happened in neuroscience and are likely to impact on the profession of psychiatry during their lifetime.'[14] He was also aware that the curriculum, overseen by the General Medical Council, was separate from the examination syllabus for Membership of the College and saw this as an opportunity to draw the two together.

Having forged a fruitful partnership with the Wellcome Trust to develop the Sainsbury Wellcome Centre, Sarah Caddick began to discuss further opportunities for collaboration with her opposite number at Wellcome, the former Head of Neuroscience and Mental Health, John Isaac. They agreed on a joint funding initiative of £400,000 to support the RCPsych's plans. The result, announced in the spring of 2016, is a three-year commission that will 'create, pilot and disseminate a model core curriculum that will train psych-iatrists to integrate a modern neuroscience perspective into their clinical work' and make the neuroscience content more 'relevant and accessible' to trainees.

The commission is co-chaired by former Dean and now President-Elect of the RCPsych, Wendy Burn, a specialist in old age psychiatry based in Leeds. 'The remit of the commission is to look at what we are doing at the moment, both what we are teaching and our methods of teaching,' she says. 'We do teach neuroscience, but what we teach is out of date, and taught in a way that is uninteresting and not uniform. Neuroscience is generally seen as boring and irrelevant by the trainees.' Co-chairing the commission is Mike Travis of the University of Pittsburgh, who leads the National Neuro-science Curriculum Initiative now under way in the USA. This has pioneered new interactive teaching methods as well as incorporating more up-to-date scientific content.

One of the challenges the commission is tackling is how to keep the course content up to date in such a fast-moving field. 'The clinical material updates itself', says Burn, 'because trainees are immersed in clinical practice. The basic material is more difficult. We would like to see more of the trainees doing neuroscience PhDs.' The college offers 'Pathfinder Fellowships' to support outstanding medical students in their final two years. 'They will become the neuroscientists of the future,' she says, 'but we want to bring them into psychiatry.'

The project will also bring to an end the anomaly that the curriculum and the MRCPsych (Member of the Royal College of Psychiatrists) syllabus are not fully aligned. Additional funding is also supporting a number of events to engage and inspire medical students, psychiatric trainees and psychiatrists with the possibility of a future in psychiatry informed by neuroscience. 'We had run twelve events by the beginning of 2017,' says Burn, 'and people have been really positive.'

'This foray into influencing psychiatry is a reflection of the way David works in other sectors,' says Caddick. She herself will sit on the commission. 'If the initiative is successful, it will transform the way psychiatrists are taught in the UK and possibly around the world,' she says. 'I think that is game-changing, for a very small amount of money. That's what we are excited about now.'

9

WHAT WORKS

Economic growth and public policy

Developing a more evidence-based approach to public policy has been one of David Sainsbury's long-term ambitions. This is the province of the think tank and the campaigning charity, many of which have formed alliances with Gatsby to pursue common ends. Almost from the very beginning, Gatsby has supported the work of influential think tanks, such as the Policy Studies Institute (PSI) (previously Political and Economic Planning) and the Institute for Fiscal Studies (IFS). For more than twenty years it was a major funder of the British Social Attitudes Survey, the annual data-gathering exercise started by Roger Jowell in 1983, and now run by NatCen, the National Centre for Social Research. The survey, based on interviews with 3,000 randomly chosen members of the public, is a major resource to guide decision-making by public bodies.[1]

Where there seemed to be a gap in the provision of good policy research, Gatsby has itself functioned effectively as a think tank, or has initiated new ones. Apart from the areas covered in the previous chapters, it has had three main areas of policy focus. The first is the relationship between universities and industry, especially in engineering and technology: from the early 1990s until 2010, 'technology transfer' and its more two-way sibling 'knowledge exchange' joined the training of engineers as concerns of Gatsby Technical Education Projects (GTEP). The second goes back to one of Sainsbury's earliest interests, the economic development of cities: in 2006, Gatsby established the Centre for Cities, which continues to provide impartial analysis of the economic drivers of urban success or failure. The third is in the practice of government, at local and national level: the Institute for Government, founded in 2007, will be the lasting legacy of David Sainsbury's experience of government from the inside.

A boost for business

Despairing of an effective industrial policy at government level, during the early 1980s Gatsby attempted to address the shortcomings of British business through academic analysis and international comparisons. Sainsbury suggested to the PSI that they commission the Boston Consulting Group to examine the industrial policy behind Japan's economic resurgence. The report, published in 1980, was authored by Ira Magaziner (who subsequently became a senior aide to Bill Clinton) and Thomas Hout.[2] 'I was very influenced by their report, and subsequently went on a couple of trips to Japan to look at their companies,' says Sainsbury.

In 1982, Gatsby made a grant to the London Business School (LBS) to establish a Centre for Business Strategy, which it continued to support until 1997. The Centre became particularly productive after the former director of the IFS, the economist John Kay, joined it as director in 1986. At the IFS, Kay had set up a research unit to develop an evidence base for the institute's work. His main aim had been to develop a tax and benefit model that would allow the IFS to produce quick analyses of the impact of changes in fiscal policy. 'We tried to get ESRC [Economic and Social Research Council] money and didn't, to my annoyance,' he says. 'So I went with [his predecessor as Director and former independent MP] Dick Taverne to see David at Sainsbury's. I talked about what we were planning, and the next day got a letter saying Gatsby would be happy to fund us, how much did we need? That model has been central to IFS work ever since.'

By 1986, Kay was looking for new opportunities to communicate serious economic research in such a way that it might inform business strategy. 'I was persuaded by people in the finance group at LBS to go there,' he says. 'The Centre for Business Strategy was a compromise between a narrowly academic environment and a more commercially oriented unit.' He saw the post as an opportunity to present modern economics research in more 'businessy language'. The main outcome of his tenure was the book Kay published in 1993, *Foundations of Corporate Success*, which is still in print and was based on a combination of the research he and his colleagues had done at the centre and the courses he had taught as a member of the LBS faculty.[3]

Communication was central to the work of the Centre under Kay's leadership. It launched a journal, the *Business Strategy Review*, in 1990, and its team of researchers published studies of industrial policy and performance both within the UK and globally. Perhaps the greatest impact of the Centre has been through its alumni: they include BBC economics editors Evan Davies and Stephanie Flanders, and Matthew Bishop, the US editor of *The Economist*. Kay himself moved on after five years, his sideline in consulting having grown to a full-time job. He cheerfully recognises that his focus on business success rather than industrial policy was somewhat at odds with Sainsbury's vision for the Centre. 'I came to realise that that was not what David wanted,' he says. 'I was doing it to get away from the public policy side.'

Saving science
Unsurprisingly, Gatsby has also supported a number of initiatives designed to improve the standing and public profile of science

and technology in the UK. Under the Conservative government of Margaret Thatcher in the early to mid-1980s, scientists became increasingly concerned about the decline in research funding in Britain relative to its competitors. So much so that Professor of Physiology Denis Noble and Professor of Physics John Mulvey, both at Oxford University, persuaded a handful of British Nobel prize winners, 100 fellows of the Royal Society and over 1,000 other supporters to contribute £20 each for a half-page advertisement in *The Times* headed 'Save British Science' (SBS). Such was the momentum that the signatories formed their own campaigning organisation under the same name, and Mulvey retired from his Oxford post to head it. In 1989, Gatsby put up the funds to set up the SBS office and pay the salaries of its small staff. SBS is still active today, having evolved in 2005 into CaSE, the Campaign for Science and Engineering in the UK.[4]

In 1989, the all-party Parliamentary and Scientific Committee, a group of MPs and peers interested in science and technology, approached Prime Minister Margaret Thatcher for funds to set up an in-house service providing well-researched scientific briefings to members of both houses of Parliament. When she asked for more evidence that it was necessary, they set up a charity and raised funds to create the Parliamentary Office of Science and Technology (POST). Again, Gatsby contributed a considerable portion of the start-up funds. The office proved to be so successful that in 1992 it was adopted and funded as a parliamentary body; it continues to flourish and is greatly valued by MPs and peers.[5]

More recently, Gatsby has made donations to Sense About Science, the charity set up by the Liberal peer Dick Taverne in 2002 to campaign for an evidence-based approach to scientific policy and the reporting of science in the media.[6] It has also supported the Science Media Centre, the independent 'press office' for the scientific community set up during David Sainsbury's tenure as science minister (see page 180).

From science to innovation

David Sainsbury's passionate interest in science has always been closely allied to a concern to see new discoveries translated into products that benefit people and contribute to the British economy. 'This is where the two streams of my life come together,' he says, 'in the sense that it always seemed to me that the link between industry and science was very important – that it was all about the contribution that science can make to society. I believe that is absolutely central.'

Unlike many politicians, however, he knows that this is a long-term process that cannot be short-circuited by trying to second-guess where applications might emerge and focusing on those. 'I hold a view, not very widely held among politicians, that you get the real breakthroughs in products that are commercialised not from doing applied research, but from doing basic research,' he says. As he found in his work on *The Race to the Top* (see page 181), the quality of research in a university correlated well with the amount of investment in spin-out companies. 'It's about how you get knowledge transfer from a research university, not about doing research in an applied university,' he says. 'I don't see any conflict between basic research and research that will aid mankind, either industrially or through medical treatment.'

Technology transfer, knowledge exchange and wealth creation are now part of the discourse of science and technology policy, but this is a relatively recent development. In the 1940s, Howard Florey thought it would be immoral to take out patents on the processes, developed by his team in Oxford, that made it possible to treat patients with penicillin, with the result that the key patent went to an American researcher who had worked out how to mass-produce the antibiotic. Scientists traditionally knew nothing about business, and business leaders often knew nothing about research. And universities were either too timid or too austerely academic to sully their hands with commercial activities. Martin Wood, an entrepreneurial Oxford scientist in the 1950s, began to manufacture superconducting magnets for sale in his garden shed because his university was so little inclined to support his venture. His company became the global maker of precision equipment Oxford Instruments.[7]

In the UK, the picture began to change in the early 1980s, and Gatsby was among the first to encourage the formal establishment of technology transfer initiatives in universities. It supported the pioneering South Bank Technopark, an initiative of the Polytechnic of the South Bank (now London South Bank University), the first such agency in London to provide flexible space for new start-ups. At the same time, for a decade it covered the core costs of CAMPUS (the Campaign to Promote the University of Salford), a charitable trust established in 1981 by the University of Salford in reaction to the savage cut of 44 per cent in its government grant announced that year by the University Grants Committee. The strategy of CAMPUS, under Salford's dynamic new vice-chancellor John Ashworth, was to develop supportive links with local industries in return for access to its researchers for consultancy services and product development. By 1989, Salford enjoyed earnings of £15.8 million from its industrial partners – 46 per cent of its total income.

Ashworth was a biologist who had previously been the chief scientific advisor in the Cabinet Office. David Sainsbury met him for the first time when visiting Salford for a political meeting, and was so impressed he asked him to become an advisor to Gatsby on science projects. Ashworth, who subsequently became director of the London School of Economics, remained an advisor for many years, also becoming a trustee of GTEP. He took a particular interest in the Gatsby plant sciences programme, helping to organise public discussions on the perceived threat of GM crops.

From the early 1990s, finding that there was still little or no national coordination of technology transfer activities, Gatsby took it up as a major area of interest. It funded a variety of experimental projects: not all were successful, but in many cases small, pump-priming grants to universities quickly created established units that could fund themselves through licensing of intellectual property or contract work, or gave individual researchers the task of building links between lab and factory.[8] As mentioned in Chapter 5, one of the more successful models was Plant Biosciences Ltd, set up jointly with the John Innes Centre in Norwich. By 2010, it had generated licensing revenue of almost £10 million and nurtured five spin-out companies.

When David Sainsbury went into government as science minister in 1998, Gatsby advertised for someone to oversee its work in technology transfer. The job went to Neil Alford, a former ICI (Imperial Chemical Industries) engineer then working on advanced materials for electronics at South Bank University and a holder of several patents, and now at Imperial College London. 'In those days, there was little government funding to do technology transfer,' he says. 'David Sainsbury was interested in finding out how universities managed their technology transfer offices, what they thought they would make out of their intellectual property, whether it could be done better, or if there needed to be government intervention.' Gatsby commissioned a number of research reports and workshops.

One of the most influential initiatives was a fact-finding tour of leading American universities for ten British vice-chancellors and other leading academics. The suggestion came from Ronald Cohen, founder of pioneering venture capital firm Apax Partners, who was aware that American universities had been much more proactive in this area than their UK counterparts. Gatsby put up £100,000 to cover the costs of the trip and the subsequent report. Among the party were Gareth Roberts, then vice-chancellor of Sheffield University, and Howard Newby of Southampton University, both of whom were knighted and went on to chair several influential bodies in academia. Both of their universities subsequently set up highly successful technology transfer operations.

The visit was an eye-opener in many respects. The technology transfer offices at universities such as Harvard, MIT and Stanford were far better resourced than those of any British university, especially in legal support for protection of intellectual property and avoiding conflicts of interest. But the greatest surprise was that American universities – mostly private institutions with large endowments – did not see technology transfer as principally about increasing their income, and indeed in some cases did not make enough to cover the costs of their technology transfer activities. These universities were united in seeing the work as part of their public service remit, bringing the fruits of university research to benefit wider society.

'British universities initially thought they would make pots of money from technology transfer,' says Alford, 'but that's not the purpose at all. The point is that it's what academics are interested in – they see it as a useful thing to be doing for the country. It takes a very long time indeed for the impact to be felt in the economy.'

The projects Gatsby funded helped to create a more positive attitude in government towards a 'third stream' of funding for university research, in addition to funds from the Higher Education Funding Council for England (HEFCE) and from the research councils, specifically targeted at projects linked to industry. The DTI showed great interest, and in 1999, when David Sainsbury was science minister, set up the University Challenge Fund (jointly with Gatsby and the Wellcome Trust), offering £40 million in fifteen regional seed funds to help entrepreneurial researchers through the difficult first years of developing a commercial product. In 2001, Sainsbury saw the University Challenge Fund incorporated into Higher Education Innovation Funding (HEIF), delivered through HEFCE ever since to universities that could demonstrate a track record in raising external funding for knowledge exchange.[9] As mentioned in Chapter 7, the initiative has been highly successful.

'Once HEIF came in, and there was much more support through other bodies, it became clear that that part of the work had been a success,' says Alford. 'We were very pleased about that.' Throughout Gatsby's technology transfer programme, which ran until 2010, its staff, trustees and advisors had taken a more conscientious approach to evaluation than had characterised some of their previous projects, commissioning several reports from Bill Wicksteed of the economic consultants Segal Quince Wicksteed (SQW). In his final report, Wicksteed wrote, 'It is quite probable that initiatives pioneered by the Gatsby Charitable Foundation played a part in raising general awareness of the importance of KTT [knowledge and technology transfer] for wealth creation. They were certainly important in galvanising energy within the institutions which were supported.'[10]

Cambridge, business and manufacturing

There is a long history of Gatsby support for education, research and technology transfer at Cambridge. David Sainsbury has an affinity with Cambridge derived from his student experience, but this is not the only reason for his interest in its work in the area of manufacturing engineering. Unusually among research universities, in 1966 Cambridge had launched an Advanced Course in Production Methods and Management (ACPMM). This innovative one-year course sent engineering graduates into companies for a series of one- or two-week, project-based placements, solving problems set by the partner company. The course was highly successful and the places were in high demand, though as a business-oriented course for many years it struggled to obtain the whole-hearted support of the central university administration. In 1987, the name was changed to the Advanced Course in Design, Manufacture and Management (ACDMM): the course was still popular, but its survival was under threat because of funding shortfalls.

Gatsby first became involved in 1990, when, as Roger Baker

recalls, a deputation led by the glass manufacturer Sir Alastair Pilkington, then chairman of Cambridge University's newly launched development campaign, came to meet David Sainsbury. He was accompanied by Alec Broers, then head of the Department of Engineering. As a result of this visit the trustees approved the suggestion that the most satisfactory way to support engineering was to put money into the ACDMM course. In 1991, Gatsby made a grant of over £1 million to Cambridge, doubling the number of ACDMM students that could be admitted.

Teaching the course at that time was Mike Gregory, himself a graduate of the 'life-changing' ACPMM, and also the creator of an innovative four-year undergraduate course, the Manufacturing Engineering Tripos. Gregory had a sabbatical coming up and wanted to travel abroad to learn more about engineering education elsewhere. Gatsby funded his trips to the USA and Japan in 1992, and on his return Gregory wrote a report setting out ten recommendations for initiatives that would develop the department from the academic study of engineering to 'something more industrially engaged'.

'Two or three months later I was summoned to meet David,' says Gregory. 'He had read my report, and invited me to pursue my ideas.' The most significant of these was to set up an Industry Links Unit (ILU) in the department, stimulating fruitful collaborations between researchers and industries. However, there was no obvious source of public funding for such an initiative. Gatsby stepped into the breach, and Baker counselled Gregory to set up a parallel commercial consultancy, Cambridge Manufacturing Industry Links (CMIL), to earn income that would support the future activities of the ILU. 'Cambridge University was not very keen at first,' says Gregory, 'but it turned out to be a good model.' ILU and CMIL eventually merged as IfM Education and Consultancy Services Ltd (IfM ECS),[11] which now turns over £6 million per year.

In 1994, having been promoted to the chair in manufacturing

engineering, Gregory began to envisage a grander plan, to create an Institute for Manufacturing (IfM). 'We wanted to link manufacturing, research, policy, and educational research and practice,' he says. The IfM came into being in 1998, and rapidly expanded, winning major grant-funded programmes from the research councils as well as developing its extensive industry networks. Gatsby continued to support it with significant grants.

Paul Christodoulou was already a beneficiary of two Gatsby initiatives when he joined the institute to head the ILU: he had done the ACDMM course and in 1998 he had taken a year out of his industrial career to do an MBA at INSEAD as a Sainsbury Management Fellow (see page 141). His first focus was on small and medium-sized enterprises (SMEs). 'Lord Sainsbury and Mike Gregory had this common hobbyhorse', he says, 'that the UK didn't have the equivalent of the German *Mittelstand'*– the collection of small to medium-sized, often family-owned, regional businesses with a long-term outlook that form the backbone of the German economy. 'They lead to competitive differentiation, and support the export economy,' says Christodoulou. 'Most of the new manufacturing companies in China have bought German equipment, because it is the best.'

The ILU's Growmore project, which Gatsby funded, researched the sticking points that arrested the development both of high-technology start-ups, and small businesses that had potential to expand. It developed a programme of intervention, using trained consultants, to help the businesses diagnose their problems and implement strategies to overcome them. By 2006, the intervention tools had been codified in such a way that they could be rolled out regionally, and eventually nationally, through the Regional Development Agencies. More recently they have been refined and applied to the aerospace, nuclear and marine industries, with support from Innovate UK and Rolls-Royce. 'There have been hundreds or even thousands of interventions, involving a team of highly experienced practition-ers with academic backing,' says Christodoulou. 'It was seeded by Gatsby, but from 2006 it generated its own momentum, which was always Lord Sainsbury's desire.'

IfM ECS, as the consultancy arm is now called, is by no means exclusively focused on SMEs, and has carried out a wide range of research and consultancy on the complex, extended manu-facturing and supply chains that now constitute the 'footprint' of large, global businesses.[12] For example, the IfM's consultants worked over seven years to help the international manufacturer of earth-moving equipment, Caterpillar, with a turnover of $47 billion in 2015, to develop an optimum production network that would be robust both at times of low and high demand.

In 2009, the institute moved out of its 'grotty, semi-subter-ranean digs' in the centre of Cambridge to its own purpose-designed building on the university's West Cambridge campus, an environment much more in keeping with its business focus. Gatsby provided £5 million of funding towards the building, which attracted matching funding from the government's Science Research Investment Fund, and a further £5 million came from the Reece Foundation. Since 2012, Gatsby has also funded another research unit within the IfM, the Centre for Science, Technology and Innovation Policy (CSTI; see Case study, page 249).

In twenty years, the IfM has grown from 50 to 200 members, and embraces education, research, consultancy and knowledge exchange. Students carry out 150 projects per year in factories around the country. IfM research has contributed significantly to questions not only about manufacturing techniques but also about such problems as the sourcing of materials, the location of factories, networks of distribution and raising finance. It has a strong programme in sustainable manufacturing, and includes a Centre for Innovative Manufacturing in Industrial Sustainability. All the knowledge gained through research work is available to businesses through IfM ECS, profits from which in turn support further research.

Mike Gregory retired as director of the IfM in 2015, to be succeeded by Andy Neely. Gregory's assessment of Gatsby's contribution, cumulatively amounting to over £10 million in financial terms but a great deal more in encouragement and advice, is unequivocal: the IfM 'would not exist without Gatsby,' he says. Paul Christodoulou goes further, attributing to David Sainsbury's supportive schemes for engineering and industry a correction of the economic policy shift to financial services, and an improvement in the standing of manufacturing business within a balanced UK industrial policy. 'Right back to his first engagement through ACPMM,' he says, 'he has promoted the fantastic opportunities for career development in technology-based industry. And all this during a period of incredible change in the global manufacturing picture, with internationalisation, offshoring and outsourcing. I'd like to think the UK still has a strong role in that picture, and it's in part down to those initiatives.'

Cambridge and MIT

The IfM is one of the best examples of Gatsby funding that has been well spent, and resulted in a robust, self-perpetuating organisation and a very wide range of influence in the field concerned. One cannot say quite so much for another Cambridge initiative that Gatsby helped to fund, but over which it had little, if any, control. In the late 1990s, having established the University Challenge Fund, the Chancellor of the Exchequer, Gordon Brown, was determined to set up a major centre to carry the message of technology transfer across the country, and generate economic benefit from Britain's universities. The result was the Cambridge-MIT Institute, an £80 million public investment designed to share the expertise in technology transfer of the USA's top technological university with its British counterparts.

The scheme was hatched in the Treasury; most of the details were in place before officials in the DTI, who had relevant expertise, were able to intervene. Gatsby was persuaded to contribute an additional £5 million to the project.

The transatlantic institute ran for just seven years, having been bogged down in its early stages over legal agreements on intellectual property. Reports by the National Audit Office and the consultancy Technopolis suggest that it successfully established the principle that technology transfer and knowledge exchange required suitably qualified professions to support it. The training body it set up, Praxis, continues (as PraxisUnico) to represent professionals in the area and to offer training worldwide.[13] Major projects funded included a three-year, collaborative university–industry 'Silent aircraft initiative', whose findings have been incorporated into more recent commercial aircraft design; and a successful regenerative medicine spin-out, Orthomimetics, was sold for £14 million to the Belgian firm TiGenix in 2008.

However, the evidence that collaboration on its own has led (as Gordon Brown envisaged at its launch) 'to the establishment of hundreds of new businesses in the UK' is thin, especially as many other initiatives in support of technology transfer came into being at the same time. In his report on Gatsby's technology transfer projects, Bill Wicksteed suggested that the institute's principal backers had expected too much change too quickly. 'The factor behind much of the success achieved can be succinctly summarised as – it's the people, stupid,' he wrote.[14]

Growth and the city

Gatsby had supported a number of small initiatives in urban policy in the 1970s (see Chapter 2), an interest David Sainsbury developed as, from the Sainsbury's headquarters in Southwark, he watched London's Docklands transform into a metropolitan mecca for services, retail and leisure activities. The revival was ultimately driven by the market, not by any strategic decisions taken by planners. Sainsbury thought there was a case for an urban policy studies centre that would analyse the economic drivers that make cities successful, and disseminate its results. But by the time he entered government in 1998, other projects had taken priority.

The Centre for Cities was incubated outside the Gatsby office, but has become one of its flagship projects. While he was a government minister, someone was needed to manage his 'pro bono' giving, donations from his own pocket to political think tanks and campaigns that could not be made through Gatsby because they were not charities. The person who took on the task was Susan Hitch, whose eclectic career was characterised by a particular skill in establishing networks and brokering agreements.

An Oxford academic who had facilitated contacts between the UK and the new leaders of former Central and Eastern bloc regimes, she joined Sainsbury's private office part-time soon after he took up his ministerial appointment. There she worked alongside Christopher Stone, who ran the private office as well as being a Gatsby trustee. Before he went into government, Sainsbury had talked to Stone about setting up a centre to research and advise on the economy of cities. Stone passed the job to Hitch. 'Urban studies had previously been focused on dysfunction and how you mitigate it,' says Hitch. 'We thought it was better to study what works.'

One of the long-term beneficiaries of Sainsbury's project-directed donations was the Institute for Public Policy Research (IPPR), whose work had fed into much of the 1997 Labour government's policy. Although the Centre for Cities was neither a political organisation nor a campaign, it seemed a good fit with the IPPR's interests in the economy, industrial strategy, regional policy, local government and housing. 'We incubated the Centre for Cities within IPPR', says Hitch, 'to benefit from its legal governance, experience, offices and services.' Together with the institute, she recruited Dermot Finch, former policy advisor at the Treasury, as the Centre's first director, and established a board with local government representatives from all parties, academics and businesspeople. Property developer Tom Bloxham of northern loft-living pioneers Urban Splash was its chair – Bloxham had helped to transform the centre of Manchester with his redevelopment of industrial buildings.

Within two years the Centre for Cities had established itself independently of IPPR and was working effectively with local and national government across the country. 'Dermot Finch was an enthusiast with a terrific eye for an opportunity and good PR,' says Hitch. 'He and Tom Bloxham made sure the Centre for Cities made space for itself in the world.' Since 2008, the Centre's *Cities Outlook* report has published comparative data available from no other source, giving an authoritative annual health check on the UK's 63 largest towns and cities, accompanied by readily interpretable infographics. Its headline conclusions are guaranteed widespread news coverage: for example, the 2016 edition highlighted the fact that 'almost half of the UK's biggest cities have low-wage, high-welfare economies', emphasising the scale of the challenge facing the then chancellor George Osborne in his ambition to make Britain a 'higher-wage, low-welfare economy'.[15] Between these annual updates, any minister, councillor or civil servant can make use of the Centre's online data tool to ask questions about business, housing, skills or a number of other indicators in a particular town or city, and represent the results as accessible charts and graphs.[16]

The new Charities Act of 2006 made public benefit a key test of charitable status; since then, the Centre, which has always been credibly impartial, no longer warrants the cautious approach taken when it was first set up. Since 2009, it has received core funding from Gatsby. It is in demand as a consultant to local authorities and businesses, and earns additional income from project grants and fees. Since 2010, it has been chaired by influential developer Nigel Hugill (credited with identifying the

In November 2014, Deputy Prime Minister Nick Clegg launched
a summit, Northern Futures, in conjunction with the Centre
for Cities, to promote growth in the north of England.

Stratford East site for London 2012's Olympic Park), with policy
specialist Alexandra Jones, previously leader of the Ideopolis
project at the Work Foundation, as chief executive.

Jones feels that the Centre plugs a critical gap in the policy
landscape. 'More central government money was going into the
regions,' she says, 'but policy didn't consider why Cambridge
was successful and Hull struggling, for example. Our role is to
ask what's needed to help Cambridge thrive and make Hull more
successful? We wanted to do work that was not just academic,
but practical and policy-oriented – that would make a difference
to decisions taken in government.' There is plenty of evidence
that it does make a difference, at both local and national level.
When Derby found itself rated low on the Centre's index of
skills, the city authorities invested specifically in raising their
position in that area.

A strong message that has come out of the research is that every city is different, and so centralised policies don't work. A key concept that has entered the national consciousness as a result of the Centre's work is that the unit of focus should be a 'city region' – defined less by geography than by the behaviour of the people who live and work there. 'It's been good to see a wider shift in government policy to look at cities and devolution,' says Jones. 'I was having conversations with ministers in the 2010–2015 coalition to make sure they were tailoring policy to places, rather than making places fit into national policy. We have been pushing the idea of giving cities more power, but the wider environment has made it possible for us to be heard.' The landscape is rapidly changing: in 2017, six combined authorities including Greater Manchester and Peterborough/Cambridgeshire elected 'metro mayors', with devolved responsibility for areas such as housing, transport and skills. In another major shift to cities, locally raised business rates will be retained for spending by local authorities by 2020.

Jones continues:

> London's problems are not the UK's problems. Particularly post-Brexit, resentment of London and the southeast continues, and we need to respond to those concerns. We are continuing to work hard to ensure that policy and practice change as a result of what we do. We have made it easier to access data about cities, and now we want to ensure that it is used by local and national government.

The data has also made it possible to identify groups of cities with common interests. The Centre supported the formation of a 'Key Cities' group of mid-sized cities, initially Sunderland, Preston, Coventry, Derby and Wakefield, and since expanding to twenty-six cities working on the common challenges they face. It also supported the formation of a 'fast growth cities group', consisting of Oxford, Cambridge, Milton Keynes, Norwich and Swindon, so that they can work together on shared concerns such as housing. 'Both groups are now running themselves, and that's how we wanted it to be,' says Jones.

In 2013, the Centre for Cities was dubbed the 'One to Watch' in the *Prospect* magazine Think Tank Awards, while two years later it was shortlisted for the Economic and Financial Award along with the eventual winner, the IFS. 'The Centre for Cities has clearly hit a bullseye,' said one judge, adding that 'the returned government's plans to devolve more power to city-level institutions places the Centre's work at the core of one of the most important debates in British policymaking'.

How to govern well

On 26 January 2017, the Institute for Government (IfG) launched its fourth *Whitehall Monitor* report, subtitled 'The civil service as it faces Brexit'. This analysis of Whitehall's staffing, funding and performance outlined the massive challenge faced at that time by a diminishing workforce with a burgeoning workload, in easy-to-follow infographics.[17]

Whitehall Monitor is 'data journalism', a handy product that is of genuine value to Whitehall watchers while raising the profile of the Institute and positioning it as an independent and trustworthy source. It also illustrates the genuine efforts made by the apparatus of UK public administration to become more transparent. But the Institute's work goes much deeper than this. With a staff of around forty, it delves into the practicalities of policymaking and implementation, looking for evidence of effectiveness – or the opposite – and publishing detailed reports. It also coordinates high-level advice to ministers and the most senior civil servants on effective leadership. Within a few years of its foundation by Gatsby in 2008, it had become, to quote its former director, the former political journalist Peter Riddell, 'part of the conversation' in Whitehall about how to govern effectively.

Sainsbury's experience in government was a major factor in the Institute for Government's foundation. He says:

> If you are a businessman and you come into government, and there is someone called the head of the civil service, you imagine he is running the civil service. It took me five years to realise that not only did he not run it, he was not even supposed to run it. Why isn't government joined up? It's because it's no one's job to join it up. Instead there is a series of baronies, with no capability at the centre for basic functions such as personnel or data processing.

Towards the end of his time in office, Sainsbury was drawn into discussions with Tony Blair's chief of staff Jonathan Powell about the possibility of co-funding a public policy institute with the business magnate and philanthropist Leonard Blavatnik. 'We had very interesting discussions,' he says. 'Should it be part of a university or should it be free-standing? What sort of things should it do?' After leaving government Sainsbury was invited, together with his advisor Susan Hitch, to attend a meeting at Blavatnik's opulent home in London, but the discussions went no further. 'It became clear that what he wanted was a kind of Kennedy School [at Harvard] that would train young people from abroad in how government worked,' says Sainsbury, 'whereas what I thought was interesting was how to make British government work better.' (The Blavatnik School of Government subsequently opened at Oxford University in 2010.)

Sainsbury began to talk to his advisors, principally Hitch and Gatsby trustee Andrew Cahn, about founding a new kind of research and professional development body, close to government but independent from it. He invited David Halpern, formerly head of the Prime Minister's Strategy Unit, to work with Hitch and Cahn to scope out such a body. Having reviewed national and international programmes that were operating in the area, Halpern wrote *A Blueprint for the Institute for Government*. 'It needed to do two things,' says Halpern, who was to join the Institute as its first research director: 'To support the professional development of ministers and senior civil servants; and to help to build internal expertise and institutional memory. It was to focus on the nuts and bolts of government: not about developing policy, but about how to make policy.' The blueprint built on the advice of senior civil servants: preparatory work included testing the ideas at a gathering chaired by the cabinet secretary and attended by all permanent secretaries. Representatives from each of the three main political parties also joined the steering group. 'It was designed with key figures', says Halpern, 'so they had a sense of ownership.'

The Institute was to address four questions. First, what is the relationship between the centre and the departments? As Sainsbury had observed, the head of the civil service currently has no resources to maintain oversight of the departments. Second, how is accountability parcelled out between the minister and the permanent secretary? 'At the moment this is ludicrously unclear,' says Sainsbury. 'Officially the minister is responsible for everything, but clearly a newly appointed home secretary cannot be blamed every time a set of records goes missing.' Third, what is the role of the minister in relation to non-departmental agencies and public bodies – over 900 in total, from the Administration of Radioactive Substances Advisory Committee to the Youth Justice Board, taking in the Bank of England, the British Museum and the Medical Research Council on the way? 'They all have different legal constitutions,' says Sainsbury. 'We need to have some way of classifying them, and clarifying the role of the minister.' Finally, how do governments make policy? 'I was led to believe that people in government were brilliant at policymaking, and that it was implementation that was bad,' says Sainsbury. 'But policymaking is incredibly bad. There is no corporate memory – no one ever remembers what happened under previous governments, or evaluates it properly, so the same mistakes keep getting made.'

The Institute opened in 2008, getting straight to work with a report on the use of targets. Former Permanent Secretary at the Department for Education and Employment Michael Bichard was subsequently appointed its director. It occupied rooms in the Royal Academy of Engineering in Carlton House Terrace, while Gatsby's officers searched for appropriate premises conveniently close to Whitehall. In 2009, it moved into the stuccoed elegance of 2 Carlton Gardens, just a stroll through St James's Park from Whitehall and Westminster, the interior of which had been discreetly modernised by the architect Stefanie Fischer. In 2010, academic, journalist and former government minister Andrew Adonis succeeded Bichard as director. The institute has since built up a committed, and generally young, staff of researchers, many of whom move on after a few years but are soon replaced by equally able successors.

Four successful initiatives put the institute on to the political and institutional map in the run-up to the 2010 election. First, the Institute set up a professional development programme for the shadow front bench – the Conservatives had been out of office for thirteen years, and few had ministerial experience. Similar programmes were also set up for Labour ministers and the Liberal Democrats. Second, the institute's researchers presciently brought out a report on minority governments, drawing lessons from recent experience in Canada, New Zealand and Scotland. It was required reading for the Conservative and Liberal Democrat coalition partners who came into office in May 2010, and was a key factor in the IfG being named Think Tank of the Year at the *Prospect* awards in 2011. Third, IfG brought in the former prime ministers of Sweden and Canada to give their personal perspectives on dealing with fiscal shortfalls such as then faced the UK, each having had to deal with budget deficits of the order of 8 per cent during the 1990s. These seminars were eye-opening for civil servants, who were fascinated to learn of the contrasting strategies the two leaders had pursued. Fourth, the Cabinet Office commissioned the IfG to produce a report on the application of behavioural theory to public policy. This was one of Halpern's key areas of expertise, and with colleagues he produced a discussion document setting out the current state of knowledge and practice on how to 'nudge' people into changing their behaviour, from giving up smoking to driving more safely. Following the report Halpern was persuaded to return to the Cabinet Office and Number 10 to head the Behavioural Insights Team, nicknamed the 'nudge unit', now an independent social purpose company.[18]

Since those early days, the Institute has continued its multiple roles of research, providing public and private space to discuss the problems facing government, and development and preparation for office for future and new ministers. Peter Riddell, former chief political commentator at *The Times*, became a part-time Fellow in 2008, and succeeded Adonis as director in 2011. 'There's an important difference between the institute and other think tanks,' he says. 'The core funding we get from Gatsby gives us the freedom to be independent. People know we don't come with an agenda.' Instead, the Institute turns the spotlight on the institutional weaknesses of government. For example, senior researcher and historian Catherine Haddon has investigated the failure to consolidate knowledge and expertise. She says:

> In 2010, a large section of the civil service had not experienced anything other than a Labour government. There's a high turnover of people, so long-term memory is diffused, difficult to access, hidden away in filing cabinets – there's no systematic way to know who has deep knowledge or expertise. New people come in to handle a policy problem or a reform, and are often reinventing the wheel. Looking back has a real impact

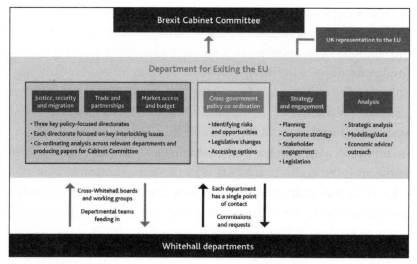

The Institute for Government makes use of infographics, such as this one describing the Department for Exiting the European Union, to help inform the press and public about the workings of government.

on being able to look forward, and IfG reports have helped a lot. But our primary goal is to make government more effective, not to comment on how it was or wasn't effective.

In 2015, the institute provided preparation for government to the Labour front bench before the election in May. 'We had also done a lot of work with senior civil servants in Whitehall, and with constitutional commentators, on what should happen if there was another hung parliament, as many expected,' says Riddell. 'Of course, the Conservatives won a majority and we immediately shifted to the agenda of the new government.' It is not the role of the institute to criticise policy, but to provide guidance on how to implement policy effectively. 'For example, we don't take a view on what the level of the public sector deficit should be,' says Riddell, 'but we do explore how we might improve the practices of government given a certain level of cost-cutting.'

This independence, together with the service it provides, gives the IfG's researchers unprecedented access to the movers and shakers, not only in Whitehall but also in the devolved governments in Edinburgh, Cardiff and Belfast. Head of the Civil Service Sir Jeremy Heywood, who frequently speaks at Institute events, has said that it 'fills a big gap'. Data from its reports are reproduced daily in the media. It reports regularly on its impact to a governing body, which, exceptionally among his many projects, is chaired by David Sainsbury himself.

Even in the short time the IfG has been in operation, there are beginning to be visible signs that their focus on specific, practical goals is working. A reform programme for non-departmental public bodies got under way in 2010. The review body accepted that the landscape was 'complex and confusing', and since 2016 the number of different types of arm's-length bodies has been reduced to three, with clear criteria for classification. The government has published a transparency clause, based on one developed at the IfG, to be used by departments in complex outsourcing contracts. Policy implementation units have been set up in departments, and their staff networked across Whitehall. It has been accepted that functional leadership at the centre of government in areas such as digital services, human resources and finance needs to be strengthened. Select committees are working with IfG staff on improving the impact of their scrutiny of government. The principal challenge, of improving the overall leadership of the civil service, has proved a tougher nut to crack. 'I think we have had a modestly positive impact,' says Riddell. 'There are many other factors. But we have held a mirror up to government, and we have done some good things. It's a long haul.'

2016 was a tumultuous year in British politics, with the EU referendum opening a completely uncharted way ahead for political leaders and civil servants. Able to respond quickly, the IfG launched a major programme of work on its implications, while at the same time welcoming a new director, Bronwen Maddox, formerly editor of *Prospect* magazine. Asked a few weeks into her appointment why she took the job, she says:

> The question of whether democracies can solve their own problems is a live one, and Western democracies are very much on the back foot in saying, 'Look, this is a good way to run a country and a society.' I was interested in those issues. David Sainsbury said, 'So many of these decisions of government are catastrophes of process' – we were talking about quite technical things like the very high rates of return the government had accepted on projects such as HS2 [High Speed Two] and Hinkley Point, and what that said about the government's understanding of risk. His phrase 'the catastrophe of process' stuck with me. And the spectacle of bright people making bad decisions repeatedly struck me as not only an interesting one but a very important one to try to get engaged with. I thought the Institute was doing a unique and credible thing in trying to make the government work more professionally in the very complex circumstances of the twenty-first century.

Case study: Making policy for innovation

Treating technological innovations or emerging industries as 'black boxes' that can all be covered by the same policy initiatives is one of the reasons that British industry has failed to capitalise on the country's world-leading record in research, according to Eoin O'Sullivan, director of the Centre for Science, Technology and Innovation Policy (CSTI), part of the Institute for Manufacturing at the University of Cambridge.[19] 'We lack institutions that are developing the enabling infrastructure to allow innovative designs to become mass market products,' he says. CSTI operates in this intermediate zone, analysing the need for state- or industry-supported infrastructure and exploring how institutions in other countries are tackling the same problem.

The Centre, funded by Gatsby since 2012, grew out of the foundation's long-standing relationship with the IfM. O'Sullivan joined the IfM as a research fellow in 2007, having previously been part of the team that set up Ireland's research council, Science Foundation Ireland. He became involved in research at IfM, comparing different countries' approaches to scaling up new manufacturing technologies; much of this work fed into UK innovation policy at the time David Sainsbury was writing his report for Gordon Brown, *The Race to the Top*. 'We tried to ground our research in real technocratic process', says O'Sullivan, 'and benchmark systematically against what's going on around the world. We continue to do this in a very structured, systematic way.'

The idea of creating a centre within IfM dedicated to this area of policy research was Sainsbury's own. On one of his regular visits he spent time in conversation with O'Sullivan hearing about work he was doing in association with the Technology Strategy Board on support for emerging industries, such as quantum electronics and regenerative medicine. 'At the end of the meeting he asked if I planned to continue doing this, and said that if so I should consider sending in a project proposal,' says O'Sullivan. 'I put together a modest plan for a couple of post-docs and PhD students, and Gatsby awarded me a five-year grant.' In 2016, the Centre received an extension to the grant that will enable it to expand, as well as endowing O'Sullivan's post as the Babbage Fellowship in Technology and Innovation Policy.

O'Sullivan acknowledges that having a policy unit in an engineering department is unusual: normally such work is done in economics departments or business schools. But he believes the Centre's location within the IfM is crucial. He says:

> The kind of thing we do is different. We open up the black boxes of technologies, manufacturing processes and sectors, and the complexity in the structure of supply chains, which are not acknowledged in a lot of innovation policy research but that are absolutely critical. The IfM does research into everything from advanced manufacturing technology, through operations management, to sustainability. Policymakers need to understand all those things. So it's a rich environment to be in, and it's why we can do things that business departments can't do.

In some respects, the Centre operates as a think tank rather than a conventional academic research centre. It selects topics for research according to what is most likely to be useful to civil servants and their advisors in agencies such as Innovate UK, and has seen a regular traffic of staff between the two. 'Traditional innovation policy work wasn't having an impact on policy practice,' says O'Sullivan. 'The interesting thing is how you scale up technologies that are going through a transition from applied science to engineering and need to be industrialised. The UK has not been very good at that.'

The Centre has helped to convene a series of workshops at which government, agency and industrial representatives from different countries meet and share best practice. A recent example, held in the White House in Washington, DC, discussed the network of advanced manufacturing institutes set up in the USA under the title Manufacturing USA.[20] 'The US institutes are so much more than technology R&D institutes,' says O'Sullivan. 'They get involved in skills and advisory support to small firms, they're connected to universities, they address the innovation bottlenecks. Our international comparisons have helped shape how people think about what those institutions should be.'

10

FOR ART'S SAKE

A family passion

As a gawky, easily embarrassed, 15-year-old schoolboy, David Sainsbury was deposited by his parents in the Paris studio of the sculptor Alberto Giacometti in September 1955 and left to sit for his portrait. His discomfiture increased when, after sketching for a while, the imposing artist put his face in his hands and groaned. When the couple returned, they pronounced themselves delighted with the drawings and asked to buy three of them. Giacometti refused, on the grounds that they were not good enough. Eventually Lisa Sainsbury struck a deal: in exchange for the drawings, she undertook to buy a raincoat for Giacometti's wife Annette on her return to London. The drawings are still in the collection at the Sainsbury Centre for Visual Arts (SCVA). So is the receipt for the Aquascutum raincoat (£27.6s.0d, equivalent to about £675 in today's money).[1]

The SCVA and its unique collection of modernist and world art represents the extraordinary legacy of Robert and Lisa Sainsbury. However, it would not exist in its current spectacular form were it not for the unstinting support, through Gatsby, of their son. David Sainsbury is not himself a collector, and his personal priorities as a philanthropist are predominantly in the fields of science and society. He did not, for example, join his

David Sainsbury was sketched by Alberto Giacometti
when he visited the artist with his parents in 1955.

cousins in contributing to the massive extension to the National
Gallery, now known as the Sainsbury Wing, which opened in
1991. However, he was devoted to his parents, and remains full
of admiration for the way they built up their beautiful art collection. He credits them with inspiring the approach to philanthropy that he has developed over fifty years. 'It's not just about
writing a cheque,' he says. 'It's about supporting causes you
really care about, getting to know the people involved, sticking
with it and making it work. That's how my parents worked, and
I've picked it up from them.'

That filial pride and respect has led Sainsbury to take the

SCVA under Gatsby's wing, caring for it as if it had been his own project. Gatsby defines the aims of its arts programme as 'to support the fabric and programming of institutions with which Gatsby's founding family has connections'. The definition also embraces performing arts institutions introduced and passionately supported by Sainsbury's wife Susie, principally the Royal Shakespeare Theatre (RSC), the Royal Academy of Music (RAM) and the Chamber Orchestra of Europe (COE). With total arts funding running at sums between £5 million and £10 million per year for the past decade, Gatsby is a major contributor to the cultural life of the country.

The Sainsbury Centre for Visual Arts

Sainsbury had grown up immersed in his parents' art collection. In the early 1930s Robert Sainsbury (always known as Bob) developed a passion for the strong, uncompromising shapes shared by modernist sculpture and drawings, and carvings from the cultures of Africa, Oceania and the Americas. He particularly favoured works based on the human form. The first sculpture he bought was a disembodied head, *Baby Asleep* (1902–4) by Jacob Epstein, whose rejection of classical aesthetics had caused uproar in the art world. As he was to do with other protégés, Bob later became a trusted friend to Epstein and quietly helped him with his finances. Henry Moore's equally shocking *Mother and Child* (1932) was also among his first purchases. When David Sainsbury was born in 1940, Moore became his godfather. *Mother and Child* stood at the foot of the curving staircase in their tall townhouse in Smith Square, near Westminster, while another Moore sculpture lived under the sink in David's bedroom, as one of the few places in the house where the floor was strong enough to support its weight.

When Bob married his second cousin Lisa van den Bergh in 1937, buying art together became their passion: as a mutual wedding present, they bought Amedeo Modigliani's *Portrait of*

Baranowski (1918). Lisa had the deeper grounding in connoisseurship and art history and preferred painting over sculpture, but despite their different backgrounds they discovered that they loved many of the same things. Their purchasing was never calculated, either on financial grounds or to 'fill gaps'. They bought what they loved, and lived surrounded by what they had bought.

However, their spending was tempered by prudence. After the Second World War, by which time they had two children (two more were born subsequently), they set up an 'Art Account' that limited their annual purchases to £1,000: as the family firm was still a private company, it paid only modest dividends. The restriction, though the limit was gradually increased, forced them to be selective. 'The history of the collection', writes Steven Hooper in his introduction to the catalogue of the Sainsbury collection, 'is the story of the application of limited resources to the acquisition of the unfashionable until these things become fashionable – and expensive – when attention was turned to other possibilities.'[2]

The Sainsburys' patronage of two further leading twentieth-century artists, Alberto Giacometti and Francis Bacon, epitomised this approach. Having grown up in Paris and being fluent in French, Lisa was at home among the community of artists and gallery owners there, one of whom introduced the couple to Giacometti. They first bought his drawings in 1949: Bob formed a strong bond with the artist, despite the fact that they shared no mutual language. A decade later they bought their first Giacometti sculpture, persuading the artist to cast in bronze the elongated, emaciated *Standing Woman* (1958–9) that they had seen in plaster in his studio.

Both Bob and Lisa were captivated by Francis Bacon's *Study of a Nude* (1953) when they saw it in London; it became the first of thirteen Bacon paintings they would eventually acquire (to the horror of many of their friends) for a total of £8,000. From

1955, they became Bacon's friends and patrons, guaranteeing his overdraft so that he could travel abroad when London became too oppressive. (Soon afterwards they established the Sainsbury Awards, bursaries of £500 given to new art school graduates so that they could focus on their work while they found their feet in the harsh commercial art world.) With a reputation for irascibility and wildness, Bacon never treated the Sainsburys with anything other than gratitude and respect. He painted portraits of both of them: the portrait of Bob was undertaken to commission, something he never did for anyone else.[3]

David Sainsbury says:

My parents collected three of the greatest artists of the twentieth century – Moore, Giacometti and Bacon – all when they were unknown, and became friends with all of them. You often find a collection where the owner has collected one famous artist, or one movement, such as the Impressionists. What is extraordinary about my parents is that they collected three people who came from completely different artistic backgrounds. It wasn't a case of buying one of each of the famous people – it was, 'These are people whose paintings we love.' My father always used to say that if you can't tell one person's taste through a collection, then it isn't a collection, it's just an assembly of pieces.

Their attitude to what used to be known as 'tribal art', and more recently 'world art', was the same. They bought beautiful things not as ethnographic curiosities, but because they were taken with the beauty of their forms. These ranged from West African masks, to ivories from Alaska, to figure sculptures from Polynesia. Many smaller pieces occupied a wall of shelves and most of the surfaces in Bob's study at Smith Square, as well as a special cabinet called 'Bob's toy department' by the children.

After Bob's retirement from Sainsbury's in the late 1960s, he and Lisa began to think about the collection's future. Asked by his father whether he would like to inherit upwards of 400 priceless objects, David took the view that they could no longer sensibly be kept in a private house, and suggested that his parents should give the collection to a museum. Bob considered the University of Cambridge, but withdrew when told that the university would split the collection between its fine art and anthropological museums, and leave most of the objects in storage.

Meanwhile, he and Lisa had got to know the founding vice-chancellor of one of Britain's new universities, Frank Thistlethwaite at the University of East Anglia. UEA was built on a greenfield site on the River Yare in Norwich, with striking modernist concrete halls of residence by Denys Lasdun known as the 'ziggurats'. Thistlethwaite had decided to try to build up an art collection for the university and wrote to ask if Bob and Lisa might 'consider the loan to us of a few pictures or prints from your collection'. They duly obliged, and also made financial donations to the new school of fine arts at UEA.

At a private dinner in 1968, Bob announced that he and Lisa had decided to leave their entire collection to the university. At first, he envisaged that UEA would raise the funds for a building to house the collection; but when, after five years, there had been no progress, the couple instead proposed to donate the collection outright, together with a 'dowry' of £3 million, half for a building and half as an endowment for future purchases that they might make during their lifetimes.

It was 1973: that year, Sainsbury's went public and the family sold off 15 per cent of its holding of ordinary shares. The value of their remaining shares went through the roof. The bonanza went not to Alan and Bob Sainsbury but to their sons, who had been given most of the shares in the company when their fathers retired. This was David Sainsbury's opportunity to express his admiration for all that his father had achieved. He agreed to donate £3 million of his windfall to set up a specific fund within Gatsby, which was gradually transferred to UEA to build the Sainsbury Centre for Visual Arts (SCVA) and form its endowment for purchases.[4] Gatsby also made annual, six-figure donations to the Robert and Lisa Sainsbury Charitable Trust.

Bob Sainsbury, however, retained full control of the building's design. As architect he chose Norman Foster, then aged thirty-eight and beginning to make a reputation with his modernist designs for industrial and commercial buildings. After a period of intense engagement with the Sainsburys and their collection, Foster produced an extraordinary double-walled, glass and steel structure, its severely rectangular plan defining a single space, full of natural light and affectionately known as 'The Shed'. It was unlike anything the British museum world had seen when it finally opened in 1978. 'The appointment of Norman Foster, who was largely unknown at the time, was a remarkable decision,' says Sainsbury. 'He had a wonderful partnership with my parents.' The partnership is reflected in the central 'Living Area' of the museum, where pieces from different traditions, periods and geographical regions are exhibited together as they would have been in Bob and Lisa's home.

Bob Sainsbury was sensitive to the collection's presence within an academic community, and concerned that it should provide a focus for continued study and interpretation. He promised UEA that the collection would come with a 'proper catalogue': he himself had edited a short interim catalogue for the opening in 1978, but as the collection continued to grow it had become out of date. To take on the task he approached Steven Hooper, an expert on Pacific art who had contributed to the 1978 catalogue and had published a comprehensive catalogue of his own grandfather's collection. They first got to know him when he had been a research assistant at the British Museum. Bob gave him a full-time job and an office in the Sainsbury headquarters, and they worked on the catalogue together for fifteen years (the collection kept expanding, so completion was a moving target). It finally came out, in three volumes, in 1997.[5]

In 1986, the Sainsburys endowed a research unit for the arts of Africa, Oceania and the Americas at UEA, under Hooper's direction. 'Oceanic art was Bob's favourite of the non-Western traditions,' says Hooper. 'World art was popular with the undergraduates, but there was nowhere in Europe where you could undertake advanced study.' The Sainsbury Research Unit (SRU) continues to flourish today: though it has remained small, with ten master's students per year and a complement of about twenty PhD students, it is recognised worldwide for its quality and its graduates now hold senior positions in a wide range of international museums. Since 2003, the original endowment has been supplemented by regular funding from Gatsby to cover additional staff and research costs.

On Friday 24 October 1986, the extended Sainsbury family gathered to celebrate Bob Sainsbury's eightieth birthday. David had struggled to think what to give his father. What do you give someone who has already given away one of the world's greatest art collections? He eventually decided to present him with a drawing and a model, both created by Norman Foster, to show how the SCVA might be extended at some point in the future. 'My father was immensely pleased with his present,' David Sainsbury told the architectural historian Witold Rybczynski. 'He took it as a sign that I would look after the museum in the future.'[6]

Sainsbury did not realise how soon that future might come. A week later, over lunch, his father suggested they go ahead right away. 'It turned out to be a very expensive birthday present,' he told Rybczynski wryly. In 1989, Gatsby donated almost £2 million towards the construction of the Crescent Wing, glass-walled and ingeniously set into a grassy slope below the main building so that it did not detract from its impact. It housed many of the back-office functions that had not been given sufficient space in the original design: storage, workshops, conservation facilities and offices for staff, as well as offices and teaching space for the new SRU.

The entrance to the Crescent Wing was down a ramp, open to the elements. Visiting one rainy day, when she was almost ninety years old and wheelchair-bound, Lisa Sainsbury complained about getting wet. Her son once again asked Foster to produce a design for a canopy that would protect the entrance from the rain. Instead, Foster proposed to tunnel between the original building and the extension. At the same time Stuart Johnson, the project manager appointed to oversee the development, pointed out that, at twenty-five years old, the building's services needed a complete overhaul. When the museum reopened in 2006, it included a new basement shop and education studio, and additional temporary exhibition space in alcoves off the underground corridor known as 'The Link'. The scheme took nearly two years and cost £12.5 million – nearly three-quarters of the cost of the original building at 1978 prices.

Although Johnson had also instituted a regular programme of maintenance, by 2010 the building was no longer meeting the more stringent levels of environmental monitoring and control that had become standard in museums. With Gatsby's partial financing, the museum took the opportunity to execute another upgrade that would create a continuous suite of galleries for temporary exhibitions. This required the shop to be moved from the basement into the main space and combined with the reception area, and converting the Sainsbury Collection 'study reserve' space in the basement into a temporary exhibition gallery. The existing blinds on the huge glass wall at one end, which had ceased to function, were replaced with light-sensitive, computer-controlled versions, allowing in more daylight and an attractive view to the east whenever light levels do not exceed conservation requirements. As before, Foster + Partners designed the upgrade, ensuring that it stayed true to Foster's – and the Sainsburys' – original vision. The building received a Grade II* listing from English Heritage in December 2012. It is a lasting monument to the dedication of Bob and Lisa Sainsbury, their generous wish to share their collection with the world, and their son's love for his parents. Bob died at the age of 93 in 2000, and Lisa in 2014 aged 101.

As well as works by Moore, Bacon and Giacometti, the Sainsbury collection includes Edgar Degas's bronze *Little Dancer* (1880–81), and works by (among others) Pablo Picasso and Modigliani. These nineteenth- and twentieth-century pieces sit comfortably alongside treasures from ancient Greece and Rome, and from the cultures of North and South America, Africa, India, Japan and the Pacific. Since Lisa Sainsbury's death there have been no further acquisitions for the Sainsbury Collection – and there will be no disposals. The museum also holds the separate Lisa Sainsbury Ceramics Collection (works by studio potters such as Lucie Rie and Hans Coper), UEA's own expanding collection of abstract and constructivist art, and the Art Nouveau collection of Colin Anderson, who was a friend of Robert Sainsbury – thousands of works in total. As funds permit, the museum continues to acquire objects that relate to the central collections or complement them.

Compared with national institutions such as the Victoria and Albert Museum, the Tate or the British Museum, SCVA's collection is small. The current director, Paul Greenhalgh, is in no doubt that it makes up for its modest size by the quality of its holdings, and is unique in its juxtaposition of modernism with the world art that inspired so many modernist artists. However, the museum's location in largely rural East Anglia means that attracting visitors from beyond the local area presents a challenge. One way it has addressed this challenge is through temporary exhibitions that are sufficiently spectacular to tempt the art critics out of London.

In 2006, when the Centre reopened after the creation of the underground link, Steven Hooper curated 'Pacific Encounters', an exhibition of more than 270 Polynesian objects including loans from national museums, which was the outcome of a three-year research project funded by the Arts and Humanities Research Council (AHRC).[7] 'It was the first time these objects had been presented as art,' says Hooper. 'It was very successful – later the whole exhibition went to the Musée du Quai Branly in Paris, at their expense, and the British Museum also showed an exhibition of the many objects they had loaned.' The *Daily Telegraph*'s reviewer called the exhibits 'as strange, moving, and mysterious as any I've seen anywhere, ever'. The first exhibition after the reopening in 2013 was 'Masterpieces: Art and East Anglia',[8] in which curator Ian Collins brought together prehistoric, Roman and Viking artefacts, paintings by Constable and Turner, and the modernist masterpieces of the Sainsbury collection. The critical response was equally glowing. In 2014, SCVA stepped on to the international stage in a hugely ambitious partnership with the Hermitage Museum in St Petersburg, loaning its Bacon paintings and borrowing masterpieces from the Hermitage in return (see Case study, page 272).

There are currently three institutions affiliated with UEA that were founded by Bob and Lisa. In addition to the SCVA and the SRU, the Sainsbury Institute for the Study of Japanese Arts and Cultures (SISJAC) opened in 1999 in Norwich city centre: Japanese art was a particular interest of Lisa Sainsbury. SRU and SISJAC each has a research library at its heart, named respectively after Robert and Lisa Sainsbury. Also housed in the SCVA is UEA's highly ranked Department of Art History and World Art Studies, which claims credit for coining the term 'world art' and founded the academic journal *World Art* in 2011.

As part of UEA, SCVA receives an annual allocation from HEFCE to support its teaching and research activities, but has also received regular top-ups from Gatsby. Representing Gatsby in its relations with the Norwich institutes is Alan Bookbinder, chief executive of the SFCT. 'David has been very generous and committed,' he says. 'He takes a great interest in what goes on, and visits regularly.' However, any shortfalls in funding have to be made up by UEA, which like all universities has many calls on its resources. Accordingly, the Centre and associated institutes have had to work hard to attract alternative sources of funding.

SISJAC has been particularly successful, developing a wide range of outside sponsors and strengthening its connections with Japan. With the resources of the institute to support it, UEA opened a Centre for Japanese Studies in 2011, which coordinates undergraduate and graduate teaching across a range of multidisciplinary programmes – tongue slightly in cheek, UEA makes much of its claim to be the 'British university nearest to Japan'. A plan is currently under way to move SISJAC from its city centre location into the SCVA, bringing it closer to the Centre for Japanese Studies and creating the possibility of co-housing its academic library with that of the SRU.

'Successive vice-chancellors have been quick to see how important SCVA is to the profile of the university,' says Bookbinder, 'but some deep thinking is having to go on about the extent to which the university is prepared to fund it more substantially. The SCVA has developed in recent years from being an interesting backwater to having ambitions to be a major player.'

Setting the stage

The SCVA is the largest but by no means the only one of Gatsby's beneficiaries in the arts. Recognising his wife Susie's passion for the theatre, David Sainsbury asked her to advise the trustees on applications in this area. Through her advocacy, Gatsby funding has embraced music and theatre as well as the visual arts. Susie Sainsbury has particularly championed performing arts institutions in which she herself has a close interest. The most significant is the Royal Shakespeare Company (RSC); she personally led the transformation of its Stratford theatres in the late 2000s.

Brush up your Shakespeare

Throughout the 1980s Gatsby made occasional small grants to theatre companies and music ensembles that had come to Susie's attention. She herself was a regular theatregoer, to be found in the audience of most if not all of the RSC's productions at the Royal Shakespeare Theatre (RST) in Stratford-upon-Avon or London's Barbican Theatre. In the early 1990s, Geoffrey Cass, then chairman of the RSC, invited her to join the board of governors. By this time her daughters were in their teens and she was looking for some outside occupation. She not only became a governor but joined the council and the foundation board, set up to create an endowment fund. It was at this point, in 1995, that the artistic director Adrian Noble dropped the bombshell that his future vision for the company involved demolishing the RST and building a new theatre. Fundraising for an endowment turned into fundraising for a huge capital project.

Actors had complained for years that the 1932 theatre designed by modernist architect Elisabeth Scott was deeply unsympathetic to the interaction between actor and audience: the acoustics were poor and most of the seats were a huge distance from the stage. Noble proposed that instead the company should build a new, flexible theatre that could mount productions in both thrust stage and proscenium arch configurations. The Arts Council agreed and offered a £50 million grant, on condition that the RSC's archaic governance structure was reformed.

'It was the most useful thing anyone has done for the RSC,' says Susie Sainsbury, who did all she could to encourage the chairman to push through the reforms. Eventually the governors were whittled down from an unwieldy 75 (13 of them over 80) to a more manageable 45, with a new charter and an executive board of fewer than 20. Susie emerged on to the board in 2000 as deputy chair, a position she held until December 2016. Through her energetic advocacy, Gatsby became the most significant private donor to the RSC's Transformation project: together with private contributions from David and Susie, donations had reached £26 million by 2014.

The RSC's finances were often on a knife-edge. While waiting for the Arts Council to release the first tranche of its grant, Susie had boosted the capacity of the fundraising team and begun the process of planning for the redevelopment. She ensured that there was a steady flow of funds from Gatsby to the RSC. In 1998, the Gatsby trustees formally introduced a funding category for 'The Arts', largely restricted to support for the SCVA and the RSC. 'David could see the point of what I was doing at the RSC,' says Susie. 'He was extraordinarily generous.'

The transformation did not go smoothly at first. With an architect appointed and several million pounds spent, Noble's vision of a complete rebuild faced strenuous local opposition. In 2003, Noble, who had just had a major success with his production of *Chitty Chitty Bang Bang* in the West End, decided that after holding various roles with the RSC for more than twenty years it was time to move on. His successor, Michael Boyd, favoured a different and no less difficult solution: to preserve most of the outer fabric of the RST and rebuild it from the inside, creating a thrust stage and tiered galleries in the style of theatres of Shakespeare's day.[9] Once they had established that English Heritage would accept some alterations to the listed building as long as certain Art Deco features were retained, the board enthusiastically embraced this plan. Boyd, Susie Sainsbury, the new chairman Sir Christopher Bland and the new chief executive Vikki Heywood became the Transformation project committee, joined in 2005 by the project director Peter Wilson and chaired by Susie. Only at this point did the Arts Council begin to release its promised grant, eventually amounting to £53 million.

Heywood says:

Susie had been involved in the previous failed project. She knew it could not fail again. It made her more able to recognise that inevitably in any arts project there will be a number of people with strong feelings about what it should be like. She had to find a way to negotiate that, to find a conclusion that everyone was happy with – including herself. She and I became partners to manage the thing so that it came into port. She is a hard taskmaster – she expects everything to be right, but I like that. It was something the five of us agreed on.

From the first, Susie supported Michael Boyd's vision of what the theatre should be. Heywood continues:

It wasn't only about what happened on the stage, it was a whole philosophy about how he wanted the RSC to be. She really enjoyed that and encouraged us to take risks. When I said, 'We'll have to build a temporary theatre [while the rebuilding took place],' she said 'Right, that's what we'll have to do.' Timescales were ridiculously tight. But if Susie was up for something, then it jolly well happened.

In six weeks, architect Ian Ritchie, who was an RSC governor, had a design for a 1,000-seat theatre ready to go to the planners. It was a towering, rectangular shed, made of COR-TEN steel that would rust to exactly the colour of Stratford red brick. It would be built adjacent to The Other Place, the RSC's theatre for experimental productions across the road from the RST: the original spaces of The Other Place would become the foyer and café of the new theatre. 'Susie is obsessed with buildings and how they work, and how to make them better,' says Heywood. 'That was another reason she was part of the team – she was as knowledgeable as anyone about how to build a building.' The 'temporary' Courtyard Theatre, built in just a year for a budget of £6 million, opened in 2006 with a thrust stage of the same type envisaged for the revamped RST. The first production there was *Henry VI, Part 1*, the first play in Boyd's 'Complete Works' festival, a staging of all thirty-seven of Shakespeare's plays over one year and making use of the Courtyard, the RST and the smaller Swan Theatre. The following year a production of *Coriolanus* was the last to take place in the old RST, and a four-year reconstruction programme began, at a total cost of £112.8 million.

Private donations were essential to the completion of the project, and Susie Sainsbury led by example. Heywood says:

> You can never underestimate the effect that a major supporter like Susie has on the confidence that it gives other donors. All arts funding projects suffer from the chicken-and-egg problem of not being able to start until you've got the money, and not being able to raise the money until you've started. Having someone like Susie who is endlessly prepared to get on aeroplanes and fly to the US, host dinners, see all the work – she probably saw more RSC productions than I did – it makes all the difference to the degree of confidence someone has when they decide to give. There are very few donors who give, but also work hard on the project they are supporting, who are there for the bad times as well as the good. That defines both her and Gatsby.

The RST reopened to its first full-scale production, *King Lear*, in early 2011. Actors, critics and audiences love it, and designers have used the three-dimensional opportunities with increasing boldness: 2016's production of *The Tempest* used animated projections and live-motion capture with spectacular effect. With its shop, restaurants, cafés and viewing tower, the theatre has transformed not only the experience of actors and audiences, but its whole relationship between the theatre and the public at large. 'One of the gifts Susie wanted to give to Michael was that the building would sum up his vision: it has a lot of entrances, it is open and welcoming, there are lots of things going on,' says Heywood. 'Now thousands of people have been through the building as part of something to do when they come to Stratford, in a way they never would have done before. That goes on forever, and that was her gift. It's an easy thing to say, but it's true: it simply would not have happened without her.'

Susie has continued to give financial support to the company; in particular Gatsby's donations to the RSC's Artists' Development Programme have provided professional development opportunities to over 1,000 company members. In the Queen's Birthday Honours in 2010, she was awarded a CBE for services to the RSC and to the Arts, and in 2014 she received the Prince of Wales Medal for Arts Philanthropy. The medal citation commented that, while she was one of 'the UK's greatest cultural philanthropists', much of her work happened 'under the radar'. Typically, other than appearing in lists of other private donors, the Sainsbury and Gatsby names are nowhere to be seen in the new RST. 'We had a conversation which was an "unnaming",' says Heywood. 'I said, "The auditorium is going to be called the Royal Shakespeare Theatre, and that's your gift." She protected it from being called anything else, which suited us down to the ground.'

In 2016, Susie made the first small concession to a public recognition of her role. The Other Place, the RSC's small performance space, has been reincarnated within the steel shell of what was formerly the Courtyard Theatre, together with new rehearsal spaces and a costume store. The Other Place's public café bar is called Susie's.

Making music

In 1980, the Sainsburys' neighbours in Notting Hill, company director Peter Readman and his wife Victoria, returned from their honeymoon in Salzburg. There they had met the conductor of the European Community Youth Orchestra, James Judd, who had asked them to help set up a new chamber orchestra consisting of forty of the 23-year-old 'graduates' of the Youth Orchestra. The Readmans had agreed to canvass for support. The Sainsburys, through Gatsby, gave them £5,000, when most other responses, says Readman, 'ranged from the pityingly dismissive to the ribald'.[10] At the inaugural fundraising concert at London's Barbican Centre in 1981, the Chamber Orchestra of Europe (COE) bowled over its audience with the quality and enthusiasm of its playing under conductor Claudio Abbado.

The Orchestra has flourished ever since on a unique model: a chamber orchestra without a principal conductor, fixed geographical base or public funding. Now with a core of sixty musicians from all across Europe, it undertakes around ten to twelve tours per year, having worked with international conductors including Bernard Haitink and Nikolaus Harnoncourt, and with soloists such as Stephen Kovacevich, András Schiff and Murray Perahia. Regarded as one of the finest chamber orchestras in the world, COE has made numerous award-winning recordings under its own record label. Gatsby has continued to make annual donations to its core costs, which the Orchestra acknowledges are essential to its survival.

With her links to COE, Susie Sainsbury was well known in the musical as well as the theatrical world. In 2000, she was invited to join the governing body of the Royal Academy of Music (RAM), one of the world's top conservatoires for the training of professional musicians. Just as with the RSC, she has been, according to the principal, Jonathan Freeman-Attwood, a 'transformational presence'. Generous in her philanthropy, her contribution, says Attwood, goes far beyond the philanthropic. 'I know no one who combines the rigours of governance and a delight in successful creative output more effectively and profoundly (and with a greater range) than Susie,' he says, citing her passion for 'giving opportunity to talented people who might otherwise not realise that talent.'

Susie has supported a series of internationally recognised recordings of Academy students playing with top conductors such as Trevor Pinnock and Oliver Knussen. In 2017, a joint CD with the Juilliard School in New York will be released, alongside Stravinsky's *Soldier's Tale* with Dame Harriet Walter. The Sainsbury Royal Academy Soloists are an elite ensemble of young international string virtuosi who perform regularly in major venues, including the Wigmore Hall. The RAM has also offered her another opportunity to get stuck in to her favourite occupation: nourishing a new capital project. 'Susie's most critical role in recent years has been her comprehensive involvement in the feasibility, fundraising and delivery of a new theatre and recital hall at the Academy,' says Freeman-Attwood. 'Her contribution, from the overall vision to the right colour of the seat numbers, speaks volumes for her inimitable sense of belonging to the place and going that extra mile.'

The architect of the new theatre, due to open in 2018, is Ian Ritchie. The space will be built within the walls of the existing theatre, part of a listed building, but offer much better facilities for performance. 'We demonstrated that a redesigned theatre for opera and musicals could have a 40 per cent increased capacity, larger orchestra pit, and for the first time a stage wing and fly tower, as well as a new recital hall on the top of the theatre roof,' says Ritchie, and that is what is currently being built.

Going backstage

From 2012, as the Gatsby trustees sought to focus the foundation's work on fewer, more directly managed projects, they ceased to support the many other small arts organisations that had previously benefited from Susie Sainsbury's advocacy. However, at David Sainsbury's suggestion, Gatsby makes an annual £1 million donation to a new charity, the Backstage Trust, of which Susie is the settlor. The trust's focus is on the performing arts, principally theatre, but 'not the glitz', says Susie: 'We seldom fund productions.' She mentors a number of young theatre directors who find themselves in the unfamiliar position of having to manage a team and interact with a board of directors. 'Business is something they know little about, but are suddenly faced with,' says Susie, and Backstage funds them to obtain the necessary training and consultancy. Backstage also continues Susie's early interest in using theatre and performance to help children communicate.

In the summer of 2014 an extraordinary installation, 'Blood Swept Lands and Seas of Red' by artist Paul Cummins and designer Tom Piper, arrived in the moat of the Tower of London. Ceramic artist Cummins created 888,246 life-sized ceramic poppies, one for every British and colonial soldier who died in the First World War. Piper is a stage designer with whom Susie worked for years at the RSC. The individual poppies that made up most of the installation, which originally ran from July to November 2014, were to be sold in aid of six service charities, and two sculptures, *Wave* and *Weeping Window*, were to be dismantled when the installation was over.

'I happened to be in New York with Tom the week that was due to happen,' says Susie. 'As a theatre designer, he was used to seeing sets broken up. But these sculptures being dismantled was different, and it seemed such a terrible waste for them to disappear from public view.' In the ensuing days she decided to help 'rescue the whole thing' for the nation. Five million people had been to see the installation, many travelling long distances at great expense. Susie helped to put in motion plans for a tour of the two sculptures to sites throughout the British Isles. Aided by Vikki Heywood, both of them used to working within the tight timescales of theatre productions, she put the plan into place without delay.

Through her Backstage Trust, Susie bought *Weeping Window*, and was delighted when Dame Vivien Duffield, of the Clore Duffield Foundation, agreed to buy *Wave*. 14–18 NOW, a five-year programme of arts projects commemorating the centenary of the First World War, took on the task of selecting suitable locations around the country where the sculptures could be displayed. 14–18 NOW (of which Susie is now president) is hosted by the

Imperial War Museum and funded by the National Lottery through the Heritage Lottery Fund, Arts Council England and the Department of Culture, Media and Sport. The Poppies tour was launched in July 2015, less than nine months after the sculptures were set to be destroyed.[11] *Wave* and *Weeping Window* will continue to tour until November 2018, when they will be donated to the Imperial War Museum London and the Imperial War Museum North.

The response in the first few venues was phenomenal, with the small Woodhorn Museum in a former colliery in Northumberland receiving 100,000 visitors in four weeks. Other venues have included Lincoln Castle, St George's Hall in Liverpool (where volunteers went to sign up in 1914) and St Magnus Cathedral in Kirkwall, Orkney. 'It could have been the daftest thing I've ever done,' says Susie, but few works of art can have had so great an impact. She is thrilled to have been part of it.

Vikki Heywood left the RSC in 2012 to take up the chair of the Royal Society for the Encouragement of Arts, Manufactures and Commerce (RSA for short). 'With Susie, you always felt that you had her undivided attention – it was like being an only child,' she says. 'It was only after I left that I discovered she had similar relationships with lots of other organisations.' Realising that at the RSA she had access to a 'neutral space', in 2015 she held a party there to bring everyone that Susie had supported together to thank her. The list included not only the RSC, the COE and the RAM, but also the Bristol Old Vic, the Hightide Festival, the Donmar Warehouse, and the Bush, Tricycle, Soho, Royal Court and Rose theatres. 'When I said, "Let's do this thing for Susie," they all said, "Absolutely, I'll clear my diary,"' says Heywood. 'It was just such a lovely evening – it opened their minds to all the other things she was doing, and having all those people in the room summed her up better than any speech could.'

Case study: 'Francis Bacon and the Masters' at the State Hermitage Museum

On the floor stood Michelangelo's *Crouching Boy* (1530–31), every bone, muscle and sinew apparently straining through the marble. On the wall nearby hung Bacon's *Two Figures in a Room* (1959), the central figure in an almost identical attitude, knees bent and head bowed, naked torso stretched and exposed. For the first time, the modern painting and the early masterpiece that inspired it were exhibited together. For David Sainsbury, it was a particularly heart-stopping moment: the Bacon had hung outside his bedroom in his parents' home. Now they were both in St Petersburg for the opening of a remarkable exhibition.

The current director of the SCVA, Paul Greenhalgh, joined in 2010, having worked for many years at the V&A in London, and most recently been Director of the Corcoran Gallery of Art in Washington, DC. Before he left the USA, he had got wind that the Hermitage's curators were interested in mounting a Bacon exhibition, and that the head of the Hermitage Foundation, Thierry Morel, was energetically developing international collaborations. The idea they initially discussed was that SCVA would loan its thirteen Bacon paintings to the Hermitage, in return for loans of some of their works at a later date.

'David [Sainsbury] was hugely supportive of the idea that his mother and father's collection would be in the world's greatest museum,' he says. Gradually a team developed: Morel was joined by Elizaveta Renne, Curator of British and Scandinavian Painting at the Hermitage; SCVA's chief curator Amanda Geitner, its head of collections Calvin Winner and its deputy director Ghislaine Wood all collaborated to imagine what the exhibition could become, and then bring it into being. The team began to conceive an audacious idea: to create a single exhibition, juxtaposing the Bacons (the thirteen paintings from the Sainsbury Collection and another seventeen loaned from elsewhere) with the works that inspired the artist – though many of them he had only ever seen in books. The exhibition would open in St Petersburg, as part of the Hermitage's 250th anniversary celebrations, and then travel to Norwich.

David Sainsbury during the setting up of the exhibition
'Francis Bacon and the Masters' at the Hermitage Museum in
St Petersburg, where Michelangelo's *Crouching Boy* (foreground)
was juxtaposed with Bacon's *Two Figures in a Room* from the SCVA.

Greenhalgh says:

Every aspect was subject to extraordinary levels of negotiation. Mikhail
Piotrovsky, a great director, stuck with it. Other figures were hugely helpful to us, including Neil MacGregor [director of the British Museum]: when
all the pressure was on about whether we do business with the Russians,
he was totally with us. As were colleagues at the Tate, the V&A and the
Science Museum – everyone stepped up to defend it.

David Sainsbury came to the Hermitage personally to hang Bacon's
portraits of his parents with two great Rembrandts of an old man and an

old woman. 'It was a very moving experience – David is rightly protective of his mother and father's heritage,' says Greenhalgh. 'He's quite modest about it, but he is also acutely aware of modernism and modern art, and how it evolved. He stood up and gave a number of impromptu talks during the Bacon exhibition, without notes, and showed a detailed knowledge.'

The 'Francis Bacon and the Masters' exhibition received international press coverage, so that when it reopened at the SCVA in the spring of 2015 it attracted attention at a level not previously experienced by the museum. 'It put us into a different league,' says Greenhalgh. 'We had major museum directors from Paris coming here, asking, "Where on earth is this?" And then they come in here, and everything's easy.' The British press was divided on the exhibition itself: for the *Financial Times* it was 'the UK's most stimulating, alluring, unexpected and insightful current exhibition';[12] for the *Guardian*, it was 'a massacre, a cruel exposure, a debacle … The jaw-dropping master-pieces by the likes of Picasso, Titian and Rodin that so nearly make this show five-star unmissable also, to my dismay, to my shock, make Bacon seem a small, timebound, fading figure.'[13] But no one was indifferent, and there was no doubting its impact.

'It changed the game for the Centre,' says Greenhalgh, 'so that when my colleagues Claudia Milburn and Calvin Winner did a modest but beautiful Giacometti show in 2016,[14] it was automatically reviewed in *The Times*, the *Telegraph* and so on. The quality of the collection is such that it deserves to be there.'

DOING GOOD, GIVING BETTER

A living legacy

In 2013 David and Susie Sainsbury joined a group of billionaires who have pledged to give away more than half their wealth. The Giving Pledge was established in 2010 by Warren Buffett and Bill and Melinda Gates, with forty American dollar billionaires signed up in the first year. The founders' aim was 'to help address society's most pressing problems by inviting the wealthiest American families and individuals to commit to giving more than half of their wealth to philanthropy'. The idea was not just to increase the amount of money donated, but, by making the pledges publicly, to 'inspire conversations, discussions, and action, not just about how much but also for what purposes' money should be raised. In 2013, the founders extended the pledge to non-Americans, and the Sainsburys were among the first to sign up.

'We do not believe', they wrote in the letter accompanying their pledge, 'that spending any more money on ourselves or our family would add anything to our happiness. However, using it to support social progress we have found deeply fulfilling. We focus on a few areas which require investment and which we care about deeply, and seeing these projects develop and bring major benefits to people has been a life-enhancing experience.' The pledge, in their case, was less a commitment for the future than a public acknowledgement of what was already the case: by 2013, the Sainsburys had already given more than £1 billion to Gatsby.

In 2005 David had declared his ambition to give away £1 billion in his lifetime. As part of that process, he wished the trustees to wind up the foundation after his death 'so that its birth, life and laying to rest will reflect his lifetime choices of the priorities for philanthropic action'. Of the £1 billion that Gatsby has spent in the fifty years of its existence, a comparatively small proportion has gone into bricks and mortar: the Sainsbury Centre for Visual Arts (SCVA) and the three science laboratories in Norwich, Cambridge and London are the exceptions that will carry the Sainsbury name into the future. However, to judge the long-term legacy of Gatsby by such tangible signs would be very misleading. Long after the fund has been spent out, lives will continue to be changed as a result of the programmes it has funded.

Several institutions have been founded with Gatsby money, with independent boards of management, and generously funded. The SCVA, the Norwich and Cambridge plant science laboratories, the Gatsby Computational Neuroscience Unit and the Sainsbury Wellcome Centre, the Institute for Government, the Centre for Cities and Gatsby Africa will be in a position to make their own way in the world if their governing bodies choose to do so. Together with many other initiatives that Gatsby has launched but passed over to others to continue, such as the Centre for Mental Health, or education projects such as the Teacher Effectiveness Enhancement Programme (TEEP) and subject knowledge enhancement, they will constitute a legacy of activities that will continue to further Gatsby's mission even after it has ceased to exist.

Attempting to quantify Gatsby's overall impact in terms of lives changed is almost impossible. Some data is relatively easy to collect: the price and yield achieved by Tanzanian cotton farmers, the number of students sitting further mathematics at

A level, the number and impact factor of publications in plant sciences. Other changes may still be in the future: the children of Cameroonian women who took small loans and expanded their businesses, able to go to school for the first time; young scientists set on a career path in plant science research because of a Gatsby summer school; engineering graduates acquiring the skills to become managers – these transformations will have knock-on effects that are impossible to predict in detail.

But perhaps most important and yet least tangible is the legacy of ideas: how to do things better, how to innovate, how to disseminate new knowledge. David Sainsbury's decision to publish a book on the foundation's work over half a century was made very much in the spirit of advocacy, rather than self-promotion. 'Most people don't get the chance to spend their money until late in life' he says. 'I have had fifty years to learn how to do this, starting with small sums. That seemed a good reason for the book.'

Agents of change

As might be expected, the trustees and officers of Gatsby are acutely conscious of the environment within which grant-making operates in the UK and further afield. Behind the scenes, and working with the other Sainsbury trusts, they have been active in campaigning for a regulatory framework that enables grant-making charities to operate more effectively.

For example, the Charities Act of 1993 did not allow foundations to spend the capital that formed their permanent endowments. John Sainsbury was particularly exercised about this, arguing that it was unreasonable to define endowment as untouchable. He had taken up the issue directly with the then Home Secretary, Michael Howard, and eventually the rules were changed to create a new category of 'expendable endowment' – capital that could, if the trustees wished, be drawn on for spending to supplement a charity's income fund. When the

Houses of Parliament set up a joint committee on the draft Charities Bill of 2004, John Sainsbury joined it and spoke up for grant-making charities, as distinct from those that delivered services. The committee concluded that 'the draft Bill should include provision to ensure that the regulatory burden on grant-making charities does not discourage philanthropy'.[1]

In the first decade of the twenty-first century, several of the Sainsbury trusts, including Gatsby, decided to spend out their endowments, and this could not have been done without the change in regulation. Other charities have benefited from the change. The Tubney Charitable Trust was founded by Miles and Briony Blackwell, of the Oxford bookselling and publishing dynasty. After they died unexpectedly in 2001, the trustees executed their wishes by spending out the charity's funds within a decade. 'There is no question in our minds that "spend out" focuses the collective mind and resources of a trust in an extraordinary way and can do more to achieve a trust's long-term goals than a slow, modest, and possibly uninspired, perpetual outward flow of funds,' the trust's chairman René Olivieri told the magazine *Third Sector*.[2] 'That would not have been achievable if the Sainsbury family had not pushed for these changes,' says former SFCT director Michael Pattison.

In another example, from the late 1990s the Charity Commission increasingly sought to require charities to hold diverse portfolios of investment in order to minimise their risks. In the early days of Gatsby and the other trusts, the vast majority of their holdings were in Sainsbury's stock, but over the years they did diversify their investments. In the mid-2000s, David Sainsbury was preparing to hand over a very large tranche of his shareholding in Sainsbury's to Gatsby. However, he was concerned that if the trustees felt compelled to sell the shares in the interests of diversification, the family and its trusts could collectively lose their controlling interest in Sainsbury's and make it vulnerable to a takeover.

Judith Portrait consulted Christopher McCall QC, specialist Chancery Counsel, who had assisted with many of the Sainsbury charities over the years. With his help, together with an enlightened response from the Charity Commission, she obtained the approval of the Inland Revenue to major gifts that permitted donors of shares to retain the last word over whether or not the gifted shares should or could be sold. 'It was a terrific team effort', she says, 'and was handled in a non-confrontational and co-operative way, with all parties involved sharing the same objective to enable more funds to be passed to charity for everyone's benefit.' In 2007, David Sainsbury felt confident that he would not be putting control of Sainsbury's at any risk by donating over £180 million in shares to Gatsby, the largest gift he had made to date.

Michael Pattison was also closely involved in arguing the case, which he felt had wide implications for philanthropy in the UK. He says:

> If there is a view that more funding is desirable in the charitable sector, then you are saying to people who have been successful entrepreneurs, 'Why not put some of your wealth into a charitable trust?' If you are going to say to these people, 'and once you have placed a block of shareholdings in the company that you have created and brought to the market into the foundation, you are going to have to sell them off,' there's no incentive to do it. It's not even really about control, it's your personal identity.

Finally, before 1995 charities were required to submit only an annual balance sheet of income and expenditure. That year the Charity Commission decided to tighten up reporting standards, and established a committee to develop a Statement of Recommended Practice (SORP), which eventually ran to over 400 paragraphs. 'The grant-making sector within charities was rather a poor relation, that didn't have much of a voice,' says Paul Spokes, former finance director of the SFCT. 'We had to apply the same standards as plcs, some of which weren't very helpful.'

For example, the SORP required all grants agreed for the future to be treated as liabilities, even though they might not be fully paid until two, three or even more years in the future. Gatsby, on the other hand, routinely held only enough cash to provide for grants that were due within twelve months of the year end. 'Our statement of financial activities could show us overcommitted by £30,000 or £40,000,' says Spokes. 'Suddenly we would be refused credit, for example when booking hotels, because it looked as if Gatsby was bust when we had half a billion in capital.' When the SORP committee was reconvened in 2005 to update the regulations, Spokes joined it, and was able to represent the interests of other grant-making charities. As well as being modular and much more accessible for small charities, the SORP now allows for charities to put conditions in their grant offer letters (such as 'subject to satisfactory reviews of progress'), so that future grants are not regarded as firm commitments and therefore need not be listed as liabilities. 'Most grants are moral and not legal obligations,' says Spokes, 'but nevertheless 99.9 per cent of grants are honoured.' By means such as these the Sainsbury trusts, often led by Gatsby, have subtly changed the philanthropic landscape in the UK to make it easier for grant-making trusts to operate.

From privacy to advocacy and transparency

The Sainsbury trusts are all very different in their spending priorities, each tailored to the interests of the individual settlors. However, they have some things in common. All operate on the basis of low overheads and minimal bureaucracy, and most have traditionally maintained an extremely low public profile. 'When I joined SFCT in 1995, the Sainsbury family was probably the most significant example of sustained family philanthropy in the last quarter of the twentieth century in Britain,' says Pattison, 'but they belonged to a culture in which personal philanthropy on that scale was seen as a private activity. The line I used to take in conversation was that the people I work for have a unique role in philanthropy in the UK in this era, but they don't choose to shout it from the rooftops.' The primary reason they did not want publicity was that, when the four largest charities were set up, the three Sainsbury brothers and their cousin were all still actively involved in the business. The trusts were vehicles for supporting things about which they were personally passionate. 'The last thing they wanted', says Pattison, 'was for people to say, "This is all about the Sainsbury's brand and selling extra cans of baked beans."'

The Sainsbury name had therefore been used very sparingly in relation to the charitable activities of the family. On David's side of the family the SCVA in Norwich, his parents' largest charitable project, was an early exception, joined in 1987 by Gatsby's Sainsbury Laboratory in the same city. His cousins, also major supporters of a variety of causes, preserved their low visibility until they jointly funded the redesigned extension to the National Gallery, which opened in 1991. Given the history of the controversial project and the Sainsbury commitment following the Prince of Wales's criticism of the original design, anonymity was not an option. 'Prior to that most Sainsbury grant-making was done far removed from the Sainsbury name,' says Pattison. 'There was no secretiveness with the people to whom the awards were being made, but it was not done for publicity, it was done out of interest in the cause.'

The Sainsbury Wing at the National Gallery brought the family's philanthropy into the public eye to a greater degree than had either of the Norwich institutions, and led many to jump to the very conclusion the family had sought to avoid. 'There was then a universal assumption that there was some enormous institution called "the Sainsbury Foundation" which was a by-product of the company,' says Pattison. 'It got thoroughly confusing – even most of the people I knew had difficulty under-standing I was not employed by Sainsbury's.' Negative publicity became a serious issue from 1997, when David Sainsbury became a target of both right- and left-wing media on his elevation to the House of Lords and subsequent appointment as a government minister (see Chapter 7). And all the while there was a rising chorus, even from within the charitable sector itself, questioning the right of private foundations to spend the tax foregone by the Treasury as they pleased, with no public scrutiny.

The Gatsby officers and trustees saw that there was a case for a modest increase in public communications by the trusts: as mentioned previously, Gatsby's annual reports were developed from 1999 to include illustrated reviews of the work funded. 'I felt there was a very positive story to tell about these trusts,' says Pattison. 'Public relations wasn't something that the family members chose to do, so we weren't in the business of PR campaigns and press releases, but we were trying to use the annual reports to provide some context.' The introductions to these reports often included statements of the broad philosoph-ical position taken by settlor, trustees and officers. For example, the 2001 report stated that 'Foundations can and should lead social progress. They have the potential to make more effective use of scarce resources than either individual donors or govern-ments ... The capacity to act strategically in defined territory over a prolonged period, irrespective of external pressures, is a special privilege of those who take part in the work of a foundation.'

At the same time, Gatsby began to participate in a general movement to encourage philanthropy in the UK, not just by example, but by active engagement with specific projects. For example, it supported the Association of Charitable Foundations in setting up a networking and research project to promote new giving, Philanthropy UK, headed by consultant Theresa Lloyd. Two publications that resulted from this project, *A Guide to Giving* and *Why Rich People Give*, proved to be invaluable resources for charities seeking funding.[3] Philanthropy UK subsequently amalgamated with the European Association for Philanthropy and Giving and the Philanthropy Advisors' Forum to form a new charity, Philanthropy Impact.[4]

An opportunity to help increase the overall pot available for charitable purposes arose in 2003. Michael Thomas, a financial executive then seconded to the Bank of England, and Piers Le Marchant, legal director for Lehman Brothers, met the Gatsby trustees and Michael Pattison and asked for their help with a project they were planning. 'They explained that there was a lot of money in dormant bank accounts, often left there for decades,' says Stone. 'And they thought there was an opportunity to liberate that money for philanthropy.'

It would require a change in law and banking practice, and they were looking for funds to support the preparatory work. The organisers registered a new charity, for which Gatsby provided initial funding, called the Balance Charitable Foundation for Unclaimed Assets, which was run from the SFCT office. Banks transferred unclaimed assets to the foundation, but were covered by an insurance policy so that, should the owners of the assets turn up, they could be paid back. In its five years of operation the Balance Foundation made grants of £8 million, mostly for causes related to social exclusion and educational disadvantage. The project coincided with a commission on unclaimed assets chaired by the venture capitalist Ronald Cohen, which included Susan Hitch from David Sainsbury's private office among its membership. In 2008, Parliament passed the Dormant Bank and Building Society Accounts Act, since when unclaimed assets have been channelled through the Big Lottery Fund, using the same insurance mechanism that Balance had trialled so successfully.

Advocacy, and dissemination of lessons learned, have gradually been recognised as key contributors to Gatsby's effectiveness. Across all the programmes, as described in the previous chapters, those involved with Gatsby-funded projects maintain close links with relevant government departments. They also share their experience with other funders operating in the same area, partly through speaking at conferences but mostly through direct, one-to-one contact, sometimes leading to partnership. Within the areas that Gatsby funds, there will be no other charity or government department that does not know that it is a major player, or understand its strategic priorities. Certain projects, notably the Centre for Cities and the Institute for Government, execute their missions partly through maintaining a high media profile.

Gatsby's approach to grant-making has also been disseminated through former staff who have gone on to work for other charities. Victoria Hornby now runs the Royal Foundation of the Duke and Duchess of Cambridge and Prince Harry. Asked about the main lessons she took from Gatsby, she focuses on what a grant-maker expects from their beneficiaries. 'A lot of grant-makers are damaging to organisations', she says, 'when they demand outcomes in three years with no sense of what will happen next. Gatsby has always taken a long-term view, because it seeks to make long-term change.' There is a preoccupation among the new generation of 'entrepreneur philanthropists' with metrics on impact and value for money. Gatsby itself has increasingly taken care to collect data on outcomes, partly because it needs the data to persuade others to become involved, as well as wanting to ensure that its money is well spent. However, Hornby argues that there is a balance to be struck. She says:

> Other grant-makers will try to drive their wishes through an organisation by endless monitoring and forms. Our sense was always that it was a conversation. We were all aiming for the same thing, and wanted to have really open conversations

about how it was going. That was unique, and I still think is the right way to be. I would rather not include the cost of hiring someone to tick our boxes and count our beans. From my time at Gatsby, but also having received money, I have a sense of what is useful and what is pointless in grant management. And David has had a brilliant approach to risk.

The foundation itself, while not embracing the full panoply of public and media relations, is now much more accessible than it was in its early days. Since 2010 the official annual reports have reverted to their previous unvarnished appearance. However, at the same time Gatsby brought in designers to create a new logo – a running figure, inspired by the final sentence of *The Great Gatsby* – and a new website, launched in 2011.[5] The site is packed with information and images, giving access to reports on all the projects currently funded. In addition, attractively designed printed reviews appear at approximately two-yearly intervals. Gatsby Education even has a Twitter account (@GatsbyEd) – something unthinkable in the early days of the SFCT, even had Twitter existed at the time.

This shift to greater transparency is very much in tune with recent thinking in philanthropy. Cathy Pharoah, Visiting Professor of Philanthropy and co-director of the Centre for Charitable Giving and Philanthropy at the Cass Business School in London, is the initiator and author of *Foundation Giving Trends*, a publication reporting on the performance of the foundations sector that has appeared annually since 2009.[6] It is jointly published with the Charities Aid Foundation, and supported by the Pears Foundation. 'There was no data unless the sector collected it,' she says. 'I felt there was a great evidence gap. The concept of families giving back is not so strong here compared with the US. I was interested in using the report as a tool for raising awareness among donors: I thought the evidence on some wealthy families would encourage others.'

There is also a public interest in knowing how philanthropic money is spent, especially when it influences public policy. Pharoah says:

> Bigger foundations have more capacity to come in as equal funding partners with government in specific areas. They have more clout to try and change policy. The government have to understand that if they want people to give more, they have to acknowledge their contribution and make sure they use it well. I don't think government has worked this out yet. We should be benefiting from the successes and skills of our entrepreneurs. They have insight, knowledge and contacts, and using that for society is very important. It would be hard to say that government could spend that money better.

A new generation

It would be impossible to conclude an assessment of the philanthropic legacy of David and Susie Sainsbury without mentioning the commitment of their three daughters – Clare, Lucy and Francesca (known as Fran) – to their own charitable causes. All three have become philanthropists in their own right – by choice. 'It's never, ever felt like an external pressure or a sort of penitential "duty",' says Clare, the eldest.

This commitment developed through their childhood without any direct lecturing on either parent's part, or indeed much understanding of the detail of David and Susie's own philanthropic activities. It was more a sense of 'the right way to be in the world' that led all three to become active volunteers in their teens: Clare with the Terrence Higgins Trust, Fran with homelessness charities and Lucy with children with special needs.

Although their parents left it very much to them to decide when to set up their charities and for what purpose, there were trustees on hand to take care of the legal and financial aspects. As the eldest, Clare was the first to set up her trust. At the age of 20 she had been diagnosed with Asperger's syndrome and had subsequently volunteered in schools and playschemes for children with autistic spectrum conditions. She set up the Three Guineas Trust in 1996, choosing the title of a favourite book – Virginia Woolf's extended essay on war, women's education and women's employment – as her father had done. 'We've all picked causes that are significant to us personally,' says Clare. 'I started out with autism and Asperger's syndrome, because of my obvious first-hand experience, but also the second-hand experience of working in schools and playschemes.' Her plan was for Three Guineas eventually to focus on poverty and women's issues as well as autism.

Lucy, the Sainsburys' second daughter, had known for many years that she wanted to work with children with special needs. After graduating she spent some time in Kenya working in a home for AIDS orphans. She gradually became aware that it was effectively a children's hospice – many of the children were dying of HIV/AIDS. On returning, she trained as a teacher, moving into teaching children with complex needs before teaching in a children's hospice. In 2001, she set up the True Colours Trust – inspired by the lyrics of Cyndi Lauper's 1986 song, which spoke strongly to her belief that everyone deserves the chance to reach their true potential and that more opportunities need to be given to children with complex needs and disabilities to ensure this happens. The True Colours Trust was set up to support children with special needs and their families, and to support people with life-limiting and/or life-threatening illnesses, both in the UK and in Africa.

Fran, the youngest daughter, set up her charity in 1999 and called it the Indigo Trust. She didn't want a name that committed her to a particular area of work, and she had been reading Oliver Sacks's description of his search for the elusive colour indigo. 'For the first few years we funded projects in homelessness, literacy, women's empowerment,' she says. 'It was very unfocused, I had no strategy, and I got very frustrated and anxious about whether I was spending effectively.'

In 2008, Fran stopped making any new grants, and after intensive training with the Philanthropy Workshop she decided to focus her charity's efforts on technology-driven projects to bring about social change in sub-Saharan Africa, particularly in the areas of transparency, accountability and citizen empowerment. For her work with the charity she was named Philanthropist of the Year at the Spear's Wealth Management Awards in 2011.

All three of the Sainsbury daughters have in common with their father an interest in supporting 'complex, gritty issues' that may have difficulty attracting other funds. 'We [Three Guineas] do try to fund stuff that's "unfashionable",' says Clare. 'Appeals to build schools for children on the autistic spectrum tend to do fairly well, but it's a lot harder to get funding for projects working with adults with autism who have severely challenging behaviour.' Rather than waiting for grant applications, Three Guineas increasingly solicits them from selected providers, and offers services to grant recipients. For example, they have funded a professional consultant to mentor small parents' groups that are making the difficult transition to becoming more professional organisations.

Following the example of Gatsby, they look for projects where relatively small amounts of money can have a huge impact; that can potentially change the field; and ideally have the potentiality to become independent of Three Guineas. 'Where possible, we expect projects to include people with autistic-spectrum conditions in running them,' says Clare; 'the "nothing about us without us" disability rights principle.'

Changing political circumstances have influenced Clare and the trustees to move into the wider area of support for the rights of people with disabilities. This area of work emerged from examination of and support for projects helping disabled women who had experienced domestic violence, beginning with a substantial grant to Beverly Lewis House in East London – the only specialist refuge for women with learning disabilities in the UK.

'The devastation of the disability benefits system has had an especially severe impact on people with autistic-spectrum conditions and/or mental illnesses,' says Clare. 'So in the last few years we've been funding services providing legal support to people trying to get their benefits reinstated at tribunals, work with the Disability Benefits Consortium, and so on. It's not autism-specific, but it's relevant and necessary work.'

With True Colours, Lucy has taken a strategic approach to effecting long-term, systemic change. For example, in 2014 the World Health Assembly for the first time passed a resolution urging member states to recognise palliative care as a component of comprehensive care throughout life. True Colours has provided long-term funding both to the International Children's Palliative Care network and to the African Palliative Care Association, both of which had lobbied energetically for this recognition. Working with national governments in Africa, the charity has helped to integrate palliative care services into the public health system throughout Malawi, and piloted the introduction of morphine for pain relief into hospices in Zambia.

The charity also made a ten-year commitment to the multi-agency Every Disabled Child Matters campaign in the UK, which led to changes in policy and funding of services across the country. Following many conversations about what the charity could most fruitfully do to change the profile of paediatric palliative care in the UK, True Colours funded the first professorship in children's palliative care, at Great Ormond Street Hospital and University College London. This has helped to ensure that there is a single voice for the sector and a focus for research.

The True Colours trustees recognise that policy change takes time. Its small grants programmes are designed to meet the immediate needs of children and families, such as buying accessible minibuses, building hydrotherapy pools, equipping multi-sensory rooms and supporting work with siblings. 'Small sums of money in the right pair of hands can achieve a great deal,' says Lucy, 'and local people are often best placed, and best qualified, to solve local problems.' A third strand of support, for medium-term funding to organisations with complementary aims, has provided financial certainty to creative arts organisations working with people with learning disabilities, such as Oily Cart and Heart'n Soul.

Fran, meanwhile, has made what she calls 'the journey from privacy to advocacy', becoming a champion of transparency in philanthropic giving. As she became more expert in open data through her work for Indigo, she was impressed with the work of the International Aid Transparency Initiative, in which donor governments publish their spending down to project level so that they can coordinate their activities. The Indigo Trust funded some data scientists to develop an open data standard for philanthropy, and she began to spend her time persuading other grant-makers to publish their grants. In 2015, she founded the charity 360Giving to promote the standard and offer an online tool that allows anyone to find out exactly what grant-giving bodies have funded previously, without having to wait a year or more for the annual report to appear.[7]

Within a year, twenty-seven charities (including the Big Lottery Fund, Comic Relief, the Esmée Fairbairn Foundation and Gatsby) had adopted the standard and published details of almost 200,000 grants; more are in the pipeline. 'The real benefits are to charities who need to research donors,' says Fran. 'It stops them applying for things that will get turned down.'

The fact that the three Sainsbury sisters' trusts are all run from the SFCT offices does not detract at all from their passionate independence as donors. They very much appreciate the model – unique in the world, it seems – of a common family office for seventeen very different charities. 'On a concrete, practical level, the way the SFCT can pool resources is very helpful,' says Clare. 'Three Guineas shares the time of a staff person with a couple of the other family trusts.' Fran agrees that the fifth generation in particular are more likely to discuss issues such as ethical investment. 'The nice thing about the wider trusts', she adds, 'is that there's no inter-family lobbying. The only thing that's funded collectively is the Sainsbury Archive' – the collection of photographs and documents on the history of the Sainsbury's retail empire held at the Museum of London Docklands. 'It's also been nice to feel that my sisters and I have been going through the process of building our trusts at the same time,' says Clare. 'We're all in the same boat.'

'We've always known that Gatsby is Dad's,' says Fran, 'and we don't have to inherit that responsibility.' But the sisters are happy to accept that their work is part of the legacy of what Gatsby has achieved, and will achieve. 'With a lot of family trusts the children take over, and that's very much what he *didn't* want,' says Lucy. 'But there is a family legacy: the excitement about philanthropy, getting involved in something that you care about and making a difference, rather than to carry on what he was doing. What the three of us are doing is very different, but the ethos and principles behind it are very similar.' Clare agrees. 'I think Dad's also been a wonderful role model for philanthropy as a creative activity,' she says. 'It's not "charity" in the sense of patronisingly handing out coins to the needy. It's complicated and interesting and rewarding work which is trying to change the world for the better.'

The political and the personal

David Sainsbury is a firm believer in the welfare state, as an organisation that has the right mechanisms for delivering health, education and social care. 'I want these things to be thought of as rights, not individual bounty from someone,' he says. The role of philanthropy, in his view, is to do those things that government is not good at. 'Philanthropy should focus on new ideas, new innovations: the projects that government finds difficult to do *because* they are innovative. Going into government reinforced my view that government is very bad at innovation, partly because it has to admit it is not doing everything perfectly now.'

The other major obstacle to innovation is an extreme reluctance to embrace financial risk. 'The Treasury would say, "What proof can you give that this is good use of public money?" The point about innovation is that you have no proof.' The whole basis of the philosophy that underlies the way Gatsby works is that this is where private money can help. 'Quite a lot of the Gatsby projects are constructed on the basis that if they work they are something that government can pick up, but are best developed outside government,' he says. 'There will always be gaps in the welfare state or new things that need to be done. So, however perfect government might be – and I don't think this is a very big danger – there would still be a role for philanthropy.'

As a former minister, Sainsbury is uniquely well placed to judge where those gaps are, and how to balance political and personal intervention to effect change. He says:

> I have always thought of philanthropy and politics as parallel tracks in my life, which are about the same thing: how do you create a better society? The best thing about political life is that you can achieve change on a scale that you can never reach as a private individual – though it can be hard work and very frustrating. The advantage of philanthropy is that you don't have to argue through ten committees – you can just say, 'I think this is a good idea,' back your judgement and do it.

It is a high-risk strategy, but that, to some extent, is the point. He continues:

You can choose to do something in circumstances where there is no conceivable way you can prove that this is a good thing. We took on plant science in the 1980s, for instance, thinking disease resistance in plants was an interesting and important subject. I could just say, 'Let's do it,' in a way that even our good research councils found it difficult to do.

This belief in risk-taking underpins the decision Sainsbury took to arrange for Gatsby to wind down after his death. 'If you become a long-term foundation, beyond the lifetime of the funder, then you tend to lose that quality,' he says. 'The trustees are looking at preserving your reputation. Other charities can do it a different way, but you should understand that your charity will cease to do the kind of risk-taking that you can do when the funder is the person running it.'

The idea that the founding settlor's commitment, drive and passion is fundamental to a foundation's effectiveness is also illustrated in the way the Sainsbury family has organised its charitable activities: not as a single family foundation, as many other wealthy families have done, but as up to eighteen separate foundations (now down to seventeen) sharing a common office. 'It wasn't very carefully thought through,' says Sainsbury, 'but that's where we got to. The very important lesson is that everyone has their own personal agenda of things they would like to change in society and what they would like to do, and that applies as much to your children as to brothers in a business. Letting them set up their own charities, even if small-scale, is much better than those poor kids that you see being dragged into their parents' charities.'

The proof that this approach works lies in the amount of time and energy that every member of the family has committed to their philanthropic activity. Sainsbury says:

This is a beautiful thing that gives me enormous pleasure. It goes back to my parents: all the things they did they cared passionately about and got hugely involved in. I've always been hugely involved in Gatsby. Susie's just come to the end of her time as deputy chairman of RSC, she's done it for twenty-three years, and she's been passionately involved in everything. And then my daughters are also involved in the same way in their projects, which is lovely.

A reckoning

The fiftieth anniversary of Gatsby's foundation in 1967 seems a suitable opportunity to review its activities and evaluate its success, which is what this book has set out to do. However, there is no sense in which 2017 marks an end point. At the time of writing major projects are in full swing in all the foundation's areas of interest.

David Sainsbury is pleased to have been reminded about some of his early ventures in the medical field, such as his support for the Liverpool School of Tropical Medicine: it had not been obvious to him at the time how influential Rex Fendall and his colleagues had been in the field of primary health care in the developing world. The work on mental health achieved a great deal in developing models for the care and welfare of people with severe mental illness in the community. Ultimately it will be up to the NHS and local authorities to implement such models and fund them adequately.

Sainsbury is particularly satisfied with the outcome of his decision to support plant science. He says:

What the TSL has achieved in taking forward that whole agenda on disease resistance is amazing. One of the few things I believe very strongly is that in a hundred years' time people will say, 'At the beginning of the twenty-first century there was a revolution that transformed agriculture in the world, because for the first time we were able to genetically engineer plants to increase their productivity.' It's taken thirty years, but TSL has been able to achieve it.

The neuroscience research programme has been in place for barely ten years, but he has equally high hopes that the same approach – hiring some of the world's brightest scientists and giving them the freedom to follow their hunches – will have an equally successful outcome.

Many of the projects initiated during the initial twenty-five years of the science and technology education programme have been incorporated into initiatives now led by other bodies and funded from a variety of sources, including the Department for Education. Reform of technician training, a goal that has eluded countless well-intentioned educationists and others over decades, at the close of 2016 seemed finally to be within reach.

The Africa programme has transformed the lives of thousands of smallholders and small-scale entrepreneurs: its current sector development and technology transfer projects have the potential to make that millions, although in such a challenging environment success is not guaranteed. Gatsby Africa has, however, developed an unparalleled body of experience in working in sub-Saharan Africa, and a network of influential individuals in the countries concerned, that makes it a sought-after partner for any other donor organisation seeking to set up projects.

Among the social and economic projects Gatsby has funded, the Centre for Cities and Institute for Government (IfG) have already established themselves as authoritative voices, speaking out in public through the media and directly through advocacy and consultancy, in changing thinking in local and national government. 'The IfG is doing good stuff after seven or eight years,' says Sainsbury. 'Whether they will make a real change, we won't know for twenty to twenty-five years.' And in the arts, he is immensely proud to have been involved in funding the transformation of the Royal Shakespeare Theatre. 'The creation of a wonderful theatrical space dedicated to the work of one of the world's greatest playwrights, which is what Susie helped to achieve, has given me enormous pleasure,' he says.

Looking back, Sainsbury attributes much of the success of Gatsby to the 'incredibly smart' people who have worked for the foundation. In particular, he attributes the success of Gatsby's science projects to the extraordinary scientific insight of Roger Freedman, and the way he has carefully managed the major projects over thirty years. But in all the areas there have been outstanding individuals who have taken 'often half-formed ideas and aspirations' and turned them into effective projects.

'If there are lessons to be learned, they are these,' he says. 'First, fund only projects you care enough about to put in the necessary thought and effort to make them work. Secondly, be realistic about timeframes and costs. It's neither clever nor commercial to set unrealistic targets. And thirdly, if you are going to fund large, transformative projects, make certain you have smart and creative people to help you.'

NOTES

Preface

1. Pharoah, C., Jenkins, R., and Goddard, K. (2016), *Giving Trends Top 300 Foundation Grant Makers 2015*, report, Centre for Giving and Philanthropy/Charities Aid Foundation, www.acf.org.uk/downloads/publications/Foundation_Giving_Trends_2015.pdf, accessed 28 June 2016.

1 A time of gifts

1. Acts of the Apostles, 20:35.
2. *Spectrum Market Insights Report 2015*.
3. Ferreira, F. H. G., et al. (2014), *A Global Count of the Extreme Poor in 2012: Data Issues, Methodology and Initial Results*, World Bank Policy Research Working Paper 7432.
4. www.oxfam.org/en/research/economy-99
5. *Giving USA 2016: The Annual Report on Philanthropy for the Year 2015*, Giving USA Foundation.
6. *Million Dollar Donors Report 2015*, Coutts, http://philanthropy.coutts.com, accessed 1 July 2016.
7. Pharoah, C., Jenkins, R., and Goddard, K. (2016), *Giving Trends Top 300 Foundation Grant Makers 2015 Report*, Centre for Giving and Philanthropy/Charities Aid Foundation, www.acf.org.uk/downloads/publications/Foundation_Giving_Trends_2015.pdf, accessed 28 June 2016.
8. See note 5.
9. *UK Giving 2014* (2015), Charities Aid Foundation.
10. http://givingpledge.org

11. Piff, P., Kraus, M. W., Coté, S., Cheng, B. H., and Keltner, D. (2010), 'Having less, giving more: the influence of social class on prosocial behavior', *Journal of Personality and Social Psychology*, 99, 771–784.

12. www.carnegie.org

13. www.facebook.com/chanzuckerberginitiative/

14. National Center for Charitable Statistics, http://nccsweb.urban.org/PubApps/profile1.php?state=US, accessed 28 June 2016.

15. Foundation Center, http://foundationcenter.org/findfunders/topfunders/top100giving.html, accessed 28 June 2016.

16. See note 7.

17. Ibid.

18. For example, see Bishop, M., and Green, M. (2008), *Philanthrocapitalism: How the Rich Can Save the World*, Bloomsbury.

19. Singer, P. (2009), *The Life You Can Save*, Random House; Singer, P. (2015), *The Most Good You Can Do*, Yale University Press.

20. MacAskill, W. (2015), *Doing Good Better*, Guardian Faber.

21. Sargeant, A., and Shang, J. (2012), *Risk and Philanthropy*, report to the Resource Alliance/Rockefeller Foundation.

22. See note 7.

2 Family business

1. Williams, B. (1994), *The Best Butter in the World: A History of Sainsbury's*, Ebury Press.

2. Fendall, N. R. E. (1972), 'Auxiliaries and primary medical care', *Bulletin of the NY Academy of Medicine*, 48, 1291–1300.

3. Fendall, N. R. E. (1978), 'Declaration of Alma-Ata', *Lancet*, 16 December, 1308.

4. World Health Report 1998, WHO, www.who.int/whr/1998/media_centre/executive_summary6/en, accessed 17 March 2016.

5. www.sfct.org.uk/the-trusts/

6. ITDG Annual Report 1974–1975, Intermediate Technology Development Group.

7. Davis, J. (1978), *Technology for a Changing World*, Intermediate Technology Publications Ltd.

8. ITDG Annual Report 1975–1976, Intermediate Technology Development Group.

9. Davis, J., and Bollard, A. (1986), *As Though People Mattered: A Prospect for Britain*, Intermediate Technology Publications Ltd.

10. Ibid.

11. URBED (1980), *Local Economic Development: A Guide to US Experience,* URBED.
12. http://urbed.coop

3 Balm of hurt minds
1. Mental Health Research in the UK: MQ Landscape Analysis 2015. https://wellcometrust.files.wordpress.com/2015/04/mq2.png, accessed 5 July 2016.
2. Powell, E. (1961), quoted on www.slam.nhs.uk/about-us/art-and-history/our-history/1900–2000, accessed 19 April 2016.
3. National Institute for Mental Health in England (2003), *Cases for Change: Policy context*, NIMHE.
4. Bouras, N., Tufnell, G., Brough, D. I., and Watson, J. P. (1986), 'Model for the integration of community psychiatry and primary care', *Journal of the Royal College of General Practitioners*, February, 62–66.
5. Craig, T. K. J., Bayliss, E., et al. (1995), *The Homeless Mentally Ill Initiative: An Evaluation of Four Clinical Teams*, London: Department of Health.
6. Muijen, M. (1992), 'Research and Development for Psychiatry (RDP): the role of an Independent Evaluation Unit', *Journal of Mental Health*, 1, 85–89.
7. Minghella, E., Ford, R., Freeman, T., Hoult, J., McGlynn, P., and O'Halloran, P. (1998), *Open All Hours: 24-hour Response for People with Mental Health Emergencies*, SCMH.
8. SMCH (1988), Report to the Gatsby Trustees (internal document).
9. Muijen, M., and Hadley, T. (1995), 'The initiatives war', *Health Service Journal*, 9 March, 24–26.
10. SCMH (1998), *Keys to Engagement: Review of Care for People with Severe Mental Illness who are Hard to Engage with Services*.
11. SCMH (2001), *The Capable Practitioner: A Framework and List of the Practitioner Capabilities Required to Implement the National Service Framework for Mental Health*.
12. SCMH (2002), *Breaking the Circles of Fear: A review of the relationship between mental health services and African and Caribbean communities*.
13. Ibid.
14. SCMH (2009), *Briefing 37: Doing What Works: Individual Placement and Support into Employment*.
15. Durcan, G. (2008), *From the Inside: Experiences of Prison Mental Health Care*. SCMH.

16. SCMH (2009), *Diversion: A Better Way for Criminal Justice and Mental Health*.
17. Bradley, K. (2009), *The Bradley Report*, Central Office of Information for the Department of Health/NHS England.
18. www.mentalhealthalliance.org.uk
19. Khan, L., Parsonage, M., and Stubbs, J. (2015), *Investing in Children's Mental Health: A Review of the Costs and Benefits of Increased Service Provisio*n, Centre for Mental Health.
20. Department of Health (2015), *Future in Mind: Promoting, Protecting and Improving our Children and Young People's Mental Health and Wellbeing*.
21. Mental Health Policy Group (2015), *Improving England's Mental Health: The First 100 Days and Beyond*.
22. www.centreformentalhealth.org.uk/News/spending-review-2015. Accessed 3 May 2016.
23. http://mentalhealthintegration.com. Accessed 27 April 2016.
24. Parsonage, M., Grant, C., and Stubbs, J. (2016), *Priorities for Mental Health: Economic Report for the NHS England Mental Health Taskforce*, Centre for Mental Health.
25. www.schoolhomesupport.org.uk
26. Berridge, D., Dobel-Ober, D., Harker, R., and Sinclair, R. (2004), *Taking Care of Education: An Evaluation of the Education of Looked After Children*, National Children's Bureau.
27. www.ican.org.uk
28. http://acecentre.org.uk
29. www.bigwidetalk.org
30. Rose, D. (2001), *Users' Voices: The Perspective of Mental Health Service Users on Community and Hospital Care*, Sainsbury Centre for Mental Health.

4 Growing Africa

1. www.oecd.org/dac/stats/final-oda-2014.htm
2. http://povertydata.worldbank.org/poverty/home
3. *MDG Report 2015: Assessing Progress in Africa Toward the Millennium Development Goals*, Economic Commission for Africa. See www.undp. org/content/undp/en/home/librarypage/mdg/mdg-reports/africa-collection.html, accessed 15 August 2016.
4. For example, see Sharples, N., Jones, T., and Martin, C. (2014), *Honest Accounts? The True Story of Africa's Billion Dollar Losses*, Health Poverty Action and other NGOs; McGoey, L. (2015), *No Such Thing as a Free Gift: The Gates Foundation and the Price of Philanthropy*, Verso.

5. Cockcroft, L. (1989), *Africa's Way: A Journey from the Past*, I. B. Tauris.
6. Fischler, M. (2010), *Impact Assessment of Push-Pull Technology Developed and Promoted by* icipe *and Partners in Eastern Africa*, icipe Science Press, www.push-pull.net/Impact_Assessment.pdf, accessed 4 July 2016.
7. Pretty, J. (2009), *Reaping the Benefits: Science and the Sustainable Intensification of Global Agriculture*, Royal Society.
8. Gatsby Charitable Trust (2000), *Building from the Base: The Work of the African Gatsby Trusts*, Gatsby Occasional Paper.
9. www.farmafrica.org/enterprise-fund/enterprise-fund
10. Pinto Y., Poulton, C., Frankenberger, T., and Ajayi, O. (2014), *African Agriculture: Drivers of Success for CAADP Implementation*, African Union, www.firetail.co.uk/reports/Drivers%20of%20Success%20Synthesis%20 Report.pdf, accessed 17 August 2016.
11. African Union (2014), *Decisions, Declarations and Resolution*, Assembly of the Union 23rd Ordinary Session, 26–27 June, Malabo, Equatorial Guinea, au.int/en/sites/default/files/decisions/9661-assembly_au_dec_517_- _545_xxiii_e.pdf, accessed 17 August 2016.
12. http://saili.org.za/website, accessed 17 August 2016.
13. www.sainsbury.org.za, accessed 17 August 2016.
14. DFID (2008), *Growth: Building Jobs and Prosperity in Developing Countries*.
15. www.tdu.or.tz
16. http://fch.cl/en
17. Booth, D., Cooksey, B., Golooba-Mutebi, F., and Kanyinga, K. (2014), *East African Prospects: An Update on the Political Economy of Kenya, Rwanda, Tanzania and Uganda*, Overseas Development Institute.

5 The power of plants

1. UK Plant Sciences Federation (2014), *UK Plant Science: Current Status and Future Challenges*, January, www.rsb.org.uk/images/pdf/UK_Plant_ Science-Current_status_and_future_challenges.pdf, accessed 25 May 2016.
2. Society of Biology (2014), *UK Plant Science: Current Status and Future Challenges*.
3. Hourihan, M., and Parkes, D. (2016), 'Federal R&D in the FY 2016 budget: an overview', American Association for the Advancement of Science, www.aaas.org/fy16budget/federal-rd-fy-2016-budget-overview, accessed 7 July 2016.

4. Haverkort, A. J., et al. (2008), 'Societal costs of late blight in potato and prospects of durable resistance through cisgenic modification', *Potato Research* 51, 47–57.

5. Baulcombe, D. (2004), 'RNA silencing in plants', *Nature* 431, 356–363.

6. www.scientificamerican.com/slideshow/10-nobel-snubs, accessed 20 May 2016.

7. www.tsl.ac.uk/news/jic-tsl-top-plant-animal-science, accessed 25 May 2016.

8. Jones, J. D. G., et al. (2014), 'Elevating crop disease resistance with cloned genes', *Philosophical Transactions of the Royal Society* series B, 369, 20130087, DOI: 10.1098/rstb.2013.0087, published 17 February.

9. www.geneticliteracyproject.org/2016/01/14/fda-approves-gmo-potato-resists-blight-caused-irish-potato-famine, accessed 25 May 2016.

10. Witek, K., Jupe, F., Witek, A. I., Baker, D., Clark, M. D., and Jones, J. D. G. (2016), 'Accelerated cloning of a potato late blight-resistance gene using RenSeq and SMRT sequencing', *Nature Biotechnology*, DOI: 10.1038/nbt.3540, published 25 April.

11. Lacombe, S., et al. (2010), 'Interfamily transfer of a plant pattern-recognition receptor confers broad-spectrum bacterial resistance', *Nature Biotechnology* 28, 365–369.

12. For example, see www.theguardian.com/environment/2014/jul/21/genome-editing-crops-restricted-eu-rules-scientists-warn, accessed 26 May 2016

13. www.bbc.co.uk/news/world-38330452

14. Flavell, R. (1989), 'Plant biotechnology and its application to agriculture', *Philosophical Transactions of the Royal Society of London*, series B, *Biological Sciences*, 324(1224), 525–535.

15. Kawashima, C. G., et al. (2016), 'A pigeonpea gene confers resistance to Asian soybean rust in soybean', *Nature Biotechnology*, DOI: 10.1038/nbt.3554.

16. Yang, W. et al. (2016), 'Regulation of meristem morphogenesis by cell wall synthases in *Arabidopsis*', *Current Biology* 26, 1–12.

17. Bennett, T., et al. (2016), 'Connective auxin transport in the shoot facilitates communication between shoot apices', *PLOS Biology*, http://dx.doi.org/10.1371/journal.pbio.1002446.

18. www.saps.org.uk

19. Saunders, D., et al. (2014), 'Crowdsourced analysis of ash and ash dieback through the Open Ash Dieback project: a year 1 report on datasets and analyses contributed by a self-organising community',

bioRxiv preprint, first posted online 25 April 2014; DOI: http://dx.doi.org/10.1101/004564.

20. Rallapalli, G., et al. (2015), 'Cutting edge: lessons from Fraxinus, a crowd-sourced citizen science game in genomics', *eLife* 2015;4:e07460, accessed 26 May 2016.

6 Skills for the twenty-first century

1. Barnett, C. (1986), *The Audit of War: The Illusion and Reality of Britain as a Great Nation*, Macmillan.
2. Finniston, M. (1980), *Engineering Our Future*, summary of the Report of the Finniston Committee of Enquiry into the Engineering Professions, HMSO.
3. www.etrust.org.uk
4. www.data.org.uk
5. www.mindsetonline.co.uk
6. Smithers, A., and Robinson, P. (2005), *Physics in Schools IV: Supply and Retention of Teachers*, Carmichael Press.
7. https://getintoteaching.education.gov.uk/explore-my-options/teacher-training-routes/subject-knowledge-enhancement-ske-courses
8. Prais, S. J. (1996), 'Reform of mathematical education in primary schools: the experiment in Barking and Dagenham', *National Institute Economic Review*, 157, 3–8.
9. Muijs, D., and Reynolds, D. (2000), 'Mathematics: some preliminary findings from the evaluation of the Mathematics Enhancement Programme (Primary)', *School Effectiveness and School Improvement*, 11, 273–303.
10. Department for Education (2011), *The National Strategies 1997–2011*.
11. Mullis, I. V. S., Martin, M. O., Foy, P., and Hooper, M. (2016), *TIMSS 2015 International Results in Mathematics*, Chestnut Hill, MA: TIMSS & PIRLS International Study Center, Boston College.
12. www.teep.org.uk
13. *TEEP Impact Report 2016*, Schools, Students and Teachers Network (SSAT).
14. *STEM Programme Report* (2006), DTI/DfES.
15. www.stem.org.uk
16. *Overseeing Financial Sustainability in the Further Education Sector* (2015), House of Commons Committee of Public Accounts, www.publications.parliament.uk/pa/cm201516/cmselect/cmpubacc/414/414.pdf

17. New Economy (2015), *Mapping of Engineering and Manufacturing Training Facilities in Greater Manchester*, neweconomymanchester.com/media/ 1457/mapping_of_engineering_and_manufacturing_training_facilities_ in_greater_manchester_final.pdf
18. www.utcolleges.org
19. SCORE (2015), *Changes to the Assessment of A-levels in the Sciences: What Do They Mean for Higher Education Admissions?*, May.
20. Sainsbury, D. (2016), *Report of the Independent Panel on Technical Education*, Department for Business, Innovation and Skills.
21. *Post-16 Skills Plan* (2016), Department for Business, Innovation and Skills/Department for Education, July.
22. Holman, J. (2013), *Good Career Guidance*, Gatsby Charitable Foundation.
23. www.compass-careers.org.uk
24. http://furthermaths.org.uk

7 A new agenda

1. Sainsbury, D. (1981), *Government and Industry: A New Partnership*, Fabian Society.
2. Sainsbury, D. (2013), *Progressive Capitalism: How to Achieve Economic Growth, Liberty and Social Justice*, Biteback.
3. Giles, J. (2006), 'Sainsbury: Labour's lab lord', *Nature*, 19 July, www. nature.com/news/2006/060717/full/news060717-12.html
4. *Competing in the Global Economy: The Innovation Challenge* (2003), DTI, HMSO.
5. Lord Sainsbury of Turville (2007), *The Race to the Top*, HMSO, 55.
6. *UK Research and the European Union: The Role of the EU in Funding UK Research* (2015), Royal Society.
7. House of Lords Select Committee on Science and Technology (2000), *Science and Society: Science and Technology Third Report*, HMSO.
8. www.sciencemediacentre.org
9. 'UK science minister quits', *Nature*, www.nature.com/news/2006/ 061110/full/news061106-20.html
10. 'UK Science minister resigns', *Science*, www.sciencemag.org/ news/2006/11/uk-science-minister-resigns
11. www.nature.com/news/ we-are-still-saving-british-science-from-margaret-thatcher-1.12800
12. Lord Sainsbury of Turville (2007), *The Race to the Top*, HMSO.
13. For example, *Competing in the Global Economy: The Innovation Challenge* (2003), DTI, HMSO.

14. http://carnegiemedals.org/medalists/
15. *Annual Report and Accounts 2006*, Gatsby Charitable Foundation.
16. www.sfct.org.uk/the-trusts

8 Between brain and mind

1. Knapp, A. (2012), 'How much does it cost to find a Higgs boson?', *Forbes*, 5 July. www.forbes.com/sites/alexknapp/2012/07/05/how-much-does-it-cost-to-find-a-higgs-boson/#6a3be8f764f0 Accessed 12 July 2016.
2. Mead, C. (1990), 'Neuromorphic electronic systems', *Proceedings of the IEEE*, 78, 1629–1636.
3. Rumelhart, D., Hinton G., and Williams, R. (1986), 'Learning representations by back-propagating errors', *Nature* 323, 533–536.
4. Hinton, G. E., Osindero, S., and Teh, Y. (2006), 'A fast learning algorithm for deep belief nets', *Neural Computation*, 18, 1527–1554.
5. For a list of the GCNU's many publications, see www.gatsby.ucl.ac.uk/publications
6. www.theguardian.com/technology/2014/jan/27/google-acquires-uk-artificial-intelligence-startup-deepmind, accessed 18 July 2016.
7. http://cbs.fas.harvard.edu/science/connectome-project, accessed 19 July 2016.
8. http://eyewire.org, accessed 19 July 2016.
9. http://wireddifferently.org, accessed 19 July 2016.
10. Isaacson, J. S., and Scanziani, M. (2011), 'How inhibition shapes cortical activity', *Neuron* 72, 231–243.
11. Dayan, P., and Abbott, L. F. (2001), *Theoretical Neuroscience: Computational and Mathematical Modeling of Neural Systems*, MIT Press.
12. Ferry, G. (2017), *Neural Architects: The Sainsbury Wellcome Centre from Idea to Reality*, Unicorn Publishing.
13. Bullmore, E., Fletcher, P., and Jones, P. B. (2009), 'Why psychiatry can't afford to be Neurophobic', *British Journal of Psychiatry* 194, 293–295.
14. www.rcpsych.ac.uk/usefulresources/rcpsychenewsletters/enewsletters2016/march2016/invitation-lecture.aspx

9 What works

1. www.bsa.natcen.ac.uk
2. Magaziner, I. C., and Hout, T. (1980), *Japanese Industrial Policy: A Descriptive Account of Postwar Developments with Case Studies of Selected Industries*, Policy Studies Institute.

3. Kay, J. A. (1993), *Foundations of Corporate Success: How Business Strategies Add Value*, Oxford University Press.
4. www.sciencecampaign.org.uk
5. www.parliament.uk/post
6. www.senseaboutscience.org
7. Wood, A. (2001), *Magnetic Venture: The Story of Oxford Instruments*, Oxford University Press.
8. Wicksteed, B., and Herriot, W. (2000), *Six United Kingdom Case Studies in Technology Transfer*, SQW.
9. www.hefce.ac.uk/kess/heif
10. Wicksteed, B. (2010), *Experience from 16 Years of Support to Knowledge and Technology Transfer and Exchange Projects by the Gatsby Charitable Foundation*, Gatsby.
11. www.ifm.eng.cam.ac.uk/services/overview
12. *Making the Right Things in the Right Places* (2007), Institute for Manufacturing, University of Cambridge.
13. www.praxisunico.org.uk
14. Wicksteed, B. (2010), *Experience from 16 Years of Support to Knowledge and Technology Transfer and Exchange Projects by the Gatsby Charitable Foundation*, Gatsby.
15. www.theguardian.com/business/2016/jan/25/north-heads-list-of-low-wage-high-welfare-cities
16. www.centreforcities.org/data-tool
17. www.instituteforgovernment.org.uk/publications/whitehall-monitor-2017
18. www.behaviouralinsights.co.uk
19. www.ifm.eng.cam.ac.uk/research/csti/
20. www.manufacturing.gov

10 For art's sake

1. Winner, C. (2016), 'Alberto Giacometti and Robert and Lisa Sainsbury', in *Alberto Giacometti: A Line Through Time*, Bloomsbury, 95–103.
2. Hooper, S. (1997), Introduction, in Hooper, S., and Austin, J. (eds), *The Robert and Lisa Sainsbury Collection*, Yale University Press.
3. Ibid.
4. Rybczynski, W. (2011), *The Biography of a Building*, Thames & Hudson; Gatsby Charitable Foundation annual reports.
5. Hooper, S., and Austin, J. (eds) (1997), *The Robert and Lisa Sainsbury Collection*, Yale University Press.

6. Ibid.
7. Hooper, S. (2006), *Pacific Encounters: Art and Divinity in Polynesia 1760–1860*, British Museum Press.
8. Collins, I. (ed.) (2013), *Masterpieces: Art and East Anglia*, Sainsbury Centre for Visual Arts.
9. Ward, D. (2011), *Transformation: Shakespeare's New Theatre*, RSC Enterprise Ltd.
10. www.coeurope.org/the-orchestra/about-us/the-coe-story
11. www.1418now.org.uk/commissions/poppies/
12. Wullschlager, J. (2015), 'Francis Bacon: at home with history', *Financial Times*, 24 April.
13. Jones, J. (2015), 'A cruel exposure of a con artist', *The Guardian*, 14 April 2015.
14. Milburn, C., and Winner, C. (2016), *Alberto Giacometti: A Line Through Time*, Bloomsbury.

11 Doing good, giving better

1. www.publications.parliament.uk/pa/jt200304/jtselect/jtchar/167/167.pdf
2. www.thirdsector.co.uk/spend-out-trusts-meet-goals-effectively-says-charity/fundraising/article/1106202
3. Breeze, B., and Lloyd, T. (2013), *Richer Lives: Why Rich People Give*, Directory of Social Change.
4. www.philanthropy-impact.org
5. www.gatsby.org.uk
6. www.acf.org.uk/policy-practice/research-publications/foundation-giving-trends-2016
7. www.threesixtygiving.org

ACKNOWLEDGEMENTS

It has been a privilege to work on this book. My thanks go first to the trustees, staff, advisors and beneficiaries of Gatsby who have been so generous with their time in giving me interviews and reviewing drafts. They are all named in the text. In particular I should like to thank present and former Gatsby trustees Judith Portrait, Christopher Stone, Andrew Cahn and Joe Burns who read the entire text, as did former director of the Sainsbury Family Charitable Trusts Michael Pattison. Gary Wilson and Jessica Roberts at Gatsby have provided invaluable assistance, Gary chasing down images and Jessica smoothing my way to interviews.

Others who gave constructive comments on whole chapters or sections include Matt Muijen, Andrew McCulloch, Andy Bell, Thomas Jamieson-Craig, Matthew Williams, Laurence Cockcroft, Justin Highstead, David McNicoll, Roger Freedman, Jonathan Jones, Ottoline Leyser, Nigel Thomas, Sarah Caddick, Peter Dayan, Alexandra Jones, Susan Hitch, David Halpern, Peter Riddell, Steven Hooper, Alan Bookbinder and Susie Sainsbury.

I have been very fortunate in my agent, Felicity Bryan, who was hugely supportive, and in the publishing team at Profile, particularly Andrew Franklin, Paul Forty and copyeditor Nikky Twyman, whose professionalism has made this a better book.

Finally, I am truly grateful to David Sainsbury for realising that there was a story to tell about the growth and development of his charitable foundation, and for commissioning me to tell it. He has taken a close interest throughout the project, read numerous drafts, and made time for a fruitful series of discussions about his personal approach to philanthropy. His high seriousness, sense of purpose and willingness to take risks, exercised with the utmost modesty and discretion, are an example to philanthropists everywhere.

Georgina Ferry
May 2017

ABBREVIATIONS

Acronyms and abbreviations do not aid readability, and I apologise that this book contains so many. It is a fact of life that the areas of life with which Gatsby has been most concerned, including science, health care, education, public policy and charities, have been particularly productive in generating such terms.

AAC	African Agricultural Capital
AACF	African Agricultural Capital Fund
ACDMM	Advanced Course in Design, Manufacture and Management
ACME	Advisory Council on Mathematics Education
ACPMM	Advanced Course in Production Methods and Management
AFRC	Agricultural and Food Research Council
AGRA	Alliance for a Green Revolution in Africa
AHRC	Arts and Humanities Research Council
AI	artificial intelligence
AIDS	acquired immunodeficiency syndrome
ALINe	Agricultural Learning and Impacts Network
ANC	African National Congress
ASE	Association for Science Education
AT-UK	Alternative Technology in the UK
BBSRC	Biotechnology and Biosciences Research Council

BEIS	Department for Business, Energy and Industrial Strategy
BEST	Better Engineering, Science, Technology
BIS	Department for Business, Innovation and Skills
CERN	European Organisation for Nuclear Research
CGF	Cameroon Gatsby Foundation
CMIL	Cambridge Manufacturing Industry Links
COE	Chamber Orchestra of Europe
CSci	Chartered Scientist
CSTI	Centre for Science, Technology and Innovation Policy
DANIDA	Danish International Development Agency
DATA	Design and Technology Association
DfE	Department for Education
DfES	Department for Education and Science
DFID	Department for International Development
DTI	Department of Trade and Industry
EATI	East African Tea Investments
EES	Engineering Education Scheme
EFR	elongation factor Tu receptor
EF-Tu	elongation factor Tu
EngTech	Engineering Technician
ERC	European Research Council
FDT	Forestry Development Trust (Tanzania)
GCNU	Gatsby Computational Neuroscience Unit
GM	genetically modified
GMFL	Gatsby Microfinance Ltd
GTEP	Gatsby Technical Education Projects
HEFCE	Higher Education Funding Council for England
HEIF	Higher Education Innovation Fund
HHMI	Howard Hughes Medical Institute
HIV	human immunodeficiency virus
HLS	Huntingdon Life Sciences
HON&V	Herbert Oppenheimer, Nathan & Vandyk (law firm)

HS2	High Speed Two (train)
ICFC	Industrial and Commercial Finance Corporation (later 3i)
icipe	International Centre of Insect Physiology and Ecology (Kenya)
ICN	Institute for Cognitive Neuroscience
IfG	Institute for Government
IfM	Institute for Manufacturing
IfM ECS	IfM Education and Consultancy Services Ltd
IFS	Institute for Fiscal Studies
IITA	International Institute of Tropical Agriculture (Nigeria)
ILU	Industry Links Unit
INIBAP	International Network for Improvement of Banana and Plantain
IPPR	Institute for Public Policy Research
ITDG	Intermediate Technology Development Group
JIC	John Innes Centre
JII	John Innes Institute
KGT	Kenya Gatsby Trust
KMT	Kenya Markets Trust
LBS	London Business School
LEAF	Leading European Architects Forum
LEP	Local Enterprise Partnership
LET	Local Enterprise Trust
LSS	Learning Skills for Science
LSTM	Liverpool School of Tropical Medicine
MEI	Mathematics in Education and Industry
MEPP	Mathematics Enhancement Programme Primary
MIT	Massachusetts Institute of Technology
MRC	Medical Research Council
MRCPsych	Member of the Royal College of Psychiatrists
MRI	magnetic resonance imaging
MUFFA	Mutuelle Financière des Femmes Africaines

NAHAT	National Association of Health Authorities and Trusts (now NHS Confederation)
NARO	National Agricultural Research Organisation (Uganda)
NatCen	National Centre for Social Research
NCB	National Children's Bureau
NIESR	National Institute of Economic and Social Research
NIMHE	National Institute of Mental Health in England
NKAT	North Kensington Amenity Trust
NSF	National Service Framework
NSLC	National Science Learning Centre
NUPRD	National Unit for Psychiatric Research and Development
NVQ	National Vocational Qualification
ODA	Overseas Development Administration
ODI	Overseas Development Institute
OECD	Organisation for Economic Cooperation and Development
PAMP	pathogen-associated molecular pattern
PBI	Plant Breeding Institute
PBL	Plant Biosciences Ltd
PEP	Political and Economic Planning (later PSI)
PEP	Physics Enhancement Programme
PET	Psychiatric Emergency Team (Birmingham)
POST	Parliamentary Office of Science and Technology
PSI	Policy Studies Institute
QTC	quantum tunnelling composite
RAEng	Royal Academy of Engineering
RAM	Royal Academy of Music
RCPsych	Royal College of Psychiatrists
RDP	Research and Development in Psychiatry
RI	Royal Institution
RITTech	Registered IT Technician
RNA	ribonucleic acid

RSA	Royal Society for the Encouragement of Arts, Manufactures and Commerce
RSC	Royal Shakespeare Company
RSci	Registered Scientist
RSciTech	Registered Science Technician
RST	Royal Shakespeare Theatre
SAILI	Scientific and Industrial Leadership Initiative
SAPS	Science and Plants for Schools
SATIS	Science and Technology in Society
SATs	standardised assessment tasks
SBS	Save British Science
SCMH	Sainsbury Centre for Mental Health
SCVA	Sainsbury Centre for Visual Arts
SDP	Social Democratic Party
SEP	Science Enhancement Programme
SETNET	Science, Engineering and Technology Network (later STEMNET)
SFCT	Sainsbury Family Charitable Trusts
SfN	Society for Neuroscience
SISJAC	Sainsbury Institute for the Study of Japanese Arts and Cultures
SKE	Subject Knowledge Enhancement
SLC	Science Learning Centre
SLCU	Sainsbury Laboratory Cambridge University
SMEs	small and medium-sized enterprises
SMF	Sainsbury Management Fellow
SORP	Statement of Recommended Practice
SQW	Segal Quince Wicksteed
SRU	Sainsbury Research Unit
SSAT	Specialist Schools and Academies Trust, now Schools, Students and Teachers Network
STEM	Science, Technology, Engineering and Mathematics
SURE	Service User Research Enterprise (at King's College London)

SWC	Sainsbury Wellcome Centre for Neural Circuits and Behaviour
TALEN	transcription activator-like effector nuclease
TCB	Tanzania Cotton Board
TDU	Textile Development Unit (Tanzania)
TEEP	Teacher Effectiveness Enhancement Programme
TEP	Technology Enhancement Programme
TGT	Tanzania Gatsby Trust
TI	Transparency International
TSL	The Sainsbury Laboratory (Norwich)
UCL	University College London
UEA	University of East Anglia
UGT	Uganda Gatsby Trust
UMDS	United Medical and Dental Schools of Guy's and St Thomas' Hospitals
UNIDO	United Nations Industrial Development Organisation
URBED	Urbanism, Environment and Design
USAID	United States Agency for International Development
UTC	University Technical College
V&A	Victoria and Albert Museum
WEB	Women's Education in Building
WHO	World Health Organization

INDEX

Italic page numbers refer to black-and-white illustrations and their captions. Colour plates are indicated by Pl.